剑桥高级英语语法
在情境中学语法

［美］**John D. Bunting**
［巴西］**Luciana Diniz**　　编著
［美］**Randi Reppen**

U0095193

GRAMMAR AND BEYOND
ESSENTIALS **4**

外语教学与研究出版社
FOREIGN LANGUAGE TEACHING AND RESEARCH PRESS
北京 BEIJING

京权图字：01-2023-0269

图书在版编目 (CIP) 数据

剑桥高级英语语法：在情境中学语法 ／（美）约翰·D. 邦廷（John D. Bunting），（巴西）卢恰娜·迪尼斯（Luciana Diniz），（美）兰迪·瑞潘（Randi Reppen）编著. —— 北京：外语教学与研究出版社，2023.9
书名原文：GRAMMAR AND BEYOND ESSENTIALS 4
ISBN 978-7-5213-4802-6

I. ①剑… II. ①约… ②卢… ③兰… III. ①英语－语法－自学参考资料 IV. ①H314

中国国家版本馆 CIP 数据核字 (2023) 第 174970 号

出版人　王　芳
项目策划　刘　旭
责任编辑　李　青
责任校对　张红岩
出版发行　外语教学与研究出版社
社　　址　北京市西三环北路 19 号（100089）
网　　址　https://www.fltrp.com
印　　刷　河北文扬印刷有限公司
开　　本　787×1092　1/16
印　　张　16.5
版　　次　2023 年 9 月第 1 版 2023 年 9 月第 1 次印刷
书　　号　ISBN 978-7-5213-4802-6
定　　价　46.00 元

如有图书采购需求，图书内容或印刷装订等问题，侵权、盗版书籍等线索，请拨打以下电话或关注官方服务号：
客服电话：400 898 7008
官方服务号：微信搜索并关注公众号"外研社官方服务号"
外研社购书网址：https://fltrp.tmall.com

物料号：348020001

目　录

"剑桥英语语法——在情境中学语法"系列介绍

"剑桥英语语法——在情境中学语法"系列在科学研究的基础上编写而成，是一套内容丰富的英语语法学习用书，适合初级至高级水平的学习者使用。本系列书着重讲解最为常用的英语语法结构，并通过真实、多样的交际语境训练学生的听说读写四项技能；既可用于课堂教学，也可供自学使用。

基于研究

本系列书中所讲解的语法点，是通过对大学讲座、教材、学术论文、高中课堂、师生交流中所用的书面及口头英语进行广泛分析研究后总结确定出来的。通过这项研究，以及对剑桥国际语料库（Cambridge International Corpus）中超过 10 亿词的书面及口头语言数据进行分析，编者们能够：

- 准确呈现英语书面语及口语中真实使用的语法规则
- 对书面语和口语中的语法差异进行有效区分和讲解
- 更关注书面语及口语中的常用语法结构，而较少关注不常用的结构
- 帮助学生规避英语学习者最常犯的错误
- 精心选择话题内容，自然地引出所要讲解的语法结构
- 将学术词汇表（Academic Word List）中的重要词汇有机融入书中

系列特色

呈现真实在用的语法

书中的语法知识通过简明的表格进行呈现。这些语法点经过了剑桥国际语料库中收录的真实语料的检验，真实呈现了英语语法的实际使用情况。

实际使用数据分析

书中大部分的"语法讲解"及"语法应用"部分都包含了"实际使用数据分析"这个特色板块。它给出的是对语料库数据分析研究后发现的一些具体的、有用的语法应用信息，这些知识点会在后面的练习题中进行练习。

常见错误提示

每一单元均包含"常见错误提示"部分，提示英语学习者容易犯的错误，为学生提供发现和纠正错误的机会，帮助他们避免在语言使用过程中犯同样的错误。这一部分的错例取材于剑桥学习者语料库（Cambridge Learner Corpus）中的真实语料。该数据库收录了超过 3500 万词的语料，其中包括英语非母语学习者撰写的论文和经验丰富的授课教师所提供的语料。

学术性词汇学习

本系列书的每一单元都包含了学术词汇表中的一些重要单词。这一词汇表基于研究统计编写而成，所列出的都是在英语学术文本中高频出现的词和词族。这些词分别与各单元主题紧密相关，在每单元的开篇文章中首次出现，在单元内的语法表及练习中反复出现，贯穿整个单元。学生完成每一级别语法学习的同时，也学到了一系列经过编者精心挑选、与其级别相适应的学术词汇以及与不同学科内容相关的词汇。

系列级别与适用水平

下表列出了本系列语法书的级别划分和大致的难度。需要指出的是，不宜将表中内容解读为精准的对应关系。

	适用水平	托福考试（TOEFL iBT）	欧洲语言共同参考框架（CEFR）
《剑桥初级英语语法——在情境中学语法》	初级	20–34	A1–A2
《剑桥中级英语语法——在情境中学语法》	中低级至中级	35–54	A2–B1
《剑桥中高级英语语法——在情境中学语法》	中高级	55–74	B1–B2
《剑桥高级英语语法——在情境中学语法》	高级	75–95	B2–C1

作者简介

John D. Bunting： 佐治亚州立大学（Georgia State University）应用语言学和英语二语系强化训练项目的高级讲师，曾在委内瑞拉教授英语；撰写了《大学词汇4》（*College Vocabulary 4*）（Cengage，2006），参与修订了《剑桥中高级词汇》（*Vocabulary in Use High Intermediate*）（Cambridge，2010）；主要研究方向是语料库语言学、词汇、学术写作、技术在语言学习中的应用和师范教育。

Luciana Diniz： 波特兰社区学院（Portland Community College）英语外语教学系主任、讲师；获得了佐治亚州立大学应用语言学硕士和博士学位，有近15年的英语外语／英语二语教学经验；主要研究方向是语料库语言学在词汇和语法教学／学习中的应用，曾多次在美国全国性和国际性研讨会上发表论文。

Randi Reppen： 北亚利桑那大学（Northern Arizona University，简称NAU）应用语言学与英语二语教学领域的教授，有20多年的英语教学和教师培训经验，其中有11年担任北亚利桑那大学强化训练项目的主任；主要研究方向是语料库在语言教学和教材编写中的应用，撰写了大量的学术文章和专著，如《语料库在语言课堂上的使用》（*Using Corpora in the Language Classroom*），合著《剑桥初级词汇（第二版）》（*Basic Vocabulary in Use*, 2nd edition）（这两本书皆由剑桥大学出版社出版）。

致谢

The publisher and authors would like to thank these reviewers and consultants for their insights and participation:

Marty Attiyeh, The College of DuPage, Glen Ellyn, IL

Shannon Bailey, Austin Community College, Austin, TX

Jamila Barton, North Seattle Community College, Seattle, WA

Kim Bayer, Hunter College IELI, New York, NY

Linda Berendsen, Oakton Community College, Skokie, IL

Anita Biber, Tarrant County College Northwest, Fort Worth, TX

Jane Breaux, Community College of Aurora, Aurora, CO

Anna Budzinski, San Antonio College, San Antonio, TX

Britta Burton, Mission College, Santa Clara, CA

Jean Carroll, Fresno City College, Fresno, CA

Chris Cashman, Oak Park High School and Elmwood Park High School, Chicago, IL

Annette M. Charron, Bakersfield College, Bakersfield, CA

Patrick Colabucci, ALI at San Diego State University, San Diego, CA

Lin Cui, Harper College, Palatine, IL

Jennifer Duclos, Boston University CELOP, Boston, MA

Joy Durighello, San Francisco City College, San Francisco, CA

Kathleen Flynn, Glendale Community College, Glendale, CA

Raquel Fundora, Miami Dade College, Miami, FL

Patricia Gillie, New Trier Township High School District, Winnetka, IL

Laurie Gluck, LaGuardia Community College, Long Island City, NY

Kathleen Golata, Galileo Academy of Science & Technology, San Francisco, CA

Ellen Goldman, Mission College, Santa Clara, CA

Ekaterina Goussakova, Seminole Community College, Sanford, FL

Marianne Grayston, Prince George's Community College, Largo, MD

Mary Greiss Shipley, Georgia Gwinnett College, Lawrenceville, GA

Sudeepa Gulati, Long Beach City College, Long Beach, CA

Nicole Hammond Carrasquel, University of Central Florida, Orlando, FL

Vicki Hendricks, Broward College, Fort Lauderdale, FL

Kelly Hernandez, Miami Dade College, Miami, FL

Ann Johnston, Tidewater Community College, Virginia Beach, VA

Julia Karet, Chaffey College, Claremont, CA

Jeanne Lachowski, English Language Institute, University of Utah, Salt Lake City, UT

Noga Laor, Rennert, New York, NY

Min Lu, Central Florida Community College, Ocala, FL

Michael Luchuk, Kaplan International Centers, New York, NY

Craig Machado, Norwalk Community College, Norwalk, CT

Denise Maduli-Williams, City College of San Francisco, San Francisco, CA

Diane Mahin, University of Miami, Coral Gables, FL

Melanie Majeski, Naugatuck Valley Community College, Waterbury, CT

Jeanne Malcolm, University of North Carolina at Charlotte, Charlotte, NC

Lourdes Marx, Palm Beach State College, Boca Raton, FL

Susan G. McFalls, Maryville College, Maryville, TN

Nancy McKay, Cuyahoga Community College, Cleveland, OH

Dominika McPartland, Long Island Business Institute, Flushing, NY

Amy Metcalf, UNR/Intensive English Language Center, University of Nevada, Reno, NV

Robert Miller, EF International Language School San Francisco – Mills, San Francisco, CA

Marcie Pachino, Jordan High School, Durham, NC

Myshie Pagel, El Paso Community College, El Paso, TX

Bernadette Pedagno, University of San Francisco, San Francisco, CA

Tam Q Pham, Dallas Theological Seminary, Fort Smith, AR

Mary Beth Pickett, Global LT, Rochester, MI

Maria Reamore, Baltimore City Public Schools, Baltimore, MD

Alison M. Rice, Hunter College IELI, New York, NY

Sydney Rice, Imperial Valley College, Imperial, CA

Kathleen Romstedt, Ohio State University, Columbus, OH

Alexandra Rowe, University of South Carolina, Columbia, SC

Irma Sanders, Baldwin Park Adult and Community Education, Baldwin Park, CA

Caren Shoup, Lone Star College – CyFair, Cypress, TX

Karen Sid, Mission College, Foothill College, De Anza College, Santa Clara, CA

Michelle Thomas, Miami Dade College, Miami, FL

Sharon Van Houte, Lorain County Community College, Elyria, OH

Margi Wald, UC Berkeley, Berkeley, CA

Walli Weitz, Riverside County Office of Ed., Indio, CA

Bart Weyand, University of Southern Maine, Portland, ME

Donna Weyrich, Columbus State Community College, Columbus, OH

Marilyn Whitehorse, Santa Barbara City College, Ojai, CA

Jessica Wilson, Rutgers University – Newark, Newark, NJ

Sue Wilson, San Jose City College, San Jose, CA

Margaret Wilster, Mid-Florida Tech, Orlando, FL

Anne York-Herjeczki, Santa Monica College, Santa Monica, CA

Hoda Zaki, Camden County College, Camden, NJ

We would also like to thank these teachers and programs for allowing us to visit:

Richard Appelbaum, Broward College, Fort Lauderdale, FL

Carmela Arnoldt, Glendale Community College, Glendale, AZ

JaNae Barrow, Desert Vista High School, Phoenix, AZ

Ted Christensen, Mesa Community College, Mesa, AZ

Richard Ciriello, Lower East Side Preparatory High School, New York, NY

Virginia Edwards, Chandler-Gilbert Community College, Chandler, AZ

Nusia Frankel, Miami Dade College, Miami, FL

Raquel Fundora, Miami Dade College, Miami, FL

Vicki Hendricks, Broward College, Fort Lauderdale, FL

Kelly Hernandez, Miami Dade College, Miami, FL

Stephen Johnson, Miami Dade College, Miami, FL

Barbara Jordan, Mesa Community College, Mesa, AZ

Nancy Kersten, GateWay Community College, Phoenix, AZ

Lewis Levine, Hostos Community College, Bronx, NY

John Liffiton, Scottsdale Community College, Scottsdale, AZ

Cheryl Lira-Layne, Gilbert Public School District, Gilbert, AZ

Mary Livingston, Arizona State University, Tempe, AZ

Elizabeth Macdonald, Thunderbird School of Global Management, Glendale, AZ

Terri Martinez, Mesa Community College, Mesa, AZ

Lourdes Marx, Palm Beach State College, Boca Raton, FL

Paul Kei Matsuda, Arizona State University, Tempe, AZ

David Miller, Glendale Community College, Glendale, AZ

Martha Polin, Lower East Side Preparatory High School, New York, NY

Patricia Pullenza, Mesa Community College, Mesa, AZ

Victoria Rasinskaya, Lower East Side Preparatory High School, New York, NY

Vanda Salls, Tempe Union High School District, Tempe, AZ

Kim Sanabria, Hostos Community College, Bronx, NY

Cynthia Schuemann, Miami Dade College, Miami, FL

Michelle Thomas, Miami Dade College, Miami, FL

Dongmei Zeng, Borough of Manhattan Community College, New York, NY

单元内容概览

现实生活中的语法

选用时新的文本素材，在真实语境中呈现各单元的语法知识。

UNIT
5

比较和对比 1：限制性关系从句；as ... as 表示比较；表示对比的常用表达

Family Size and Personality

1 现实生活中的语法

阅读这篇关于出生顺序的文章，文章讨论了孩子的出生顺序如何影响其成年后的性格。文章采用了分块比较法来组织观点，是一篇比较和对比型写作的范例。

A 读前准备 你有几个兄弟姐妹？你认为他们的某些性格特征和出生顺序有关吗？阅读文章并思考：根据文中的信息，出生顺序对性格的影响有多大？

B 阅读理解 回答下列问题。

1 How are former presidents Jimmy Carter, George W. Bush, and Barack Obama connected to the main idea of the text?

2 According to the writer, why are firstborn children usually more ambitious than their siblings?

3 Which of the different birth order types – firstborn, middle born, youngest, and only child – do you think has the fewest advantages in life? Explain.

C 语法发现 按照下列提示，找出并试着理解用 as ... as 表示比较和对比的句子。

1 阅读第 3 段中含有 as ... as 的句子。排行中间的孩子与先出生的孩子相比，是一样坚定、更加坚定还是没那么坚定？说明理由。

……

Birth Order

and Adult Sibling Relationships

What do U.S. Presidents Jimmy Carter, George W. Bush, and Barack Obama all have in common? In addition to being elected president of the United States, 5 these men all share the same birth order. Each one is the oldest child in his family. In fact, many very successful people in government and business have been "firstborn" children. While there is always some variation, some experts 10 agree that birth order can have an influence on a person's personality in childhood and in adulthood.

Firstborn children often share several traits. First, in contrast to their siblings, they are 15 more likely to be responsible, ambitious, and authoritarian. This is probably because they are born into an environment of high expectations, and they usually receive a great deal of attention. They are used to being leaders, taking 20 responsibility for others, and sometimes taking on an almost parental role.

…

50

Family Size and Personality **51**

语法发现

旨在引起学生对语法结构的关注，引导他们分析语法结构的形式、意义及用法。

引导学生不仅学习传统的语法知识，还要了解如何在真实场景中使用本单元所学的语法知识，其中包括该语法点在口语和书面语中使用时的差异。

语法讲解

首先有一个概述，以简明易懂的语言对语法进行概括性描述，然后分要点具体讲解。

2 限制性关系从句

语法讲解

关系从句（relative clauses）可用于修饰名词，置于所修饰名词之后。限制性关系从句（identifying relative clauses / restrictive relative clauses）用于提供关于所修饰名词的必要信息。这类从句可以在各种学术写作中使用，在比较和对比型写作中尤其实用，可用来描述被比较事物的特征。

Children who / that have no siblings are often very close to their parents.
People gradually behave in ways which / that are more consistent with their preferred self-image.

2.1 限制性关系从句

A 限制性关系从句由关系代词 that，which，who，whom 或 whose 引导，用于修饰名词。
限制性关系从句给出关于主句中名词或名词短语的必要信息，说明具体所指的是哪个人或事物。如果没有限制性关系从句所提供的信息，句意将不完整。

限制性关系从句
People who do not have children may not be aware of differences in birth order.
限制性关系从句
Creativity is a trait that all middle children share.

B who，that 和 whom 用于指代人。whom 在关系从句中作宾语，非常正式。在非正式的口语和书面语中，常用 that 或 who 代替 whom。

人
Researchers who / that study families have different views.
My siblings are the people in my life whom I will always trust.

......

52　Unit 5 比较和对比 1

📊 实际使用数据分析

在学术写作中，当关系代词指代人时，who 的使用频率比 that 高。

Who	▆▆▆▆▆▆
That	▆▆▆

在口语中，当关系代词指代人时，that 的使用频率比 who 高。

Who	▆▆▆
That	▆▆▆▆▆▆

💻 语法应用

练习 2.1　限制性关系从句

A 下面这段文字谈到了出生顺序。用 that，which，who，whom 或 whose 填空。有时正确答案不唯一。

Birth order researchers have discovered some interesting information [1] *that* can help us understand our colleagues better. Do you have a difficult boss [2] _____ authoritarian personality makes your life difficult? If so, your boss might be a firstborn child. Children [3] _____ are born first are often more authoritarian than their younger siblings. Do you have a co-worker [4] _____ is passive, but particularly creative and insightful? This person may be a middle child. People [5] _____ have both older and younger siblings are often passive because their older siblings were responsible for their well-being when ...

54　Unit 5 比较和对比 1

表格呈现

表内列出本单元所学语法的形式、意义及用法，清晰明了，方便课堂使用及查阅参考。

语法应用

练习题型丰富，内容新奇有趣，能让学生保持学习的兴趣与热情。

配套音频

🎧 这一图标表示相应的部分配有音频。扫描本书封底的二维码即可在线听录音，登录封底的网址可获取录音文本。

练习 3.2 更多练习: as ... as 表示比较

🎧 A Venus Williams 和 Serena Williams 是一对著名的姐妹。听一段关于她们的录音，完成表格。

	Venus Williams	Serena Williams
1 Birth date	June 17, 1980	
2 Height	6'1"	
3 Year turned professional		
4 Wimbledon singles victories (individual years)		
5 U.S. Open singles victories (individual years)		

B 根据练习 A 中的信息和下列提示，使用 as ... as 短语（almost as ... as，just as ... as，nearly as ... as 和 not quite as ... as），在一张纸上写出完整的句子。有时正确答案不唯一。

1 Serena / is / tall / Venus.

Serena is not quite as tall as Venus.

2 Serena / is / old / Venus.

3 Serena / has / experience / Venus.

4 Serena / is / important to U.S. sports / Venus.

Serena and Venus Williams

5 Serena / has / won / Wimbledon singles / Venus.

6 Venus / is / famous / Serena.

7 Serena / has had / U.S. Open singles victories / Venus.

...

58 Unit 5 比较和对比 1

真实语境中的练习

这类练习形式由封闭式转为开放式，可以相对自由地回答。让学生在真实情境中运用所学语法点组织起有意义的语言，实现沟通的目的。

常见错误提示

本部分是基于对语料库中超过 13.5 万篇学术论文的常见错误分析而给出的提示。学生可通过这一部分学习如何避免英语学习者常犯的错误，培养自主纠错的能力，由此提升自己的口语及写作水平。

词汇应用

练习 4.1 表示对比的词汇

A 下列是关于美国儿童的句子。用方框中的单词或短语填空。

differ from	major difference between	unlike
in contrast	significantly different from	

1 One _major difference between_ children in the United States in 1900 and now is that children in the past didn't get a lot of individual attention from their parents, while children today get a lot of individual attention.

2 Another way that today's children are _____ children in the past is that in the past, children often worked to help their families, but children now often work for their own extra spending money.

3 Today's children also _____ children in 1900 in that they are required to attend school.

4 Children in the past often had large families with several siblings. _____, many children today have one or two siblings or are only children.

5 In 1900, children were very independent. _____ them, children today depend on their parents a lot.

…

5 常见错误提示 ⚠

1 who 引导的关系从句不用于修饰表示无生命事物的名词。
　　　　　that
A study who showed the benefits of being an only child was published last year.

2 关系代词作主语时不可省略。
　　　　　　who
Children have older siblings tend to be somewhat dependent.

3 在关系从句中，主语和谓语动词的单复数形式注意保持一致。
　　　　　　　have
Children who has siblings often become secure and confident adults.

4 注意要用 the same as，而不要用 the same than。
　　　　　　　　　　　　　　　　　　　　　　　　　　as
Middle children often have the same level of creativity than youngest children.

改错练习

下面是一篇文章的主体段落，文章比较了现在与过去的家庭。从中找出另外 8 处错误并改正。

Families Past and Present

A major way that families have changed is the number
　　　　　　　　that
of families have only one child. The number of families had only one child was low in the United States in the 1950s

5 and 1960s. However, one-child families began increasing in the 1970s and are very common today. This is especially true in households who have only one parent. One

…

紧扣单元主题的练习

为学生提供多种语境，练习相应语法的使用，提高其英语的准确性和流利度。

登录本书封底的网址可下载查看练习的参考答案。

改错练习

为学习者提供发现并纠正常见错误的机会，培养自主纠错的能力，提升英语表达的准确性。

剑桥高级英语语法
——在情境中学语法

GRAMMAR AND BEYOND

ESSENTIALS 4

原因和结果 1：句子结构；用名词表示原因的常用句式

The Environment and You

1 现实生活中的语法

生态足迹用来衡量人类对地球自然资源的影响。阅读这篇关于生态足迹的文章。文章描述了一个原因及其导致的多个结果，是一篇因果关系型写作的范例。

A 读前准备 人们在日常生活中常做的哪些事情会影响环境？举出 3 个例子。阅读文章并思考：在作者看来，开采煤炭、石油等自然资源可能产生什么影响？

B 阅读理解 回答下列问题。

1 In your own words, what is an ecological footprint? Provide examples of activities that could cause a large and a small ecological footprint.

2 According to the essay, what are three major consequences of large ecological footprints?

3 "We do not inherit the Earth from our ancestors; we borrow it from our children" is a Native American proverb. How is this proverb related to the essay?

C 语法发现 按照下列提示，找出说明原因和描述结果的句子并回答问题。

1 在第 1 段第 11—15 行找到描述资源易获取时生态足迹的值较大的句子。用 C 标出说明原因的分句，用 E 标出陈述结果的分句，并圈出引出原因的单词。

2 在第 3 段中的第 1 个句子下面画线。这句话描述的是原因还是结果？作者使用了哪个短语来引出所描述的内容？

3 在第 3 段中找出描述向大气中排放有害气体所导致的结果的句子，并圈出引出结果的短语。

Ecological Footprints

Environmentalists are increasingly concerned about the impact that individuals have on our planet, and many people now want
5 to help protect the environment. A good place to start is reducing one's ecological footprint. An ecological footprint is an estimate of how much land, water, and other
10 natural resources are being used by a person or a group. Because resources are easily accessible in developed countries like the United States, people in these countries tend
15 to have large ecological footprints. For example, they may take long showers, leave their computers on for the whole day, buy new things they do not need, and fly frequently
20 between cities. The consequences of large ecological footprints can be disastrous.[1]

One of the worst effects of large ecological footprints is the loss of
25 natural resources, such as oil, water, and wood. These resources are being consumed so fast that the Earth does not have time to renew them. Approximately 99 million barrels of
30 oil are produced daily in the world. People use oil to run their cars, heat their homes, and create products such as clothes, paint, and plastic. Plastic is now one of the biggest threats to our

35 environment, and in fact to each of us. The naturalist David Attenborough shocked the world by showing images of sea birds attempting to feed their young on plastic shopping
40 bags. It is estimated that eight million tonnes of plastic end up in our oceans every year. Unless this stops, there will be more plastic than fish in the ocean by 2050. Already, billions of
45 people around the world are drinking water that is contaminated by plastic. The United States is the country worst affected, with 94% plastic contamination in its tap water.

50 Large ecological footprints also lead to higher greenhouse gas emissions. The mining of oil, natural gas, and coal, as well as the use of these resources in electrical power
55 plants and automobiles, releases dangerous gases into the air, where they trap[2] heat. As a result, the Earth gets warmer.

It is our responsibility to find ways
60 to decrease our impact on our planet. Even small changes can make a difference and help to protect the environment. If we do not start reducing our ecological footprints
65 right away, it may be too late for future generations to contain[3] the damage.

[1]**disastrous:** causing a lot of damage 灾难性的
[2]**trap:** prevent from leaving 留存，储存
[3]**contain:** limit 控制，遏制

2 句子结构：简单句和并列复合句

语法讲解

在因果关系型写作及其他类型的学术写作中，使用多种句型可以帮助写作者有效地表达信息。写作者可以使用简单句（simple sentences）来有力地陈述事实或观点，也可以使用并列复合句（compound sentences）来连接相关的信息，例如原因和结果。

简单句：
Lack of natural resources is one of the results of large ecological footprints.
并列复合句：
Large ecological footprints cause many problems, and it is our social responsibility to solve them.

2.1 简单句

A 简单句只包含一个分句，称为主句（main clause）或独立分句（independent clause）。与所有句子一样，简单句中必须有主语和谓语动词。	主语　　　　　　　　　　　动词 Millions of barrels of oil are produced daily.
动词可后接多种成分或词类，包括： 宾语 介词短语 形容词 副词	主语　　　　　　动词　　　宾语 Plastic pollution has devastated our oceans. 主语　　　　　　　　　　　动词 Ozone and other greenhouse gases are often 介词短语 in the news. 主语　　　动词　　形容词 The Earth is becoming warmer. 主语　　　　　　　　　　　　　　　　动词 Natural resources that provide energy will run 副词 out eventually.
B 句子的主语可以为： 形容词 + 名词 代词 名词 and 名词 名词 + 介词短语 名词 + 关系从句 动名词	Small changes can make a difference. This has devastated many oceans. Ozone and other greenhouse gases are often in the news. The health of our oceans remains critical. Natural resources that provide energy will run out eventually. Reducing our ecological footprints is crucial.

2.1　简单句（续表）

C 句子的谓语可由一个主要动词构成，可由 be，do，have 等助动词 + 主要动词构成，也可由 can，will 等情态动词 + 主要动词构成。 句子的谓语可以包含不止一个主要动词。	主要动词 The health of our oceans **remains** critical. 助动词 This **has** devastated many oceans. 情态动词 People **may** take long showers. The average temperature **rises and falls**.

2.2　简单句的用法

A 在较长的语篇中可以用简短的简单句强调重点信息。	The consequences of these footprints can be disastrous.
B 如果某个句子中缺少主语或谓语动词，那么这个句子就不完整，被称为残缺句（fragment）。 为了避免残缺句，需要确保所有的句子都有主语和谓语动词。	残缺句（缺少主语）：In the future, will probably be much warmer on Earth. 修正：In the future, **the temperature** will probably be much warmer on Earth. 残缺句（缺少谓语）：The worst effect of large ecological footprints the loss of natural resources. 修正：The worst effect of large ecological footprints **is** the loss of natural resources.
C 在学术写作中，写作者可以使用过渡词语来连接两个独立分句，以清晰地表达分句在意思上的联系。 常见的过渡词语有： as a result，consequently，furthermore，however 连接独立分句时，过渡词语之前用句号或分号，之后用逗号。	These gases trap heat in the air. **As a result**, the Earth gets warmer. These gases trap heat in the air; **as a result**, the Earth gets warmer.
D 两个独立分句之间也可用分号来连接。如果两个分句在意思上紧密相连，那么使用分号是个不错的选择。	独立分句 1　　　　　　　独立分句 2 People should buy less; they should replace items only when absolutely necessary.

2.3 并列复合句

A 并列复合句由至少两个独立分句构成，分句由并列连词（and，but，or，so，yet）连接，且并列连词之前要使用逗号。并列复合句可用于连接独立分句间的信息。

独立分句 1
Some people are concerned about the environment,
独立分句 2
so they recycle as much as they can.

B 写作中应避免出现连写句（run-on sentences）或逗号粘连（comma splices）的错误。

连写句是连接两个独立分句时，没有使用并列连词的句子。

连接两个独立分句时，可以使用逗号和并列连词。

逗号粘连是只使用逗号来连接两个独立分句的现象。

两个独立分句之间可以使用句号。

连写句： These gases trap heat in the air the Earth gets warmer.

修正： These gases trap heat in the air, **so** the Earth gets warmer.

逗号粘连： Humans are the cause of many environmental problems, it is our responsibility to resolve them.

修正： Humans are the cause of many environmental problems. It is our responsibility to resolve them.

C 在报纸文章、杂志文章等的写作中，常在句首用 and 和 but 来引出句子。但这种用法通常不宜用在学术写作中。

Natural resources are being consumed so fast that the Earth does not have time to renew them. **And** as a result, these resources are becoming scarce.
There are efforts to clean up the oceans. **But** the health of our oceans remains critical.

语法应用

练习 2.1 主语和动词

阅读下列关于冰岛能源的句子，在每个独立分句中的主语下面画线，并圈出动词。

1 Iceland has huge frozen glaciers, but it also has more than 100 volcanoes.

2 In 1998, Iceland decided to become independent from fossil fuels.

3 It began to increase its use of renewable energy sources.

4 Electricity in Iceland's homes is generated by geothermal springs, or it comes from the energy of the rivers and glaciers.

5 The water in geothermal springs is already hot, so Icelanders use it instead of fossil fuels to heat their homes.

6 Basic services such as transportation in Iceland are switching to electric vehicles, and all ships in the large fishing industry may eventually operate on hydrogen fuel.

7 Iceland satisfies its country's need for energy without relying heavily on fossil fuels.

练习 2.2 残缺句、连写句和逗号粘连

A 阅读下列关于环境的句子，用 √ 标出完整的句子，用 F 标出残缺句，用 R-O 标出连写句，并用 CS 标出出现逗号粘连的句子。

1 (a) __√__ Over time, people have destroyed the natural habitats of many plants and animals in order to build more homes and grow more food. (b) __F__ For this reason, many of our forests now gone. (c) __R-O__ Plants and animals are losing their homes they may become extinct.

2 (a) _____ Water pollution a serious problem. (b) _____ For many years, people got rid of waste by dumping it into the water. (c) _____ As a result, the quality of the water in many of our oceans, rivers, and lakes unacceptable. (d) _____ In fact, nearly about two billion people in the world do not have safe drinking water, and over two million people die each year from diseases related to water.

3 (a) _____ Environmentalists are constantly trying to come up with ideas to protect the environment nobody knows what the environment will be like in the future.
(b) _____ However, researchers believe that much has already improved.
(c) _____ Individuals are becoming more aware of the environment around them.

4 (a) _____ Trying to protect nature in various ways. (b) _____ Some people are helping to clean up the environment by driving electric cars, others are working to preserve endangered plants and animals. (c) _____ These efforts will allow future generations to have clean air and water and to enjoy the world's natural beauty.

5 (a) _____ The forests of the Earth are being cut down. (b) _____ The destruction of the forests is the result of human and natural disasters. (c) _____ Has negative consequences on the environment.

B 修正练习 A 中的残缺句、连写句以及出现逗号粘连的句子。与同伴互相检查改好的句子。

1 *For this reason, many of our forests are now gone. Plants and animals are losing their homes. As a result, they may become extinct.*

2 _____

_____

3 _____

_____

4 _____

_____

5 _____

_____

3 主从复合句

语法讲解

连接原因和结果时，还可以使用主从复合句（complex sentences）。这类句子由一个独立分句和至少一个从属分句（dependent clause）构成。

Because resources are readily accessible in developed countries like the United States, people in these countries tend to have large ecological footprints.

3.1 主从复合句

主从复合句通常由一个独立分句和一个由从属连词引导的从属分句构成。从属连词可以表明两个分句之间的关系。

常见的从属连词有：

although，after，as if，because，before，if，since，whereas，whether，while

当从属分句位于独立分句之前时，使用逗号将两者分隔开。

独立分句
Future generations will suffer
从属分句
if pollution is not reduced.

从属分句
Although people try to save energy,
独立分句
global demand for energy increases every year.

3.2 主从复合句的用法

A 在学术写作中，含有从属连词 because，if，since 和 when 的主从复合句可用于表示因果关系。

原因　　　　　　　　　　结果
If pollution is reduced, global health will improve.

B 不与独立分句连接的从属分句也是残缺句。

为避免写出残缺句，可以：

将从属分句与独立分句连接。（注意：如果从属分句位于句首，则使用逗号将其与独立分句分隔开。）

或

用过渡词语替换从属连词，将从属分句变为独立分句。

残缺句：Because energy use is high in the developed world. People there use a lot of resources.

从属分句
修正：Because energy use is high in the developed world, people there use a lot of resources.
独立分句

修正：Energy use is high in the developed world. As a result, people there use a lot of resources.

语法应用

练习 3.1 主从复合句

A 阅读下列关于白头海雕的句子，在表示原因的句子旁标记 C，在表示结果的句子旁标记 E，再使用 because，if，since 或 when 将每对句子组合起来。有时正确答案不唯一。

1 __E__ The United States government declared bald eagles an endangered species.

__C__ Bald eagles were almost extinct in the 1960s.

Because bald eagles were almost extinct in the 1960s, the United States government declared them an endangered species.

2 _____ The bald eagle showed the qualities of impressive strength and courage.

_____ The bald eagle was chosen in 1782 to be the symbol for the United States.

3 _____ The government enacted laws that included banning the use of the pesticide DDT.

_____ The bald eagle population began to recover.

4 _____ In 2007, the bald eagle was taken off the Endangered Species Act's "threatened" list.

_____ The bald eagles' numbers had greatly increased since the 1960s.

5 _____ The bald eagle population may decrease once more.

_____ The habitats of the bald eagles are not protected in the future.

6 _____ Some biologists are urging wind energy companies to develop safer turbines.

_____ The birds are sometimes killed by the blades of wind turbines.

7 _____ People can help protect the bald eagle.

_____ People volunteer to clean up the habitats where eagles nest.

B 结对练习 和同伴想出两种濒危动物，并讨论导致其濒危的原因（例如栖息地丧失、杀虫剂、过度捕捞等）以及目前采取的保护措施。接下来，根据下面的指示进行角色扮演。如有可能，请在对话中使用 because，if，since 和 when。

A 你是一位记者。就你们谈论过的一种动物对同伴 B 进行采访，询问这种动物濒临灭绝的原因以及环境政策对其产生的影响。

B 你是一位环保主义者。回答同伴 A 所提出的问题。

Partner A	*Tell me about an endangered animal that people should know about.*
Partner B	*Sea turtles are an endangered animal.*
Partner A	*Why are they endangered?*
Partner B	*One reason is the fishing industry. Many turtles die when they bite the hooks and get caught in the fishing lines.*
Partner A	*How are they today?*
Partner B	*Since there are now programs that protect the turtles, their numbers have improved in recent years.*

与同伴互换角色，再次进行角色扮演，讨论另一种濒危动物。

练习 3.2 更多练习：主从复合句

阅读下列问题，并听一段关于大城市共享单车项目的广播访谈。边听录音边做笔记，再用 because，if，since 和 when 回答问题。

1 Why are bikeshares becoming so popular in large cities?

Bikeshares are becoming popular because they are a great way to reduce pollution.

2 Why do people use a bikeshare?

_____

_____

3 What do people have to do if they want to use the bikes?

_____

_____

4 What happens when riders get a flat tire?

_____

_____

_____

5 If a city wants a bikeshare program to be successful, what two things are required?

_____

_____

6 What can bikeshare riders do in some cities when they want to find a bike or an empty space at a station?

_____

_____

7 Why do some people feel uncomfortable riding the bikes?

_____

_____

4 用名词表示原因的常用句式

词汇讲解

因果关系可以通过许多不同的方式来表示。使用名词 cause，reason 和 factor 是其中一种重要方式。	One important cause of overpopulation is lack of education. Low cost is the primary reason why many communities use coal for energy. Emissions from cars are a major factor in the increase in air pollution.

4.1　表示原因的名词：cause，reason，factor

A 含有名词 cause 的表达常用于以下含有动词 be 的句式中： 名词短语　　　　　　　名词短语 _____ is a / one cause of _____. 　　　　　　名词短语　名词短语 Another cause of _____ is _____.	A higher birth rate is one major cause of overpopulation. Another leading cause of overpopulation is the decline in death rates.
B 含有名词 cause 的表达通常用于描述负面结果。cause 通常不与表示成功或积极结果的词一同使用。	Some researchers believe that the primary cause of global warming is large ecological footprints.

C 含有名词 reason 的表达常用于以下含有动词 be 的句式中：

从句 从句
One reason (why) _____ is _____ .

从句 名词短语
One reason (why) _____ is _____ .

名词短语 从句
The reason for _____ is _____ .

名词短语 名词短语
The reason for _____ is _____ .

句子
_____ . For this reason / these
分句
reasons, _____ .

One reason (why) the population **is** growing so fast **is** that death rates have fallen dramatically.
One reason (why) the population is growing so fast **is** the decline in the death rate.
The real **reason for** our concern about overpopulation **is** that our resources are limited.
The primary **reason for** our concern about overpopulation **is** limited resources.
People are living longer, healthier lives. **For this reason,** the population has been increasing.

D 含有名词 factor 的表达常用于以下含有动词 be 的句式中：

名词短语 名词短语
_____ is a / one factor in _____ .

名词短语 名词短语
Another factor in _____ is _____ .

Mortality is one key **factor in** the current growth in population.
Another critical **factor in** water pollution **is** the increase in fertilizer use by farmers.

📊 实际使用数据分析

最常与 cause 连用的词有：
leading, probable, common, root, underlying, exact, major, likely, main, important, primary
Scholars are not sure whether poverty is an **underlying cause** of overpopulation.

最常与 reason 连用的词有：
good, major, real, main, primary, biggest
One **good reason** to recycle is to save money.

最常与 factor 连用的词有：
important, another, major, key, significant, critical
Decreasing the number of cars on the road is a **critical factor** in the effort to reduce air pollution.

词汇应用

练习 4.1 表示原因的名词

A 这是一篇关于出行方式的网络文章。用 cause / reason / factor 和 "实际使用数据分析" 中的形容词将文章补充完整。

Changing with the Times

Some experts say that one [1] *leading cause* of air pollution is the carbon emissions from cars. To reduce these emissions, many people have changed how they get around. James Kendall of Cincinnati, Ohio, sold his gas-guzzling car and purchased a hybrid vehicle. Kendall says, "One [2] _____ _____ I bought a hybrid is that it's better for the environment. However, another [3] _____ _____ in my decision was money. I spend a lot less on gas now."

Linda Wong of Los Angeles, California, takes public transportation as often as she can. "Carbon emissions from cars is the [4] _____ _____ of smog and air pollution in L.A.," she explains. "I don't want to add to that. That's the [5] _____ why I don't like to drive. Another [6] _____ _____ in my decision is that driving in L.A. is very stressful."

Pedro Sandoval of Missoula, Montana, started using a carpool to get to and from work two years ago because of his concern for the environment, but he says that the [7] _____ _____ that he has stuck with it has to do with other incentives. "I've met a lot of really nice people and saved a lot of money." He'll take public transportation, but, as he says, buses are a [8] _____ _____ of pollution, too.

B **结对练习** 和同伴一起选择 3 个与环境有关的问题，参考下面的例子，用含有 factor，reason 和 cause 的表达说明每个问题可能的原因和影响。

| noise pollution | nuclear safety | overpopulation | water pollution |

The use of medicines is a factor in water pollution. The medicines we use end up in our water. For this reason, some communities have started to collect unused medicines so that they don't end up in our water.

A 下列问题谈到了人们或城市是如何减轻对环境的影响的。用含有 cause，reason 或 factor 的句式，以及 "实际使用数据分析" 中的形容词回答问题。

1 What is one reason why some people prefer not to eat meat?

One primary reason why some people prefer not to eat meat is that they don't want animals to be killed for food.

2 What do you think is one reason for the rising interest in locally grown food?

_____

3 What are two causes of pollution in cities?

_____

4 What is one important factor in a city's decision to start a bikeshare program?

_____

5 Some cities have decided to ban the use of plastic bags in grocery stores. What do you think is the reason for this ban?

B 结对练习 和同伴轮流提问并回答练习 A 中的问题。你们同意对方的回答吗？说明理由。

I disagree that people don't eat meat because they don't want animals to be killed. I think that some people don't eat meat because they can't afford it.

5 常见错误提示 ⚠

1 为避免出现残缺句，要确保句子中有主语和谓语动词。

The result of a large ecological footprint ^is^ often pollution.

2 在学术写作中，要用 because，而不要用 cuz 或 coz。

Animals are becoming extinct ~~cuz~~ ^because^ humans have moved into their habitats.

3 注意区分 cause 和 because。

~~Cause~~ ^Because^ water pollution is widespread, there is a shortage of clean drinking water in many parts of the world.

4 在学术写作中，注意避免在句首使用 and。

Shoppers should bring their own bags to stores because paper bags lead to ~~deforestation. And~~ ^deforestation, and^ plastic bags are dangerous for birds and marine life.

改错练习

下面的段落选自一篇关于海洋污染的文章，从中找出另外 8 处错误并改正。

One significant cause of ocean pollution *is* ∧the accidental spilling of crude oil by
large ocean-going ships. The consequences of oil spills can be disastrous to both marine
plant and animal life. For example, oil that spills on the surface of the water blocks
oxygen from getting to marine plant life. Cause oxygen is necessary for survival, marine
5 plants die. And the fish that eat them can die as well. In addition, oil spills can coat
the feathers of marine birds. Oil-coated birds can become weighted down, so cannot
fly. Furthermore, oil often removes the natural coating on marine birds' feathers. As
a result, the birds can die from overexposure cuz the coating protects them from the
elements. Oil spills also affect the human food chain. This occurs coz shellfish such as
10 mussels and clams filter water through their bodies. If the water is polluted with oil, the
flesh of the shellfish becomes polluted as well. And this makes them harmful for human
consumption. Cause oil spills affect human, animal, and plant life, many people agree
that these spills one of the most serious environmental problems in the world today.

原因和结果 2：表示原因的从属连词和介词；表示结果的过渡词语；用名词表示结果的常用句式

Consumer Behavior

1 现实生活中的语法

阅读这篇谈论影响消费者购买行为的因素的文章。文章描述了多个原因及其对应的结果，是一篇因果关系型写作的范例。

A 读前准备 在过去半年里，你购买过的最贵的一件产品是什么？什么因素会影响你是否购买某件产品？阅读文章并思考：作者认为影响消费者购买行为的关键因素有哪些？

B 阅读理解 回答下列问题。

1 According to the text, what is the definition of consumer behavior? Use your own words.

2 Name one factor from the essay that might influence someone to buy more and one factor from the essay that might influence someone to buy less.

3 Why does the writer believe it is important to understand consumer behavior?

C 语法发现 按照下列提示，找出说明原因和描述结果的词语。

1 在第 1 段中找到并圈出单词 effect，再在与 effect 连用的动词、形容词和介词下面画线。作者在第 5 段中使用了两次 effect，且选择了不同的形容词进行修饰。在这两个含有 effect 的短语下面画线，并圈出形容词。

2 在第 2 段中找到描述饿着肚子对购物可能有所影响的句子，圈出下一句中引出结果的词语。

Understanding Consumer Behavior

Consumer behavior is the process consumers go through in making purchasing decisions. This process includes the steps they take from the moment they become aware of a particular need through the final decision to purchase or not purchase a product. According to marketing experts, this process includes the time spent planning where to shop and comparison shopping. Along the way, consumers are influenced by many factors, including psychological and physical ones. Many experts agree on four factors that have a significant effect on consumer behavior.

One set of factors that influence consumer behavior is physical factors – how a person physically feels when shopping. For example, being hungry when grocery shopping affects how people shop. The result is that people often buy more food than they would if they were not hungry. In contrast, feeling tired leads people to buy less.

Cultural and social factors also have an effect on consumer behavior. Some people make choices because of what their friends do. One example is the importance attached to owning a particular item, such as an expensive pair of jeans, in a person's social network. Another social factor is whether the culture encourages or discourages a behavior, such as bargaining for a lower price.

A third factor that impacts consumer behavior is a person's self-image. People often try to match their purchases, from paper towels to cars, to their idea of self.

For example, some people care very much about the environment and health of the planet. Therefore, they might choose to drive an electric car due to its low impact on the environment. Other people might see themselves as economical shoppers. As a result, they might buy only simple, inexpensive clothing in order to maintain that aspect of their self-image.

Finally, a person's own experience is a factor. Memories about a certain product or place can have a direct effect on later decisions. For instance, people will tend to go back to a restaurant because they had a good eating experience there. On the other hand, if a person becomes ill eating seafood, it might have a negative effect on his or her future desire for that kind of food.

Every day, people make choices about what to buy. However, they are often unaware of the process behind their decision making. As a result, they can become vulnerable to[1] advertising and other marketing techniques that target the factors that convince people to buy more. Consumers may want to make changes in their purchasing patterns, but they might not know how to make these changes. One important step is for them to become more aware of why they make choices. Becoming educated about their behavior as consumers is an important way for people to make better buying decisions.

---

[1] **vulnerable to:** able to be easily hurt or influenced 易受伤害的，易受影响的

2 表示原因、理由或目的的从属连词和介词

语法讲解

在学术写作中，有些从属连词（subordinators）和介词（prepositions）可以表示原因、理由或目的，也可以回答由 why 引导的疑问句。这些从属连词和介词或是单词或是短语。	Some people buy products they do not need only **because** they are on sale. We often choose what products to buy **as a result of** past experience.

2.1　表示原因、理由或目的的从属连词的用法

A 从属连词用于连接主从复合句中的独立分句和从属分句。其中，从属分句也可被称为状语从句。	独立分句 Some consumers purchase certain products 从属分句 **because** they want to maintain their self-image.
B 如 Unit 1 中提到的，从属连词 because 和 since 可用于表示原因或理由。	结果　　　　　　　　　　　原因 / 理由 Some consumers buy products **because** they want to be like their friends.
C 从属连词 so 和 so that 可用于表示目的。	目的 Some consumers buy "green" products **so (that)** they can appear environmentally aware.

2.2　表示原因或理由的介词的用法

介词 because of，as a result of 和 due to 用于表示原因或理由。与从属连词不同，这些介词后接名词短语。	结果　　　　　　　　　原因 / 理由 Some people choose products **because of** their past experiences. 结果　　　　　　　　　原因 / 理由 Shoppers will buy more food **as a result of** being hungry when they shop. 结果　　　　　　　　　原因 / 理由 Some consumers choose an electric car **due to** its low impact on the environment.

语法应用

练习 2.1 表示原因、理由和目的的从属连词

A 下列是有关消费者行为的句子。在表示原因的句子上标记 C，在表示结果的句子上标记 E，再使用括号中的词将每对句子组合起来。有时正确答案不唯一。

C	*E*

1 our decisions affect our financial future / it is important for us to make responsible buying decisions (*because*)

   It is important for us to make responsible buying decisions because they affect our financial future.

2 it is not easy to ignore advertising / consumers need to learn how to shop wisely (*since*)

3 make a list before you leave home / you do not buy something you do not need (*so that*)

4 people can get into debt easily / it is easy to buy things using a credit card (*because*)

5 children see the snack foods and ask their parents for them / stores put snack foods on low shelves (*so that*)

6 people will impulsively buy products that they don't need / stores put fun items like candy and toys by the checkout counters (*so*)

B **小组活动** 结合自己的想法，在一张纸上完成下列句子，然后将你写的句子分享给小组成员并进行解释。询问他们是否同意你的观点，并让他们说明原因。

   1 Sometimes people buy things they don't need because …
   2 Sometimes people spend more money than they make because …
   3 Manufacturers of cereals often include cartoon characters in their commercials so …
   4 Fast-food restaurants often air commercials during late-night TV so that …
   5 Stores sometimes advertise a few items at very low prices because …
   6 Some people prefer to buy products online since …
   A *My sentence is* People buy things they don't need because they want to feel better. *For example, when I have a bad day, sometimes I go out and buy something – even something small like a book – to make myself feel better.*
   B *I agree with you because I do that, too, but I think more often people buy things they don't need because they are bored.*

下文谈到了消费者的购买习惯。每个从属连词和介词都缺失了一个单词，在横线上补充所缺单词。

Consumers buy things for a lot of different reasons. Most frequently, people buy products [1] _**because**_ of their individual tastes. For example, they might buy the same snacks or cereals every time they go shopping [2]_____ to their family's likes and dislikes. They don't even think about whether or not they want those items. People also make purchases as a [3]_____ of need. They buy an air conditioner [4]_____ of severe hot weather, or they purchase fire alarms in their house [5]_____ that their family stays safe. Finally, sometimes people make impulse purchases. They buy things they haven't planned to buy and may not necessarily need or even want. Sometimes they make these purchases [6]_____ a result of effective advertising or in the case of food, because [7]_____ hunger while they are shopping. They also make impulse purchases due [8]_____ their own personalities. Some people are more prone to impulse buying than others are.

A 听一段关于 Roger 个人购物习惯的采访。先阅读下列问题，然后边听录音边针对问题做笔记，再使用括号中的词回答问题。

1 Why does Roger sometimes go shopping when he doesn't need anything?
(because) _**He goes shopping when he doesn't need anything because he's happy when he is shopping.**_

2 How does he control his spending?
(so that) _____
_____

3 Does he use a credit card or debit card for his purchases? Why or why not?
(because of) _____
_____

4 Why does he do a lot of research when he has to buy an expensive product?
(as a result of) _____
_____

5 Does he eat out a lot?

(*due to*) _____

B **结对练习** 改写练习 A 中第 2—5 个问题，然后用这些问题采访同伴，再在一张纸上记录下同伴的回答。回答时尽量使用练习 A 中所给的介词和从属连词。最后将写好的句子分享给另一组同学。你们的习惯和经历相似吗？

3 表示结果的过渡词语

语法讲解

在学术写作中，另一种连接原因和结果的重要方式是使用过渡词语。有些过渡词语常用于表示原因、理由或结果。	Sometimes people buy products that show that they are part of a social network. **Therefore,** they might choose an expensive pair of jeans because the jeans are popular with their friends.

3.1 表示结果的过渡词语的用法

A 过渡词语用于连接两个独立分句。 这两个句子之间可以使用分号或句号。 过渡词语后要加逗号。	Environmental values might affect some purchases; **consequently,** many merchants offer green products. Environmental values might affect some purchases. **Consequently,** many merchants offer green products.
B 下列过渡词语用于表示影响或结果： as a consequence，as a result，consequently，therefore，thus 注意：thus 几乎不用于非正式的口语或书面语中。	Many consumers are concerned about the environment. **As a result**, they buy products that are environmentally safe. Some consumers feel the need to be part of a certain group; **therefore**, they buy products that are expensive and fashionable.

练习 3.1 过渡词语

A 下列句子描述了广告对消费者的影响。将括号中的词语重新排序，写出完整的句子。记得在过渡词语之后使用逗号。

1 People see and hear over 2,500 advertisements per day.

As a result, people need to be aware of the effects of advertising.
<u>(of advertising / be / people / need to / aware of / the effects / as a result)</u>

2 Candy and sugary cereals are advertised during children's television shows.

_____
(for them / a desire / children / develop / as a consequence)

3 Public television does not show advertisements for sugary foods.

_____
(exposed to / not / children / are / them / as a result)

4 The effects of smoking are serious and possibly deadly.

_____
(it / not / on TV / them / legal / to advertise / is / therefore)

5 Happy people are often shown eating snack foods.

_____
(think / them / viewers / too / snack foods / happy / will make / eating / consequently)

B **结对练习** 和同伴一起选择两种不同的产品，并讨论每种产品是如何通过广告进行营销的，以及这些广告对消费者产生的影响。基于讨论内容，使用练习 A 中表示因果关系的词语，在一张纸上为每个产品写出 5 个句子。最后，将你们的想法分享给另一组同学。

The first product we discussed was an exercise shoe. Every ad shows young, thin women who are very pretty wearing the shoes. They have handsome boyfriends, and they seem very happy. Consequently, when I see the advertisements, I always think I should buy the shoes.

练习 3.2 更多练习：过渡词语

A 下列句子介绍了一些广告手法及其对消费者的购买决定所产生的影响。将左侧的原因和右侧的结果对应起来。

Causes	Effects
1 Advertisements equate high prices with effectiveness.	<u>1</u> a Consumers end up buying expensive brands.
2 Some advertisements target children.	____ b Consumers buy more than they need.
3 Prices for large quantities of food are discounted.	____ c Consumers sometimes buy products that might not be good for them.
4 Advertisements often show beautiful people.	____ d Children start to become consumers early.
5 Sometimes ads do not focus on the ill effects of the products.	____ e Consumers believe the products will make them beautiful, too.

B 用 as a consequence，as a result，consequently 和 therefore 将练习 A 中的每对句子组合起来。每个过渡词语只能使用一次。

1 *Advertisements equate high prices with effectiveness. As a result, consumers end up buying more expensive brands.*

2 _____

_____

3 _____

_____

4 _____

_____

5 _____

_____

C 小组活动 在小组内讨论你们最近的购买行为。什么因素影响了你们的购买决定？基于讨论内容，用 as a consequence，as a result，for this reason，therefore 等过渡词语写出 5 个句子，并将这些句子分享给另一个小组。

A friend of Amy's daughter had her ears pierced recently. For this reason, Amy's daughter wanted to get her ears pierced, too.

Julia Rozzio watched a very funny commercial about electric cars. As a result, when it was time to buy a new car, she decided to buy an electric one.

4 用名词表示结果的常用句式

词汇讲解

在因果关系型写作中，常用一些含有名词 effect 和 result 的表达来表示结果。	Advertising **can have a big effect on** children and teens. The increase in sales **is a direct result of** our ad campaign.

4.1 含有 effect 和 result 的表达

A 含有名词 effect 的表达常用于以下句式中：

名词短语　　名词短语
The / One effect of _____ on _____ is
名词短语
_____.

名词短语　　　　　　　名词短语
_____ have an effect on _____.

One effect of advertising **on** the public **is** overconsumption.

Advertising **can have a** significant **effect on** children and teens.

B 含有名词 result 的表达常用于以下句式中：

名词短语　　　　　　名词短语
_____ is a result of _____.

从句　　　　　　　名词短语
When / If _____, the result is _____.

名词短语
_____ have a result.

Overconsumption **is a** predictable **result of** consumers' unawareness of sophisticated advertising techniques.
When / If consumers are unaware of their behavior, **the** primary **result may be** overconsumption.
Consumer awareness of advertising techniques often **has a** positive **result**.

📊 实际使用数据分析

最常与 effect 连用的词有： no, little, significant, some	Research suggests that advertising has **little effect** on a family's food budget.
最常与 result 连用的词有： direct, positive, predictable, primary	Women's desire to be thin is a **direct result** of advertising.

词汇应用

练习 4.1　用名词表示结果的常用句式

A　下文谈到了在职父母的消费行为。从方框中选择正确的选项填空。在必要的地方添加恰当的标点符号。

a direct result can be	one effect of	effect on
a positive effect on	effect of	~~have a significant effect on~~

These days, both parents work full-time in many families. This fact can ¹ *have a significant effect on* their consumer behavior. In general, too, the behavioral change will have ² _____ the economy. Parents with full-time jobs may not have time to cook dinner when they get home from work. As a result, they may spend more money in restaurants than families with non-working parents do. Dual-income families may eat out a lot or bring prepared food home. Some parents who work full-time may want to spend a lot of time with their children when they are not working. ³ _____ that they do special activities with their children that cost money. For example, they might take their children to amusement parks or go to the movies with them on the weekends. Some parents may also have to wear business attire for their jobs, which has an ⁴ _____ their clothing expenses. Another ⁵ _____ a dual-income lifestyle may be higher commuting expenses. The working parents may have two cars or pay twice the amount in public transportation costs. In sum, ⁶ _____ a dual-income lifestyle is that it will benefit the economy.

B **结对练习** 用含有表示结果的名词的常用句式，搭配恰当的形容词，回答下列关于父母的消费行为的问题，并将你的回答分享给同伴。

1 How does having two working parents in a family affect the family's consumer behavior?

One positive effect of working parents on children is that the children need to become more responsible.

2 How does the fact that working parents may not have time to cook dinner affect their lives?

3 What effect can having a dual income have on entertainment expenses?

4 How might working parents' jobs affect a family's clothing expenses?

5 How does a dual-income lifestyle affect a family's commuting expenses?

练习 4.2 更多练习：用名词表示结果的常用句式

A 使用含有 effect 和 result 的表达，并从"实际使用数据分析"中选用恰当的形容词或限定词，回答下列关于消费者行为的问题。

1 Some stores, especially clothing stores, play loud music. If a store plays loud music, does the store have a positive or negative effect on you? Why? Would you walk into the store or not?

Music always has a positive effect on me. If I like the music, then I'll go into the store.

2 Do brand names have a significant effect on your decision to buy clothes? Why or why not?

3 Why do some people prefer to buy expensive brands? What is it a direct result of? Explain your opinion.

4 What do you think the primary result of advertising is on young children?

5 What kind of effect do consumer reviews on websites have on you as a consumer?

6 Why are some people thrifty? What could it be the result of?

B **小组活动** 将你的回答分享给小组成员，讨论出大家都一致同意的答案，并将讨论结果分享给全班同学。

5 常见错误提示

1 注意区分 affect 和 effect：affect 几乎总是用作动词；effect 几乎总是用作名词。

Product placement in movies usually has a strong ~~affect~~ ^effect^ on sales.

2 在含有 cause，result 和 effect 的表达中，注意使用正确的介词。

Cartoon characters in ads have a significant effect ~~in~~ ^on^ children.

As a result ~~on~~ ^of^ advertising on Saturday mornings, the company reached their target market – children.

3 注意区分 because 和 because of：because 后接主语和动词；because of 后接名词短语。

Advertisers are coming up with new ways to market products because ~~of~~ young consumers are paying less attention to ads.

Advertisers are coming up with new ways to market products because ^of^ young people's disinterest in ads.

改错练习

下面是一篇文章的主体段落，文章谈论了有效的广告宣传活动。从中找出另外 6 处错误并改正。

Overexposure to advertising has gradually resulted ~~on~~ ^in^ consumer inattention. In fact, studies have shown that most advertisements have little affect in consumers. One way in which manufacturers are responding to this problem is by a technique known as product placement. Rather than spending money on

5 advertisements that consumers ignore, companies place their products in TV shows or films. For example, characters drink a particular brand of soda, drive a particular type of car, or use a certain computer. An example of successful product placement is the use of Apple products in various TV shows and films. In 2010, Apple's products were present in 30 percent of that year's top 33 films.

10 This resulted on increased sales for Apple because product placement. Product placement has a second beneficial affect. Placing products in movies and TV shows allows film companies to lower production costs because of they can use products for free. For example, the TV show *My Fair Wedding* features several jewelry and makeup brands in each episode. Without product placement,

15 producers might have to purchase the jewelry and makeup. As a result on using product placement, the show's producers use the jewelry and makeup for free.

原因和结果 3：真实条件句和非真实条件句；含有 if 和 unless 的常用表达

Social Responsibility

1 现实生活中的语法

阅读这篇谈论企业承担社会责任的意义的文章。文章描述了一个原因及其对应的多个结果，是一篇因果关系型写作的范例。

A 读前准备 你认为企业履行社会责任意味着什么？企业可以如何帮助当地社区？阅读文章并思考：在作者看来，企业承担社会责任的好处是什么？

B 阅读理解 回答下列问题。

1 According to the writer, how can corporate social responsibility benefit the community?

2 Why does the writer argue that it is important that companies implement green policies?

3 Explain this sentence in the last paragraph: "Supporters say that it is not just that a company makes money, but how it makes money."

C 语法发现 按照下列提示，找出说明原因和描述结果的句子并回答问题。

1 在第 1 段中找到含有 if 从句的句子，这个句子包含了原因和结果。描述结果的是 if 从句还是主句？作者对于结果有多确定？主句中的哪个单词表明了确定程度？

2 在第 5 段中画出含有 if 从句的句子，并将这句话的含义与 1 中的句子进行比较。哪句话描述的结果更有可能发生？为什么？

3 阅读第 4 段第 38—43 行的句子，将含有 when 的句子与其后含有 if 的句子进行比较。哪句话所描述的结果更有可能发生？哪些单词给出了线索？

CORPORATE SOCIAL RESPONSIBILITY:
The Wave of the Future

Most managers would be in agreement that the main goal of a modern company is to make a profit. If a company does not make money, it will go out of business. In addition,

5 while pursuing profit, companies should be ethical in their business practices. However, more and more people believe that the ethical pursuit of profit is no longer enough for modern companies. They argue that

10 companies should also incorporate a strong sense of corporate social responsibility. This means managing a business while attempting to have a positive impact on the community. There are many reasons why companies may

15 choose to embrace social responsibility.

According to proponents of corporate social responsibility, if companies make socially responsible decisions, they can improve life in the community. For example, companies can

20 make an impact on a local community when they sponsor local cultural events or science fairs for high school students. To make a broader impact, companies can give money to charitable organizations that are connected to

25 the core beliefs of the company. An example

---

[1] ally: a person, country, or organization that provides help and support 盟友，支持者；同盟国

---

of this is People Water, which helps develop and support clean water programs around the world. Companies can also try to improve public policy. For instance, they may stop doing

30 business with companies that use child labor, even if that means higher manufacturing costs and lower profits.

Corporate social responsibility can also benefit the environment. For example,

35 companies can implement green policies, such as restricting printing to important documents, buying locally grown products, or conducting an electronics recycling fair. When companies conduct their business with an awareness of

40 the environment, they set an example for the community. If these policies are part of the culture of the company, employees are likely to follow them outside the workplace.

Finally, if a company makes social

45 responsibility part of its corporate mission, it can potentially have a better public image. A socially responsible company will be seen as an ally[1] of the community. This positive public image may set the company apart from

50 its competitors. It will also attract investors, which will improve the company's finances. Companies like Patagonia, Inc. are very aware of this benefit. They hire executives to focus on corporate social responsibility throughout

55 the business.

Many companies see the value of corporate social responsibility for the community as well as for their own organization. However, corporate social responsibility could play a

60 role in every company. Supporters say that it is not just that a company makes money, but how it makes money. They argue that if more companies embraced corporate social responsibility, there would be more instances of

65 positive social change in the world.

2 表示现在和将来的真实条件句

语法讲解

表示现在和将来的真实条件句（present and future real conditionals）可以描述现在和将来可能发生的情况及其可能的结果。学术写作中常用这两类条件句来表示因果关系。	Companies **improve** life in the community **if** they **are** socially responsible. **If** companies **follow** green policies, they **will set** a good example for their employees.

2.1 表示现在的真实条件句

表示现在的真实条件句的构成： if 从句（现在时）+ 主句（现在时）	if 从句（现在时） If companies **donate** to charity programs, 主句（现在时） they **set** good examples for other companies.
if 从句可置于主句之前或之后。if 从句在主句之前时，使用逗号将其与主句分隔开；if 从句在主句之后时，不使用逗号。 注意：可以在主句的开头使用 then，句意不变。	Companies **set** a good example for other companies if they **donate** to charity programs. If companies donate to charity programs, **then** they set a good example for other companies.

2.2 表示现在的真实条件句的用法

A 表示现在的真实条件句可用于描述普遍真理、习惯、惯例和科学事实。	If companies **recycle**, employees generally **recycle**, too.
B 在真实条件句中，if 从句用于描述主句中的行为或事件（即结果）发生所必需的行为或事件（即条件）。	if 从句：条件 If companies **contribute** to charity, 主句：结果 many programs **benefit**.
C 当所述事件为一般事实或惯例时，可以使用 when 或 whenever 代替 if。	Companies **help** the community **if** / **when** / **whenever** they are socially responsible.

2.3 表示将来的真实条件句

A 表示将来的真实条件句的构成：
if 从句（现在时）+ 主句（be going to / 情态动词 + 动词原形）

if 从句可置于主句之前或之后。if 从句在主句之前时，使用逗号将其与主句分隔开。

if 从句（现在时）
If we get a tax refund this year,
主句（be going to + 动词原形）
(then) we **are going to buy** an electric car.
主句（情态动词 + 动词原形）
We **will / might buy** a hybrid car
if 从句（现在时）
if we get a tax refund this year.

B if 从句用于描述将来可能会发生的情况（即条件），主句用于描述可能会产生的结果。

条件　　　　　　　　结果
If I get a raise, we will be able to buy a new car.

2.4 表示将来的真实条件句的用法

A 表示将来的真实条件句可用于表示预测。这类条件句可以描述将来可能发生的情况及其可能的结果。

If a company **does not make** a profit, it **will go** bankrupt.

B 主句中可以使用不同的情态动词。情态动词的选择可以表明结果发生的可能性有多大。

will = 确定的

If a company has a good public image, it **will** attract investors.

can / could = 可能的

If a company addresses social responsibility, it **can** result in a better public image.

should = 很有可能的

If the company installs solar panels at its factories, this **should** cut energy costs in half within two years.

may / might = 不确定的

Employees **might** consider ways to make their companies greener if they receive rewards for their ideas.

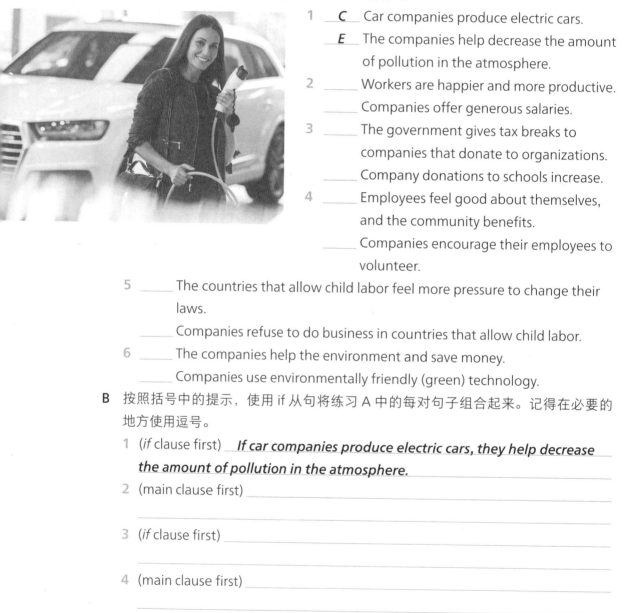

语法应用

练习 2.1 表示现在的真实条件句

A 下列每对句子都描述了公司承担社会责任的方式（条件）及其对应的结果。在描述条件的句子旁标记 C，在描述结果的句子旁标记 E。

1 **C** Car companies produce electric cars.

   E The companies help decrease the amount of pollution in the atmosphere.

2 _____ Workers are happier and more productive.

   _____ Companies offer generous salaries.

3 _____ The government gives tax breaks to companies that donate to organizations.

   _____ Company donations to schools increase.

4 _____ Employees feel good about themselves, and the community benefits.

   _____ Companies encourage their employees to volunteer.

5 _____ The countries that allow child labor feel more pressure to change their laws.

   _____ Companies refuse to do business in countries that allow child labor.

6 _____ The companies help the environment and save money.

   _____ Companies use environmentally friendly (green) technology.

B 按照括号中的提示，使用 if 从句将练习 A 中的每对句子组合起来。记得在必要的地方使用逗号。

1 (*if* clause first) ***If car companies produce electric cars, they help decrease the amount of pollution in the atmosphere.***

2 (main clause first) _____

   _____

3 (*if* clause first) _____

   _____

4 (main clause first) _____

   _____

5 (*if* clause first) _____

   _____

6 (main clause first) _____

   _____

C 结对练习 和同伴轮流朗读练习 B 中的句子。使用 when 或 whenever 替换 if，与同伴讨论句子的意思是否发生了改变并说明理由。

练习 2.2 表示将来的真实条件句

A Johnny 的鸡肉餐厅销售业绩不佳，下面是一些提高销量的建议。将左侧建议的做法与右侧的结果对应起来。

Suggested Actions

<u> f </u> **1** Offer inexpensive lunch specials.

_____ **2** Donate the profit of a sandwich to a nonprofit organization.

_____ **3** Have some vegetarian choices.

_____ **4** Create a website.

_____ **5** Install energy-efficient ovens.

_____ **6** Use bikes – not cars – to deliver food.

_____ **7** Buy local produce.

Results

a Save money on gas.

b Attract customers who don't eat meat.

c Lower its electricity bills.

d Show people that it supports local farmers.

e Improve its public image.

f See an increase in its lunch business.

g Get more online orders.

B 使用表示将来的真实条件句和最能表达括号中含义的情态动词，将练习 A 中的每对句子组合起来，为餐厅写出改进建议。

1 (strong possibility) ___*If the company offers inexpensive lunch specials, it should see an increase in its lunch business.*___

2 (possible) _____

3 (strong possibility) _____

4 (not certain) _____

5 (possible) _____

6 (certain) _____

7 (certain) _____

C 结对练习 和同伴一起想出一个目前业绩不佳的公司，在一张纸上列出导致现状的 3 条原因，并写出相应的建议。使用表示将来的真实条件句和恰当的情态动词来表明你们对这些建议是否会奏效的确定程度。接下来，与另一组同学交换句子，阅读他们给出的原因和建议。你们同意他们的想法吗？解释你们的观点。

For the problem of rude waiters, your suggestion is If you train your waiters to be kind and helpful, your business will improve. *We agree that training is helpful, but we think* could *is more accurate because we don't think training is enough to change people's behavior. We believe that employees will change if they also feel respected by management.*

3 表示现在和将来的非真实条件句

语法讲解

表示现在和将来的非真实条件句（present and future unreal conditionals）可以描述非真实的、想象的情况及其对应的结果。在因果关系型写作中，可以用非真实条件句提出不大可能发生的条件并预测在该条件下会产生的结果。	If employees became involved in the community, they would feel good about themselves. If the restaurant donated money to a community organization, its public image would improve.

3.1 表示现在和将来的非真实条件句

A 非真实条件句的构成： if 从句（过去时）+ 主句（情态动词 + 动词原形） 主句中最常用的情态动词是 would。 if 从句可置于主句之前或之后。只有当 if 从句在主句之前时，才需要使用逗号将其与主句分隔开。	if 从句（过去时） If we **were** socially responsible, 主句（情态动词 + 动词原形） we **would** attract more customers. Charitable programs **would** help more people if more companies **contributed** to their programs.
B 在正式书面语中，单数主语（包括 I）后使用 were，而不使用 was。在口语和非正式书面语中，更常用 was。	正式用法：If I **were** socially responsible, I would recycle. 常见用法：If I **was** socially responsible, I would recycle.
C 可以在主句中使用的情态动词有 would，might 和 could： would 用于表示较为确定或期待的结果，常用于非真实条件句中。 might 和 could 用于表示不太确定的结果。 could not 用于表示不可能的结果。	Communities **would** benefit if more companies donated time and money to local charities. If your company advertised more, you **might** get more business. If the organization did not receive donations, it **could not** exist.

3.2 表示现在和将来的非真实条件句的用法

A 在非真实条件句中，if 从句用于描述非真实的或想象的情况，这种情况在现在或将来可能会发生，但发生的可能性较小。主句用于描述这种情况对应的结果。	if 从句：条件 If the company **used** more resources on social issues, 主句：结果 it **would** attract more investors. （公司目前没有在社会问题上使用很多资源，未来可能会，但可能性较小。）

3.2　表示现在和将来的非真实条件句的用法（续表）

B 在因果关系型写作中常用表示现在的非真实条件句来提出与现实并不一致的情况并预测其结果。

Less energy **would** be consumed in the world **if** more companies **used** green technology.
（目前使用绿色技术的公司还不够多。句子中所描述的情况与目前的实际情况不符。）

语法应用

练习 3.1　表示现在和将来的非真实条件句

A 下文就个人可以如何承担更多社会责任给出了建议，在另外 4 个表示现在的非真实条件句下面画线。

It always feels good to help other people and know that you are making a positive difference in someone's life. Here are a few tips to get you started. First, decide who you want to help. If you want to help your community, visit a local school and ask if they need help. The school would probably appreciate your
5　help. If there were more volunteers in classrooms, teachers could spend more time with students who need special help. If there's a park or other public place near you that is full of trash, get a group of friends together and volunteer to clean it up. Your actions would have a huge impact. If these places were cleaned up, more people would visit them. As a result of all these visitors, local shops
10　would get more business and hire more staff.

If you want to help people outside of your community or country, find an organization that sends money, supplies, and clothes to troubled areas. Your contributions are crucial. If these organizations didn't get donations and help, they couldn't be as effective as they are.
15　You could also spend your time or money helping an organization that works for a special cause like cancer or heart disease. If you spent time volunteering for one of these organizations, you might learn more about the organizations and find ways to help them receive more donations. These donations could be used to fund research and lead to breakthroughs or cures. If you made a donation
20　today, you would know that your money is going toward an important cause.

B　**结对练习**　与同伴互相解释你们在练习 A 中所给答案的理由。你赞同对方的答案和解释吗？

A 听一段关于如何改善社区生活的广播访谈。边听录音边针对以下问题做笔记，再根据说话者所表达的确定程度选择情态动词 would，might 或 could，使用非真实条件句回答问题。

1 Why is it important for more people to safely recycle their old electronics?

If more people safely recycled their old electronics, it would reduce
toxins in the environment.

2 Why is it important for more people to donate their old clothes to community organizations?

_____

_____

3 Why should more people volunteer at a school?

_____

_____

4 Why should teenagers volunteer?

_____

_____

5 Why should more people donate money to community organizations?

_____

_____

B **小组活动** 以小组为单位，讨论以下问题：社区可以如何鼓励人们参与解决影响生活质量的问题？社区可以如何让更多的年轻人和老年人参与其中？什么能激励居民参与进来？解释你们认为年轻人与老年人没有参与其中的原因，再写出 5 条建议来说明激励和奖励的措施。将你们的想法分享给另一个小组或全班同学。

We think that teenagers are very busy with school, so they don't have time. But
they also want to socialize and feel accepted. Teenagers would become more
involved if the
volunteering was
combined with a
social event. The
city could ...

4 含有 unless 和 if 的常用表达

词汇讲解

unless, if ... not, only if 和 even if 也可用于描述条件。	**Unless** cities require solar panels for new construction, builders may continue to use older forms of energy delivery. People will recycle **only if** it is required by law. **Even if** companies do a lot for the community, they still need to make a profit.

4.1 否定条件: unless, if ... not

unless 可用于描述现在或将来可能的、含有否定意味的条件。当条件不被满足时，不利的或令人不愉快的结果将会产生。

if 与具有否定意义的主语（例如 no one）连用以及 if ... not 这两种结构可以表达与 unless 相同的意思。

否定条件
Unless the organization gets more donations,
不利的结果
it will have to cut some programs.
Unless someone speaks up, the city will not fix the problems. (= **If no one** speaks up, the city will not fix the problems.)
Unless more employees volunteer for the event, it will be canceled. (= **If** more employees **don't** volunteer for the event, it will be canceled.)

4.2 唯一条件: only if

only if 用于表示只有当某个特定的条件成为现实时，某个结果才会产生，而其他条件下都不会产生此结果。

当 only if 引导的从句位于句首时，从句后不用逗号，而且主句中的情态动词要置于主语之前。

Consumers will change their habits **only if** prices increase dramatically.

only if + 条件   情态动词
Only if prices increase dramatically **will**
+ 主语
consumers change their habits.

4.3 强调条件: even if

even if 强调条件并不重要。无论条件是否实现或被满足，结果都不会改变。

相比之下，if 从句表示期待改变的发生。

even if + 条件
Even if many people start driving electric cars,
不变的结果
the country's energy needs will not decrease.
（尽管条件实现了，但期待的改变仍不会发生。）
if + 条件   期待的结果
If many people start driving electric cars, the country's energy needs will be lower.（我们期待这个改变的发生。）

练习 4.1 unless，only if，even if

A 下列句子描述了一家重视社会责任的零售公司的退款和换货规定。用 unless，only if 和 even if 填空。

1 ___*Even if*___ the product is broken, offer to exchange the item for another one.

2 The customer can exchange the product _____ he or she has bought the item within the last 60 days. If it is more than 60 days, get a manager's approval before you make the exchange.

3 Offer an exchange first _____ the customer appears upset and asks for the money right away. In that case, give them the money.

4 _____ the customer has a receipt can you offer an exchange. Do not offer one otherwise.

5 Do not offer the customer a store credit _____ the product is in good condition because we need to be able to resell it.

6 Give a cash refund _____ the customer refuses an exchange and a store credit. In general, try to avoid giving full cash refunds.

7 You cannot give a full cash refund _____ you have approval from a manager. His or her approval is required.

8 _____ the customer becomes upset, stay calm and patiently explain that you are doing everything you can to help him or her.

B **结对练习** 用 if ... not 改写上面含有 unless 的句子。改写时需要对一些词进行调整。

练习 4.2 更多练习：unless，only if，even if

结合你对于所居住城市的社会责任的看法，写出表示条件或结果的分句，补全下列句子。在必要的地方使用 unless，even if 和 only if。

1 Unless the city provides free recycling pick-up, _____.

2 Even if people recycle, _____.

3 If the city doesn't clean up the parks, _____.

4 Only if the city adds more buses and subway trains, _____.

5 _____ will people volunteer in the community.

6 _____, there will continue to be crime downtown.

7 _____, children won't have a safe place to play.

8 _____, people will continue to throw litter on the streets.

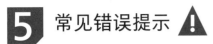 **常见错误提示**

1 在 if 从句中，主语和谓语动词的单复数形式注意保持一致。

                                          buys

The restaurant will have more customers if it ~~buy~~ local produce.

2 注意在情态动词之后使用动词原形。

                              make

If a company improves its image, It can ~~makes~~ a higher profit.

3 在真实和非真实条件句中，注意使用情态动词的正确形式。

                                        will

真实条件句：If companies use recycled paper, they ~~would~~ save money.

                          would

非真实条件句：Telecommuting ~~will~~ work if employees had laptops.

4 不要混淆 unless 和 otherwise。

                                    unless

Our dependence on oil will not decrease ~~otherwise~~ we start making more electric cars.

改错练习

下面是一篇文章的主体段落，文章描述了公司可以如何作出改变来承担更多社会责任。从中找出另外 7 处错误并改正。

Making a Better World

                                        create

    If a company allows telecommuting, it can ~~creates~~ a better working lifestyle for its employees and a better world. If a business have a telecommuting program, it not only improves the environment, but also improves the quality of life for its employees. Take, for example, an employee who usually drives to

5 the office. If he or she can works from home a few days a week, there is one less car on the road. This reduces the levels of carbon dioxide in the air. If there is less carbon dioxide, there would be less pollution in the future. Telecommuting also improves the communities that employees live in. Often employees are too busy to get involved in their communities. If employees spent fewer hours at the office,

10 they will spend more time in their communities. Employees can gets involved in local programs if they can structure their own working days. For example, many telecommuters cannot volunteer in local schools or other neighborhood activities otherwise they have some free time during the week. If more companies offered telecommuting, both the environment and our communities will benefit.

原因和结果 4：表示因果关系的现在分词短语和动词

Alternative Energy Sources

1 现实生活中的语法

阅读这篇关于太阳能的文章，文章论述了多个因果关系。为了让读者相信太阳能是一种优质的替代能源，作者引用了一些专家的观点。

A 读前准备 石油、天然气、煤炭等传统能源的优点和缺点分别是什么？阅读文章并思考：作者认为太阳能的优点是什么？

B 阅读理解 回答下列问题。

1 Why does the writer believe that it is important to switch from traditional energy sources to alternative energy sources, such as solar power?

2 What is the difference between renewable and nonrenewable resources? Give examples.

3 Does the writer believe that solar energy is a feasible alternative to traditional energy sources? Explain.

C 语法发现 按照下列提示，找出并试着理解描述因果关系的现在分词短语。

1 阅读第 45—49 行和第 54—56 行的句子，这两个句子各包含一个描述结果的分词短语。圈出作者用来引出结果的单词。

2 注意 1 中所圈单词之后的动词 -ing 形式，在该动词及其宾语下面画线，并试着用 as a result 将每个短语改写为句子。

3 再次阅读最后一段第 1 个句子中的现在分词短语。这个短语描述的是原因还是结果？其位置与 1 中分词短语的有何不同？

Making the Dream a Reality:
NEVER RUNNING OUT OF ENERGY

The demand for energy is always increasing. Currently, electricity is produced mainly with nonrenewable fossil fuels, such as coal, oil, and natural gas. Although

5 this use of fossil fuels can meet the world's current energy needs, it can potentially lead to negative consequences. These may include global warming, scarcity of[1] resources, and high prices. Environmental analysts warn

10 us that the reserves of oil in the world are gradually shrinking. Fortunately, there are other alternatives for energy sources. Many experts note that solar energy is one excellent substitute because it is feasible[2] to

15 use and is a clean source of energy.

Solar energy is feasible for several reasons. There are already solar thermal[3] power stations located in many places in the world, including in the United States, Spain,

20 Australia, South Africa, and India. In these power stations, solar energy is converted into thermal energy, providing hot water and heat for homes and offices. Representatives in the solar energy industry point out that the

25 cost of producing solar energy is decreasing. For example, it costs around $50 to produce a mega-watt hour of electricity through solar power, compared with about $100 to produce a mega-watt hour from coal. This

30 lower cost for solar energy is encouraging because it may signal the start of a change in the way we power not only our buildings, but our vehicles, too. This lower cost for solar energy will make it easier to use in more

35 places in the future.

In addition to its feasibility, solar energy is very clean, unlike fossil fuels. It does not create pollution like coal, gas, and oil. It is true that many other materials can also

40 produce energy, such as recycled automobile tires and aluminum cans. However, these materials are nonrenewable and create pollution. Solar energy consumes far fewer nonrenewable materials, making less of an

45 impact on the environment. For example, solar energy uses long-lasting solar panels to convert energy from sunlight, thereby reducing our dependence on coal, oil, and gas.

50 Being such a clean energy, solar energy is a sensible alternative to fossil fuels. It reduces our dependence on imported fuels and improves the quality of the air we breathe. The world needs energy sources

55 like solar energy that can save resources, thus preserving the environment. The rise of renewable sources of energy – solar, wind, and water energy in particular – shows that we are gradually finding ways to avoid

60 running out of energy. The United Nations Environment Programme stated that in 2017 more energy from solar power was created than any other type of energy. There is therefore reason to hope that renewables

65 will eventually win the battle against nonrenewables.

---

[1]**scarcity of**: lack of 不足，短缺
[2]**feasible**: possible to succeed 可行的
[3]**thermal**: related to or caused by heat 热的；热量的；由热引起的

2 表示结果的现在分词短语

语法讲解

现在分词短语以动词 -ing 形式开头，可在学术写作中表示结果。	Solar energy is converted into thermal energy, **providing hot water and heat for homes**. Nuclear plants are expensive to build, **limiting their desirability**.

2.1 表示结果的现在分词短语

A 表示结果的现在分词短语常置于独立分句之后。	独立分句 Solar energy is very clean, 现在分词短语 **causing less pollution**.
B 现在分词短语和独立分句之间用逗号隔开。	The government is investing large sums of money in alternative energy projects, **creating thousands of new jobs**.

2.2 表示结果的现在分词短语的用法

A 现在分词短语可用于表示独立分句中所描述情况或动作的影响或结果。	原因 Some countries give tax credits for wind energy, 影响／结果 **lowering costs for consumers**.
B 可以用 thus 或 thereby 引出现在分词短语，以强调独立分句与现在分词短语之间的因果关系。	The manufacturing of solar energy systems can create jobs, **thus** <u>stimulating the economy</u>. Most solar panels have no moving parts, **thereby** <u>lowering maintenance costs</u>.

语法应用

练习 2.1　表示结果的现在分词短语

A 听一段关于风能的讲座，将下列表示原因和结果的句子对应起来。

	Causes		Effects

<table>
<tr><td>d 1</td><td>Wind power costs about the same as coal and oil.</td><td>a</td><td>It provides low cost power to everyone.</td></tr>
<tr><td>2</td><td>The technology of wind power is improving.</td><td>b</td><td>It is a steady source of power.</td></tr>
<tr><td></td><td></td><td>c</td><td>It reduces air pollution.</td></tr>
<tr><td>3</td><td>Wind power will not involve many costs in the near future.</td><td>d̸</td><td>This makes it an affordable source of alternative energy.</td></tr>
<tr><td>4</td><td>Wind power produces zero carbon dioxide emissions.</td><td>e</td><td>It lowers the costs even further</td></tr>
<tr><td>5</td><td>Wind energy is renewable.</td><td></td><td></td></tr>
</table>

B 用表示结果的现在分词短语将练习 A 中的每对句子组合起来。记得在分词短语前使用逗号。

1 *Wind power costs about the same as coal and oil, making it an affordable source of alternative energy.*

2 _____

3 _____

4 _____

5 _____

练习 2.2 更多练习：表示结果的现在分词短语

A 下列是关于替代能源的句子。在表示原因的句子旁标记 C，在表示结果的句子旁标记 E。

1 **C** Solar energy technology continues to improve.

  E Solar energy provides more efficient and cost-effective choices.

2 _____ Solar energy reduces noise pollution.

  _____ Solar cells are silent when collecting energy.

3 _____ Solar energy helps keep our air clean.

  _____ Solar energy does not release any harmful gases into the atmosphere.

4 _____ Homeowners can sell excess electricity they create through solar energy.

  _____ Homeowners can produce extra income with no extra effort.

5 _____ Governments often give tax credits for solar power generation.

  _____ Tax credits lower the cost of installing a solar energy system.

6 _____ Solar energy provides a long-term source of energy.

  _____ Solar energy exists in the sunlight we enjoy every day.

7 _____ Wind power is another clean source of energy.

  _____ Wind power offers another renewable option for our future energy needs.

B 结对练习 在一张纸上，用 thus / thereby 和现在分词短语将练习 A 中的每对句子组合起来，并与同伴对比写好的句子。

1 *Solar energy technology continues to improve, thereby providing more efficient and cost-effective choices.*

3 表示原因的现在分词短语

语法讲解

在学术写作中，可以用现在分词短语表示原因或理由。	Producing very little waste, solar power creates an environmentally friendly source of energy. Being such a new technology, solar energy is still in the development stage in many countries.

3.1 表示原因的现在分词短语

A 表示原因或理由的现在分词短语几乎总置于独立分句之前。	Providing an almost unlimited clean source of electricity, solar energy will certainly grow in importance.
B 现在分词短语中省略的主语必须与独立分句的主语相同。	Being widely accessible, <u>hot rocks</u> deep in the earth could be an unlimited source of energy.
C 注意不要混淆现在分词短语与动名词。 动名词可以作句子的主语或宾语。	现在分词短语 Investing in alternative sources of energy, the country will be ready for increases in oil prices. 动名词短语 Investing in solar energy was once considered a high risk.

3.2 表示原因的现在分词短语的用法

A 现在分词短语可用于表示独立分句中所描述的情况或动作的理由或原因。	理由 / 原因 Using wind energy, 结果 we can lower the cost of electricity for consumers.
B 可以用介词 by 或 in 引出现在分词短语，以强调现在分词短语与独立分句之间的因果关系。by 的使用频率比 in 高。	原因　　　　　　　　结果 By <u>using solar energy</u>, we can reduce our ecological footprint. In <u>cutting tax credits for alternative energy</u>, the government has increased our dependence on fossil fuel.

 语法应用

练习 3.1　表示原因的现在分词短语

A 阅读这篇关于节约家庭能源的网络文章，在表示原因的现在分词短语下面画线，并圈出表示结果的现在分词短语。

Tips for Saving Energy

Many people want to save energy in their homes, but they're not sure how. The truth is there are several simple ways to begin saving energy and money. First, people can keep their appliances unplugged when they're not in use, decreasing small amounts of energy use with each unplugged appliance. In taking that simple step, some consumers have saved hundreds of dollars in energy costs in a single year. Along the same lines, people should not leave the lights on when they're not in a room. By making this change, people can easily save a few dollars a month on their energy bills. Also, by purchasing and installing energy-efficient appliances, people can reduce their energy use. These appliances may cost more money to buy. However, they save consumers money in the long run, using less electricity than regular appliances. Keeping doors and windows closed, people can reduce their use of air conditioning and heating. By setting thermostats lower while they are away or sleeping, people can reduce their energy costs by up to 10 percent. All consumers should take these simple steps, making a positive difference in energy use and reducing electricity bills.

B　结对练习　向同伴解释你在练习 A 中所给答案的理由。

I circled "decreasing small amounts of energy use with each unplugged appliance" because it describes the effect of unplugging appliances when they are not in use.

练习 3.2　更多练习：表示原因的现在分词短语

A　结合练习 3.1 中的信息或自己的想法，用现在分词短语及括号中的介词补全下列关于节能的句子。记得在分词短语之后用逗号。

1　(*by*) ___***By using dimmers and timers for all the lighting,***___ hospitals can bring their energy costs down.

2　(*in*) _____ restaurants can reduce their use of electricity.

3　(*by*) _____ hotels would be able to reduce energy costs.

4　(*by*) _____ offices could reduce waste and energy bills.

5　(*in*) _____ airports might be able to reduce their energy costs.

6　(*by*) _____ schools could probably reduce their energy bills.

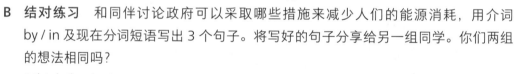

B　结对练习　和同伴讨论政府可以采取哪些措施来减少人们的能源消耗，用介词 by / in 及现在分词短语写出 3 个句子。将写好的句子分享给另一组同学。你们两组的想法相同吗？

I think that by increasing taxes on energy use, people will want to use energy more efficiently.

4 表示因果关系的动词

词汇讲解

在学术写作中，常用 cause，lead to，produce，contribute to，result in 和 result from 这些动词和动词短语来表示因果关系。	Curiously, increases in efficiency may have **led to** greater demand. Higher gas prices have **contributed to** more consumer awareness of energy issues.

4.1 表示因果关系的动词

A cause 可用于主动语态或被动语态（be + caused + by），常用于谈论灾难、危机等负面事件。

The accident **caused** a shutdown of the plant's central operations.
The slow development of alternative energy is **caused by** cheap oil.

B lead to 和 produce 也可用于表示因果关系。与 cause 相比，它们的语气更加中性，可用于讨论正面或负面的事件。

New laws **have led to** an increase in wind-generated electricity.
Overreliance on fossil fuels **could produce** an uncertain future for all of us.

C contribute to 用于表示多个原因中的一个原因。

Pollution **contributes to** many health problems.
Increased use of wind power **contributes** directly **to** a cleaner environment.

D result in 和 result from 也可用于表示因果关系。result in 用于引出结果；result from 用于引出原因。

　　　　原因　　　　　　　　　结果
Strict standards for cars **will result in** a reduction in energy use.
　　　　　结果　　　　　　　　　　原因
A reduction in energy use **will result from** strict standards for cars.

词汇应用

练习 4.1 表示因果关系的常用动词

使用括号中的表达改写下列关于能源的句子。

1 The sharp increase in oil prices in the 1970s created a surge in state-funded energy research and development. (*result in*)
   The sharp increase in oil prices in the 1970s resulted in a surge in state-funded energy research and development.

2 Growing concerns about environmental issues were a factor in the government's decision in the 1970s to promote alternative energy sources. (*contribute to*)

3 Increase in oil supplies and falling prices in the 1980s were partly a result of a reduction in U.S. rules requiring more fuel-efficient cars. (*result from*)

4 An increase in fossil fuel usage and nuclear plants was a result of a lack of consistent solar and wind energy supplies. (*was caused by*)

5 In the future, hydrogen-based energy sources could give us pollution-free cities. (*lead to*)

_____

6 Continued overreliance on oil could create political conflicts in the future. (*cause*)

_____

练习 4.2　更多练习：表示因果关系的常用动词

A 阅读下列关于国际能源问题的句子，圈出正确的选项。

1 The Japanese nuclear power plant accident in 2011 (resulted in) / was caused by widespread protests against nuclear plants.

2 Japan's position as the world's leading manufacturer of household solar technology **was a result of / produced** the Japanese government's financial assistance for solar roof panels in 1994.

3 High energy needs and low energy production **were caused by / contributed to** Japan's interest in renewable energy sources.

4 In Denmark, a high tax on electricity **produced / resulted from** an incentive for consumers to use less energy.

5 Denmark's interest in reducing dependence on foreign fossil fuels **resulted from / led to** the country's commitment to using natural sources of energy.

6 In Italy, a lack of natural resources **resulted in / resulted from** a need to import foreign electricity.

7 A desire to reduce use of foreign electricity **has been caused by / has contributed to** Italy's current focus on energy efficiency.

B **结对练习**　和同伴讨论其他国家经历过的能源危机，用练习 A 中横线上的表达解释其中的因果关系。

In Ecuador in 2009 and 2010, there was an energy crisis. Severe droughts resulted in very low water levels at hydroelectric plants. This led to many blackouts.

5 常见错误提示

1 注意用 result in，而非 result of，引出结果。

The increased demand for oil has resulted ~~of~~ _in_ higher prices for gas.

2 注意用 result from，而非 result by，引出原因。

A decrease in carbon dioxide emissions will result ~~by~~ _from_ an increase in electric cars.

3 注意要用 contribute to，而不要用 contribute for。

The use of solar energy will contribute ~~for~~ _to_ a healthier environment.

4 用 contribute to 时，主语和谓语动词的单复数形式注意保持一致。

This factor ~~contribute~~ _contributes_ to climate change.

改错练习

在下面关于替代能源的段落中，找出另外 5 处错误并改正。

Rising awareness of the dangers of carbon emissions and the limits of our natural resources has contributed ~~for~~ _to_ some creative ideas for alternative energy sources. While most scientists think of ways to use renewable resources in the environment to make energy, others are finding ways to generate electricity from
5 the movements of the human body. Michael McAlpine of Princeton University and some of his colleagues placed a material called PZT into flexible silicone rubber sheets. The PZT-filled sheets generate an electrical current when they are bent. Bending the sheets repeatedly results of a significant amount of energy. Placing these crystals in a pair of shoes or even directly into the body could result
10 of enough electricity to charge devices like cell phones or tablets.

Our body heat can help create energy, too. For example, Belgian nanotechnology engineers built thermoelectric devices that allow a person's body heat to contribute for powering medical devices such as EKG machines and brain monitors. In 2010, engineers in Paris discovered a different way to
15 use body heat to conserve electricity. The engineers developed a system that uses geothermal technology to move heat from a metro, or subway, station to heating pipes in a public-housing project above the station. Their system resulted from a 33 percent cut in carbon dioxide emissions in the housing project's heating system. Innovative approaches like these contributes to solving our
20 ongoing need for alternative energy sources.

比较和对比 1：限制性关系从句；as ... as 表示比较；表示对比的常用表达

Family Size and Personality

1 现实生活中的语法

阅读这篇关于出生顺序的文章，文章讨论了孩子的出生顺序如何影响其成年后的性格。文章采用了分块比较法来组织观点，是一篇比较和对比型写作的范例。

A 读前准备 你有几个兄弟姐妹？你认为他们的某些性格特征和出生顺序有关吗？阅读文章并思考：根据文中的信息，出生顺序对性格的影响有多大？

B 阅读理解 回答下列问题。

1 How are former presidents Jimmy Carter, George W. Bush, and Barack Obama connected to the main idea of the text?

2 According to the writer, why are firstborn children usually more ambitious than their siblings?

3 Which of the different birth order types – firstborn, middle born, youngest, and only child – do you think has the fewest advantages in life? Explain.

C 语法发现 按照下列提示，找出并试着理解用 as ... as 表示比较和对比的句子。

1 阅读第 3 段中含有 as ... as 的句子。排行中间的孩子与先出生的孩子相比，是一样坚定、更加坚定还是没那么坚定？说明理由。

2 阅读第 4 段中含有 as ... as 的句子。最小的孩子与排行中间的孩子相比，是一样富有创造力、更有创造力还是没那么有创造力？说明理由。

3 阅读第 5 段中含有 as ... as 的句子。独生子与非独生子相比，是一样聪明、更加聪明还是没那么聪明？说明理由。

Birth Order

and Adult Sibling Relationships

What do U.S. Presidents Jimmy Carter, George W. Bush, and Barack Obama all have in common? In addition to being elected president of the United States, these men all share the same birth order. Each one is the oldest child in his family. In
5 fact, many very successful people in government and business have been "firstborn" children. While there is always some variation, some experts agree that birth order can have an influence on a person's personality in childhood and in adulthood.

Firstborn children often share several traits. First, in contrast
10 to their siblings, they are more likely to be responsible, ambitious, and authoritarian. This is probably because they are born into an environment of high expectations, and they usually receive a great deal of attention. They are used to being leaders, taking responsibility for others, and sometimes taking on an almost
15 parental role.

Middle children, on the other hand, exhibit different characteristics from firstborns. They are often not as determined as firstborns. They tend to be more passive and solitary. Having to share family attention with older and younger siblings, middle children
20 have a tendency to be more realistic, creative, and insightful.

Youngest children are often more protected than their older siblings. As a result, they are more likely to be dependent and controlling. They are often as creative as middle children, but usually more easygoing and social.
25 A child with no siblings, or an "only child," also exhibits some unique characteristics. While some parents worry that an only child will have difficulties socializing and making friends, studies show that an only child is just as intelligent, accomplished, and sociable as a child with siblings. In fact, some research indicates that
30 being an only child has some benefits. These children tend to have better vocabulary, perform better at school, and maintain closer relationships with their parents than children with siblings.

Even though it is assumed that birth order dictates some personality traits, individuals can free themselves from the roles they
35 played when they were young, but it can be difficult. According to Vikki Stark, family therapist and author of *My Sister, My Self*, change requires letting go of familiar ways of being and patiently asserting new behaviors that express one's true self.

2 限制性关系从句

语法讲解

关系从句（relative clauses）可用于修饰名词，置于所修饰名词之后。限制性关系从句（identifying relative clauses / restrictive relative clauses）用于提供关于所修饰名词的必要信息。这类从句可以在各种学术写作中使用，在比较和对比型写作中尤其实用，可用来描述被比较事物的特征。	Children who / that have no siblings are often very close to their parents. People gradually behave in ways which / that are more consistent with their preferred self-image.

2.1 限制性关系从句

A 限制性关系从句由关系代词 that，which，who，whom 或 whose 引导，用于修饰名词。 限制性关系从句给出关于主句中名词或名词短语的必要信息，说明具体所指的是哪个人或事物。如果没有限制性关系从句所提供的信息，句意将不完整。	限制性关系从句 People who do not have children may not be aware of differences in birth order. 限制性关系从句 Creativity is a trait that all middle children share.
B who，that 和 whom 用于指代人。whom 在关系从句中作宾语，非常正式。在非正式的口语和书面语中，常用 that 或 who 代替 whom。	人 Researchers who / that study families have different views. My siblings are the people in my life whom I will always trust.
C whose 表示所属关系。在学术写作中，whose 后接表示有生命或无生命事物的名词。	所属关系 Researchers whose work focuses on families disagree about the importance of birth order. She cited a study whose results supported previous research.
which 和 that 用于指代事物。在学术写作中，that 的使用频率比 which 高。	事物 The study examines characteristics that / which are common in firstborn children.

2.1 限制性关系从句（续表）

D 在限制性关系从句中，关系代词可以作动词的主语。 在限制性关系从句中，关系代词也可以作动词的宾语。 注意：关系代词作宾语时可以省略，但在学术写作中最好不要省略。关系代词作主语时不可以省略。	Psychologists <u>who</u> work with only children and their parents can help the children learn to share attention.（在关系从句中，who是动词work的主语。） There are several strategies <u>that</u> parents use to help their only children.（在关系从句中，that是动词use的宾语。） The research (that) they just published on sibling order was inconclusive.
E 在非常正式的写作中，可将介词置于从句的句首。 注意：位于介词之后的关系代词不可省略。	正式写作： An older sibling is someone on whom you can always rely. 常见用法： An older sibling is someone that / who you can always rely on. Researchers studied the ways in which parents interacted with their only child.

实际使用数据分析

在学术写作中，75% 由 whose 引导的关系从句修饰的是表示无生命事物的名词。	The report included the results of a study funded by an organization **whose** mission is to help children reach their potential.

2.2 限制性关系从句的用法

A 在比较和对比型写作中，可以用限制性关系从句来提供所修饰名词的特征等信息，以显示所比较的人或事物的不同之处。	My friend who lives in Boston always remembers my birthday, but my friend who lives in New Jersey does not. Some people like to play games that involve competition, while others like to play games that encourage collaboration.
B 关系从句与其他类型的从属分句相似，须与主句一同使用，不可单独出现，否则就是残缺句。	残缺句： A recent study reports that firstborns are generally smarter than siblings. Who are born later. 修正： A recent study reports that firstborns are generally smarter than siblings who are born later.

在学术写作中，当关系代词指代人时，who 的使用频率比 that 高。	Who	██████	
	That	███	
在口语中，当关系代词指代人时，that 的使用频率比 who 高。	Who	███	
	That	██████	

语法应用

练习 2.1 限制性关系从句

A 下面这段文字谈到了出生顺序。用 that，which，who，whom 或 whose 填空。有时正确答案不唯一。

Birth order researchers have discovered some interesting information [S] ¹ **that** can help us understand our colleagues better. Do you have a difficult boss ² _____ authoritarian personality makes your life difficult? If so, your boss might be a firstborn child. Children ³ _____ are born first are often more authoritarian than their younger siblings. Do you have a co-worker ⁴ _____ is passive, but particularly creative and insightful? This person may be a middle child. People ⁵ _____ have both older and younger siblings are often passive because their older siblings were responsible for their well-being when they were young. The creativity ⁶ _____ they exhibit might be the effect of their having spent a lot of time on their own due to having to share parental attention with their older and younger siblings. People ⁷ _____ you work with ⁸ _____ are controlling may be youngest children. These people are also likely to be more social than co-workers ⁹ _____ are middle children. Of course, these are only generalizations. There are countless factors ¹⁰ _____ help form people's personalities, but birth order research may shed some helpful light on people's behavior in the workplace.

B 观察你在练习 A 中填写的关系代词，在作主语的关系代词上方标记 S，在作宾语的关系代词上方标记 O，在表示所属关系的关系代词上方标记 P。

练习 2.2 更多练习：限制性关系从句

A 下面的句子谈论的是对父母行为的看法。用限制性关系从句将每对句子组合起来。

1 Some parents often focus too much attention on their son or daughter. These parents have only one child.

   Some parents who have only one child often focus too much attention on their son or daughter.

2 Parents put a lot of pressure on their children to do a lot of activities. These parents want their children to excel.

3 Children often feel a lot of stress. Their parents have high expectations of them.

4 Sports practice and music lessons are examples of activities. Some parents expect their children to do these activities after school.

5 Parents raise more independent adults. These parents give proper emotional support to their children.

6 Some children have behavioral problems at school. Their parents both work long hours.

B **结对练习** 向同伴讲述你是否同意练习 A 中的每个观点。如有可能，请使用限制性关系从句。

   A *I don't think it's true that parents who have only one child focus too much attention on that child. I was an only child, and I don't think that I received too much attention from my parents.*

   B *I disagree. In my experience, parents who have an only child often want to give that child everything. The child doesn't realize what it's like to share, either.*

3 as ... as 表示比较

语法讲解

| 在比较和对比型写作中，说明比较对象之间的相似点与不同点时，可以使用 as ... as。 | Some people think that youngest children might not be **as mature as** their siblings. Sometimes younger children do not get **as much attention as** their older siblings. |

3.1 as ... as

| **A** as ... as 可用于以下结构中：
(not) as + 形容词 / 副词 + as

(not) as + 名词短语 + as | 形容词
Youngest children are not as **independent** as their older siblings.
副词
An only child socializes as **well** as children with siblings.
名词短语
An only child has as **many close friends** as children with siblings. |
| **B** as ... as 也可用于比较可数名词和不可数名词的量：
(not) as much + 不可数名词短语 + as

(not) as many + 可数名词短语 + as | Younger children sometimes don't get as **much attention** from parents as firstborn children.
Growing up as an only child has as **many advantages** as growing up in a large family. |

3.2 as ... as 的用法

| as ... as 可用于
强调两个事物的相同之处：
_____ (just) as ... as _____
表明两个事物略有不同：
_____ almost / nearly / about / not quite as ... as _____
强调两个事物的不同之处：
_____ not nearly as ... as _____ | Only children usually turn out **just as well as** children from large families.
Firstborn children are **almost as open to new experiences as** their younger siblings.

Genuine concern over sibling order may **not be nearly as widespread as** it seems at first glance. |

语法应用

练习 3.1 as ... as 表示比较

A 根据表格中的信息，用 as ... as 完成下列关于性格特征和出生顺序的句子。

	Firstborn Children	Middle Children	Youngest Children
Responsible	Very	Somewhat	Not Very
Social	Somewhat	Not Very	Very
Creative	Not Very	Very	Very
Realistic	Very	Very	Not Very
Dependent	Not Very	Not Very	Very

1 Middle children ___*are not as responsible as*___ (responsible) firstborns.

2 Firstborn children _____
   (social) youngest children.

3 Middle children _____
   (creative) youngest children.

4 Youngest children _____
   (realistic) middle children.

5 Middle children _____
   (dependent) firstborn children.

6 Firstborn children _____ (realistic) middle
   children.

7 Firstborn children _____ (creative) youngest
   children.

8 Middle children _____ (dependent) youngest
   children.

B 再次阅读练习 A 中表格里的信息，想一想你自己和你熟悉的人的出生顺序。表格中的信息是否准确地描述了你和他们的性格特征？请举出例子来说明。

I'm a middle child and my brother is a firstborn child. According to the chart, I'm not as responsible as firstborn children, but actually, I'm much more responsible than my brother. Maybe it's because I was given the responsibility of taking care of everyone while my parents worked. I think I have always felt responsible for my siblings. I agree with the idea that youngest children are social. My younger brother is really outgoing and has a lot of friends ...

A Venus Williams 和 Serena Williams 是一对著名的姐妹。听一段关于她们的录音，完成表格。

	Venus Williams	Serena Williams
1 Birth date	*June 17, 1980*	
2 Height	*6'1"*	
3 Year turned professional		
4 Wimbledon singles victories (individual years)		
5 U.S. Open singles victories (individual years)		

B 根据练习 A 中的信息和下列提示，使用 as … as 短语（almost as … as, just as … as, nearly as … as 和 not quite as … as），在一张纸上写出完整的句子。有时正确答案不唯一。

1 Serena / is / tall / Venus.
   Serena is not quite as tall as Venus.

2 Serena / is / old / Venus.

3 Serena / has / experience / Venus.

4 Serena / is / important to U.S. sports / Venus.

5 Serena / has / won / Wimbledon singles / Venus.

6 Venus / is / famous / Serena.

Serena and Venus Williams

7 Serena / has had / U.S. Open singles victories / Venus.

8 Venus / has had / success in business / Serena. They are both successful businesswomen.

C 结对练习　用 as … as 比较两个你熟悉的人，并讲给同伴听，然后写出 5 个关于他们的句子。如有可能，请使用形容词、副词、名词短语以及 almost，not nearly，not quite 等词语。

Younsil does not have as many children as Victoria.

Younsil is not quite as shy as Victoria.

表示对比的常用表达

词汇讲解

在学术写作中表示对比时有一些实用的词语，包括 difference(s)，differ，in contrast 和 unlike。这些词语在比较和对比型写作中很重要。	One major difference in some cultures is the role of adult children. In contrast to the past, more U.S. children now live with their parents into their early adulthood.

4.1　difference(s)，differ，in contrast，unlike

A 名词 difference 常用于以下句式：

名词短语
The difference between _____
名词短语
and _____ is ...

One significant difference between youngest children and their older siblings is that youngest children receive a lot of attention.

B 动词 differ 常用于以下句式：

名词短语　　　　　名词短语
_____ differ(s) from _____ in that ...

The results of current research differ from earlier results in that they show a definite relationship between birth order and personality.

C 短语 in contrast 常用于以下句式：

名词短语　　独立分句
In contrast to _____ , _____ .

独立分句
In contrast, _____ .

In contrast to traditional American families, young adults from Latino culture live with their parents until marriage.
Many children without siblings receive a lot of attention. In contrast, children with siblings often share their parents' attention.

D 介词 unlike 常用于以下句式：

名词短语　　独立分句
Unlike _____ , _____ .

Unlike firstborn children, youngest children are generally very creative.

📊 实际使用数据分析

最常用于修饰 difference 的形容词和数量词有： significant, major, important, many, large, small, some, minor, cultural, regional, individual	There are many cultural differences in how parents treat their children. One major difference between the siblings is that the older ones tend to be more confident.

练习 4.1 表示对比的词汇

A 下列是关于美国儿童的句子。用方框中的单词或短语填空。

differ from	~~major difference between~~	unlike
in contrast	significantly different from	

1 One _**major difference between**_ children in the United States in 1900 and now is that children in the past didn't get a lot of individual attention from their parents, while children today get a lot of individual attention.

2 Another way that today's children are _____ children in the past is that in the past, children often worked to help their families, but children now often work for their own extra spending money.

3 Today's children also _____ children in 1900 in that they are required to attend school.

4 Children in the past often had large families with several siblings. _____, many children today have one or two siblings or are only children.

5 In 1900, children were very independent. _____ them, children today depend on their parents a lot.

B **结对练习** 与同伴在一张纸上画出下面的表格，对比在你们所熟悉的文化中 20 世纪初的儿童与当今的儿童，并写出 5 条对比信息。再用练习 A 中的词语将所填信息组成句子，分享给全班同学。

Children in the 1900s	Children Now

One major difference between young children in my native country today and in the 1900s is that in the 1900s, they used to work in factories. Today that's illegal.

5 常见错误提示

1 who 引导的关系从句不用于修饰表示无生命事物的名词。

A study ~~who~~ ^{that} showed the benefits of being an only child was published last year.

2 关系代词作主语时不可省略。

Children _∧ ^{who} have older siblings tend to be somewhat dependent.

3 在关系从句中，主语和谓语动词的单复数形式注意保持一致。

Children who ~~has~~ ^{have} siblings often become secure and confident adults.

4 注意要用 the same as，而不要用 the same than。

Middle children often have the same level of creativity ~~than~~ ^{as} youngest children.

改错练习

下面是一篇文章的主体段落，文章比较了现在与过去的家庭。从中找出另外 8 处错误并改正。

Families Past and Present

A major way that families have changed is the number of families _∧ ^{that} have
only one child. The number of families had only one child was low in the United
States in the 1950s and 1960s. However, one-child families began increasing
in the 1970s and are very common today. This is especially true in households
5 who have only one parent. One reason families are smaller is the cost of living.
It is not the same than it was 40 years ago. For example, it costs about 10 times
more to send a child to college than it did 40 years ago. As a result, many parents
choose to have only one child because they do not have
enough money for more children. In addition, attitudes
10 about only children are also not the same than attitudes
about them in the past. In the 1950s and 1960s, people
avoided having only one child. At that time, many people
thought that children did not have siblings had many
disadvantages. For example, people thought that they
15 did not learn good social skills. However, recent studies
who focus on only children show a different picture.
These studies show that only children tend to have the
same social skills than children who has siblings.

6 比较和对比 2：复杂名词短语；平行结构；常用数量词

Men, Women, and Equality

1 现实生活中的语法

阅读这篇关于性别不平等现象的文章，文章谈论了男性与女性在社会上如何被区别对待。文章采用逐点比较法来组织观点，是一篇比较和对比型写作的范例。

A **读前准备** 你认为在当今社会中是否存在男性与女性被区别对待的现象？阅读文章并思考：在作者看来，男性与女性在哪些方面受到了区别对待？

B **阅读理解** 回答下列问题。

1 According to the writer, what is gender inequality and where can it be found?

2 How does the writer say that women and men are treated differently in the workplace?

3 Give two examples of how boys and girls are treated differently in U.S. society.

C **语法发现** 按照下列提示，找出作者用平行结构对比性别差异的例子并回答问题。

1 在第 25—27 行找到描述男性在工作场所被期待具有的行为特征的句子。再在第 29—32 行找到描述女性被期待具有的行为特征的句子。作者用了几个形容词来描述男性的特征？几个形容词来描述女性的特征？这两个句子还有什么共同点？

2 在第 47—49 行找到比较男孩和女孩收到的礼物类型的句子。句子中列举了几种男孩的玩具，几种女孩的玩具？

3 在第 3 段找到对比男孩和女孩被期待具有的行为特征的句子。作者用了几个形容词来描述男孩的特征？几个形容词来描述女孩的特征？这个句子中的两个分句还有什么共同点？

Gender Inequality

WE ARE EQUAL!

Although progress has been made in recent decades, it would be wrong to think that men and women today are treated equally in the United States or in other industrialized
5 nations. Historically, men in the United States have always had more financial, legal, and political power and more job opportunities than women. However, since the 1960s, there has been a progressive increase in the number
10 of women working outside the home, running their own businesses, and participating in political life. Nevertheless, despite women's increasing participation, gender inequality can still be found in the workplace as well as
15 in cultural and social aspects of life.

Women and men are not always treated equally at work. The clearest sign of inequality in the workplace is at the top levels of management. For example, the vast
20 majority of major corporations have male CEOs (Chief Executive Officers), and most of the top positions are filled by men. Another sign of gender inequality is the different expectations employers have of men and
25 women in leadership positions. Men are usually expected to be assertive, confident, and decisive. When men take a dominant role, they are often rewarded by their employers. Assertive women, on the other hand, are
30 often not well received in the workplace because they are expected to be flexible, cooperative, and deferential.[1] There are also significant differences in salary. According to the Institute for Women's Policy Research,

35 women still make less than men even when they do the exact same job. For example, in 2016, full-time female employees made 80.5 cents compared to every dollar made by male employees or, in other words, a wage
40 difference of 20 percent.

Gender differences are found in our cultural and social lives as well. Boys and girls are taught different gender roles and social expectations from birth. For example, in the
45 United States many baby boys still receive blue clothes and blankets, while many girls receive pink ones. Boys are often given cars, trucks, and toy soldiers as presents, while girls often receive dolls, dollhouses, and toy ovens.
50 In terms of behavior, in many cultures people tend to expect boys to be aggressive and dominant, whereas they generally expect girls to be emotional and subordinate.[2] As children grow up and become adults, these behavior
55 patterns are usually reinforced through social interactions.

Gender inequality has existed in the United States and other industrialized countries for many years, and it will not
60 disappear overnight. Progress has been made recently regarding the opportunities for women. However, both men and women should continue to work for equality to create a fairer environment for everyone.

---

[1]**deferential:** polite and showing respect 谦恭的
[2]**subordinate:** lower in position; following orders 下级的，从属的

2 复杂名词短语

语法讲解

名词短语（noun phrases）包括名词及其修饰语。有些修饰语，例如形容词，常置于名词之前；而有些修饰语可置于名词之后。在复杂名词短语（complex noun phrases）中，名词前后都可以使用修饰语。添加修饰语是一种有效呈现信息的方式，因此复杂名词短语常用于学术写作中。

有形容词和介词短语修饰的名词短语：

The **sensitive issue** of gender inequality has been discussed for many decades.

有形容词和限制性关系从句修饰的名词短语：

Sometimes **professional** women **who start their own businesses** have trouble getting loans.

2.1 名词之后的修饰语

A 名词之后常见的修饰语有：

关系从句

介词短语

关系从句
New York has the most women **who own businesses**.
The organization provides advice for women
介词短语
in business.

B 有些关系从句可省略关系代词和动词 be，简化为：
-ing 短语
-ed 短语

The number of women ~~who are~~ **starting their own businesses** is increasing.
Women ~~who are~~ **elected to Congress** are in the minority.

2.2 复杂名词短语的用法

A 在学术写作中，复杂名词短语通常可代替其他词类，例如动词短语。这种方式可以减少分句的数量，有效地整合句中信息。写作者也常使用复杂名词短语来连接句间信息。

动词短语
Recent research shows that there **are more mothers**
动词短语
who are working.（两个从句）
名词短语
Recent research shows **an increase in the number of working mothers**.（一个分句）
The **salary** of men and women **differ significantly** for the same job. This **significant difference** in **salary** is one indication of persistent inequality.

2.2　复杂名词短语的用法（续表）

B 复杂名词短语通常可代替动词（通常为 be）+ 形容词。此时，动词短语中的形容词成为名词短语的一部分。这种方式可以使一个句子包含更多的信息。

<small>be + 形容词</small>
The rise of women in business **has been impressive**. This indicates that traditional gender roles are being challenged.

<small>名词短语</small>
The impressive rise of women in business indicates that traditional gender roles are being challenged.

C 在比较和对比型写作中，名词修饰语可用于比较或对比事物的细节。

The boy twin received a **blue blanket with white stripes**, while his twin sister received a **pink blanket with yellow stripes**.

语法应用

练习 2.1　复杂名词短语

A 阅读下列关于性别与职业的句子，在关系从句下面画线，圈出名词后的介词短语。

1 A couple of decades ago, women <u>who were interested in studying engineering</u> were rare.

2 Today, there are more and more women in the field of engineering.

3 There didn't use to be many men who were attracted to the field of nursing.

4 Now the number of men who are working as nurses is growing.

5 Two fields that were once occupied only by men were law enforcement and firefighting.

6 These are two careers that are attracting many young women today.

7 Because of an increase in demand and services in data communications and home health-care aides, more men and women are choosing professions in these areas.

B **结对练习**　将关系从句简化为 -ed 短语或 -ing 短语，改写练习 A 中含有关系从句的句子。

1. A couple of decades ago, women interested in studying engineering were rare.

阅读下列关于职场女性的句子，将句子中的黑体词改写为名词短语。在必要的地方改变单词的形式。

1 The number of women working outside the home has **increased significantly**.
   There has been a ___*significant*___ ___*increase*___ in the number of women working outside the home.

2 It has not been easy for women to **achieve progress** toward equality in the workplace.
   The _____ of _____ toward equality in the workplace has not been easy for women.

3 The **growing** number of women in management **is recent**. This indicates that gender differences are becoming less important.
   The _____ _____ in the number of women in management indicates that gender differences are becoming less important.

4 In many companies the **roles** of men are **dominant**. This is still evident, although it is changing.
   The _____ _____ of men in many companies is still evident, although it is changing.

5 The **struggle** for women in the workplace has been **long** and **difficult**. This has resulted in many more career opportunities in recent years.
   The _____ and _____ _____ for women in the workplace has resulted in many more career opportunities in recent years.

6 Women have **increasingly participated** in the workforce; nevertheless, gender inequality continues.
   Although there is an _____ in the _____ of women in the workforce, gender inequality continues.

7 Current research shows that the number of women going to medical school and law school is **rising steadily**. This is expected to continue.
   The _____ _____ in the number of women going to medical school and law school is expected to continue, according to current research.

8 **Women's enrollment** in college has been **higher** than men's since 2000. This is due in part to the fact that more men drop out.
   _____ _____ _____ in college since 2000 is due in part to the fact that more men drop out.

9 In a recent survey, men **perceive** career advancement more **optimistically** than women. This supports the fact that men hold the majority of middle management positions.
   Men's _____ _____ concerning career advancement supports the fact that men hold the majority of middle management positions.

3 平行结构

语法讲解

当句子中列举或比较的每项内容都遵循相同的语法结构时，读者就能更容易地理解这些复杂的信息。这就是平行结构（parallel structure）。	In some cultures, men are expected to be **assertive**, **confident**, and **decisive**. In some cultures, women **spend the day taking care** of the children, while men **spend the day working** outside the house.

3.1 平行结构

A 平行结构适用于连接并列的：

形容词

                               形容词　　　形容词　　　形容词
Boys are encouraged to be **aggressive**, **outgoing**, and **strong**.
Many Vietnamese believe that marriage should promote the

名词短语

                    名词短语　　　名词短语　　　名词短语
interests of **the community**, **the family**, and **the couple**.

动词短语

                            动词短语
A Brazilian bride and groom **say their wedding vows**,
动词短语　　　动词短语
kiss, and **exchange rings**.
Many women struggle with cultural expectations

从句

                    从句　　　　　　　　　从句
when they pursue a career or **when they decide not to marry**.

B 句子中列举的每项内容通常长度一致，这使得句子所传递的信息更容易理解。

Receptions for Brazilian weddings involve **delicious food**, **much laughter**, and **constant music**.（列举的每项内容都包含一个形容词和一个名词，长度一致。）

C 写作者常用平行结构来比较或对比列举的多项内容。

Years ago, men **worked** outside the home, while women **cleaned** the house, **did** the cooking, and **cared for** the children.

练习 3.1　平行结构

为下列关于性别差异的句子选出最佳答案。

1 Men and women working together can reduce inequality slowly, carefully, and ___*significantly*___ .

  a with significance　　b significantly　　c significant

2 Unlike the past, these days women are often encouraged to go to college, have careers, and _____ .

  a invests in her future　　b investing in their future　　c invest in their future

3 Both men and women enjoy going to work, making money, and _____ .

  a provides for their families　　b providing for their families

  c they provide for their families

4 Traditionally, men have often been encouraged to become competitive, aggressive, and _____ .

  a unemotional　　b they are not emotional　　c they can't show their feelings

5 Companies that attract women tend to offer opportunities for advancement, flexible schedules, and _____ .

  a they have mentors for them　　b mentors　　c women need mentors

6 Unlike women, men are much more likely to ask for raises, bonuses, and

  _____ .

  a promote　　b promoting　　c promotions

练习 3.2　更多练习：平行结构

A 结合自己了解的情况或本单元所学内容，使用平行结构回答下列关于男性、女性和职业的问题。

1 What are three things that women can do to decrease gender inequality in the workplace?

  Women can refuse to accept unfair treatment, make men more aware of their behavior, and continue to ask for what they want.

2 What are three skills that many people thought in the past were women's skills?

  _____

  _____

3 What are two professions that men typically did in the past that are now also done by women?

  _____

  _____

4 What are three careers that women have traditionally gone into?

  _____

  _____

5 What are two different ways that some women react to having a female boss?

6 What are two possible ways that women are different from men in relationships?

B 结合自己了解的情况，使用平行结构回答下列关于男性的问题。

1 What are three things that men can do to decrease gender inequality in the workplace?
Men can be more aware of their behavior, honest in their interactions, and accepting of women as their equals.

2 What are three skills that many people believe are more suited to men than women? Why do you think most people have this belief?

3 What are three professions that women did in the past that are now also done by men? What are your feelings about having men in these professions?

4 What are two professions that people still associate with men rather than women? What are possible reasons for this?

5 In your experience, what are two ways that some men react to having a female boss?

6 In your opinion, do men in their 20s and 30s have different perceptions of women in the workplace than men who are older? Why or why not? Give two reasons for your opinion.

C 小组活动 在小组中分享练习 A 和练习 B 的回答。你是否同意其他人的观点？说明理由。

A *I say that women can refuse to accept unfair treatment, make men more aware of their behavior, and continue to ask for what they want. Those behaviors would decrease gender inequality.*

B *I don't agree with everything you say because first of all, I think that management must change and that change is difficult because it is like changing a culture's values and ideas.*

4 常用数量词

词汇讲解

数量词（quantifiers）用来表示某物的数量或程度，常用于比较和对比型的学术写作中。写作者可以通过使用数量词来使表达更加准确，从而避免作出过度概括的陈述。

Many top positions are filled by men.
Few of the top executives are women.

4.1 数量词

A 数量词用于名词之前。常用的数量词有：all, almost all, both, few, most, no, several, some。	**Most** toys are gender-specific. **Several** women hold important positions in that company.
B 数量词常用于以下结构中： 数量词 + of + the / this / that / these / those / such + 名词短语 数量词 + of + 物主限定词（my, your 等）+ 名词短语 数量词 + of + 宾格代词（it, them, us 等） 注意：以上结构中要用 none，而不用 no。	**Many of the** women in my country have two jobs. **Most of my** friends are aware of traditional gender roles. **None of us** supports inequality in the workplace.
C 以下数量词只用于可数名词之前： a few, a great many, both, few, many, several。	Only **a few** presidents of countries are women. **Both** boys and girls learn gender roles from an early age.
以下数量词只用于不可数名词之前： a great deal of, a little, little, much。	The article contained **a great deal of** information about gender roles. We have achieved **little** progress in gender equality.
D 有些数量词用于比较数量：fewer, less, more。	**Fewer** men than women work as nurses.
considerably, significantly, slightly, substantially 等副词常用于修饰比较级形式的数量词。	In the past, many men felt women could not succeed as executives. **Significantly fewer** men today believe that. In the 1970s, most lawyers were men. Today there are **substantially more** female lawyers.
E 在比较和对比型写作中，可以用数量词限定过于宽泛的表述，使之更加恰当、准确。	Men are aggressive, and women are passive.（过于宽泛） **Some** men are dominant and **some** women are passive.（更加准确）

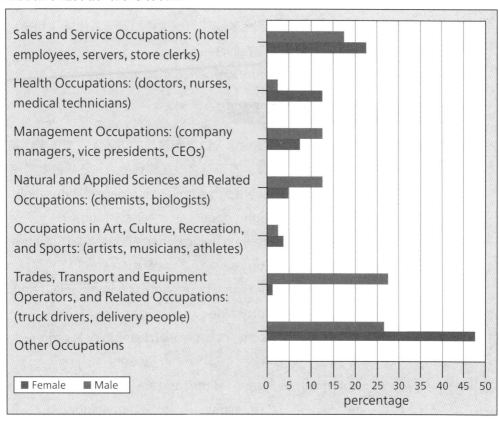

词汇应用

练习 4.1　常用数量词

A　下面的图表展示了加拿大一些主要职业群体中男性和女性的比例。结合图表信息，从方框中选择恰当的词语填空。

Sales and Service Occupations: (hotel employees, servers, store clerks)

Health Occupations: (doctors, nurses, medical technicians)

Management Occupations: (company managers, vice presidents, CEOs)

Natural and Applied Sciences and Related Occupations: (chemists, biologists)

Occupations in Art, Culture, Recreation, and Sports: (artists, musicians, athletes)

Trades, Transport and Equipment Operators, and Related Occupations: (truck drivers, delivery people)

Other Occupations

■ Female　■ Male

0　5　10　15　20　25　30　35　40　45　50

percentage

Source: Statistics Canada, Labour Force Survey. (www.statcan.gc.ca)

| ~~a great deal of~~ | most of | a slightly higher number of |
| fewer | significantly fewer | substantially more |

1　___*A great deal of*___　men are in the trades and transport areas.

2　_____ men are in management occupations than in sales and service occupations.

3　There are _____ men than women who are chemists and biologists.

4　_____ women have occupations such as artists, musicians, and athletes than those of truck drivers and delivery people.

5　_____ women than men have jobs in the trades, transport, and equipment operators sector.

6　_____ the women have jobs in occupations not listed in the chart.

Men, Women, and Equality　**71**

B 结对练习 结合练习 A 中图表里的信息，使用练习 A 中方框里的词语及其他数量词，与同伴一起写出 3 个句子，将这些句子分享给另一组同学并给出可能的解释。其他同学是否同意你们的观点？

Significantly fewer men are in health occupations. I think this may be because there are usually more women in health-care occupations such as nursing.

C 结对练习 运用你们的知识和经验，使用数量词和副词写出 4 个句子，比较你们所处文化或社会里不同职业中存在的性别差异。

In my culture, significantly more women than men are teachers.

练习 4.2 更多练习：常用数量词

A 听一段谈论美国男性和女性平均每天做家务时长的访谈。在听录音之前，先阅读下列句子，猜一猜答案并圈出来。再听录音，在横线上填写正确答案的序号。

1 _____ percent of women spent some time doing general household activities.

a Seventy-four　　　**b**Eighty-four　　　c Ninety-four

2 _____ percent of men spent time doing general household activities.

a Twenty-seven　　　b Forty-seven　　　c Sixty-seven

3 _____ percent of women did some housework (cleaning or laundry).

a Twenty-nine　　　b Forty-nine　　　c Sixty-nine

4 _____ percent of men did some housework (cleaning or laundry).

a Five　　　b Ten　　　c Twenty

5 _____ percent of women prepared the food and cleaned up.

a Fifty-eight　　　b Sixty-eight　　　c Seventy-eight

6 _____ percent of men prepared food and cleaned up.

a Twenty-one　　　b Thirty-one　　　c Forty-one

B 用下面括号中的副词和数量词写句子，比较练习 A 中的数据。

1 (significantly fewer) ___*Significantly fewer men than women spent time doing housework.*___

2 (substantially more) _____

3 (some) _____

4 (most) _____

5 (both) _____

常见错误提示

1 当一个句子中有两个或两个以上的形容词并列时，注意使用平行结构。
A study showed that elementary school teachers discriminated against children
inattentive
who were noisy, active, and ~~if they did not pay attention~~.

2 当一个句子中有两个或两个以上的名词短语并列时，注意使用平行结构。
Wedding guests include the friends of the bride, the bride's co-workers,
and the bride's family ~~is also invited~~.

3 当一个句子中有两个或两个以上的动词短语并列时，注意使用平行结构。
to run
The girls loved to play basketball, to wrestle, and ~~running~~ races, just like the boys.

4 当一个句子中有两个或两个以上的从句并列时，注意使用平行结构。
These days most married women feel that they should continue working,
have their own bank accounts, and ~~to~~ share household chores with their husbands.

改错练习

下面是一篇文章的主体段落，文章比较了过去和现在的女性角色。从中找出另外 9 处
错误并改正。

Women's Roles, Past and Present

Roles for women in the United States have changed in terms of the subjects
the careers that they choose
that women study in college and ~~they choose careers~~. Before the 1970s, most
middle-class men were expected to attend college and pursuing careers that
were both professional and they paid well. Men provided the main financial
5 support for the family. Middle-class women, however, were expected to get
married or, if they went to college, preparing for traditionally female professions,
such as teaching or to be a nurse. Women were not expected to support a family.
If a woman worked after college, she was expected to stop as soon as she got
married or to have children. Because they did not expect to support a family or
10 working for a long time, some women also studied non-career-oriented subjects
such as literature or art history. Nowadays, in contrast, most women plan to work
for most of their adult lives and they help support their families. Many women
feel that they should prepare for a job, that they should move forward in their
careers, and to find satisfaction in their work. Therefore, today, there are many
15 more women studying career-oriented subjects such as business, accounting,
and to work in law enforcement. In fact, many fields that were once thought
of as for men only, such as law enforcement, now employ women. Although
women still do not earn as much as men, they have come a long way since the
1970s in expanding their college and career opportunities.

UNIT 7

比较和对比 3：形容词和副词的比较级和最高级；冠词；描述相似性的常用表达

Family Values in Different Cultures

1 现实生活中的语法

阅读这篇文章，文章讲述了拉美文化与传统美国文化背景下的美国家庭之间所存在的文化差异。作者在文中比较并对比了这两种文化的多个方面。这是一篇比较和对比型写作的范例。

A 读前准备 family 这个词对你来说意味着什么？阅读文章并思考：作者是如何解释这一概念的？

B 阅读理解 回答下列问题。

1 How are the beliefs of Dr. Benjamin Spock related to the way many U.S. families raise their children?

2 Who might young Latino adults live with when they finish college? What about college graduates in traditional U.S. families?

3 What does the writer mean when he or she says that "it is wise not to stereotype cultures"? Do you think the writer avoids stereotyping cultures in this essay? Explain.

C 语法发现 回答下列问题，注意描述不同点和相似点的形容词比较级及其他表达方式的使用。

1 再次阅读第 2 段中第 24—26 行的句子。Spock 医生认为，随着年龄的增长，美国儿童应该变成什么样？注意句中比较级的两种形式。使用哪种形式取决于什么？

2 作者在第 45—52 行比较了哪两件事？

3 再次阅读最后一段。传统美国文化与拉美文化有何相同之处？在作者用来表达相似性的词下面画线。

What Family Means:
An Intercultural Perspective

THE DEFINITION OF FAMILY differs from culture to culture. These differences become more apparent when families from
5 diverse cultures live in the same area. For example, with the increasing number of Latinos in the United States, diversity in the culture of U.S. families has become more noticeable.
10 Differences include how family is defined, how children view themselves within the family, and what happens when children reach young adulthood.

Traditionally, in U.S. culture, when people
15 refer to their family, they usually mean their immediate family, that is, their parents and their children. Many of these families follow the basic principles of Dr. Benjamin Spock, a famous pediatrician[1] in the mid-1900s. He
20 wrote a popular book on raising children that changed the style of parenting from strict to more permissive. He believed that children should be free to set their own goals and choose their own career path. In Dr. Spock's
25 view, as children get older they should become more independent. After finishing high school, American teenagers who go to college often move out of their parents' homes and live in a college dormitory or their own apartment.
30 After college, many live on their own. Children who continue to live with their parents after high school or college might be asked to pay rent. In general, family takes on a smaller role as children enter adulthood.
35 In contrast, in many Latino cultures, when people refer to their family, they include extended family, such as aunts, uncles, cousins, and grandparents. Latino life centers on family. In fact, the largest component of Latino
40 life is usually the family. Sociologists have suggested that each family member feels a moral responsibility to help other members of the family who may be experiencing problems such as poor health, financial concerns, and
45 unemployment. It is common for Latino families to encourage longer visits from relatives, and they expect loyalty, sacrifice, and hard work from family members. Many Latino young adults live with their parents until marriage,
50 and in some cases even after marriage. This is seen as more acceptable in Latino culture than in traditional U.S. culture.

Beliefs about family relationships and expectations differ among traditional U.S.
55 and Latino cultures. Despite these differences, traditional U.S. culture is similar to Latino culture in terms of the importance of family. Understanding the cultural background of others is valuable for people living in diverse
60 communities, like in the United States. However, it is wise not to stereotype cultures. Not all Latino families stick together. Similarly, not all parents from traditional U.S. culture point to the door when their children turn
65 18. Cultural background plays a role in our relationships with family members, but culture is rarely the sole defining element for anyone.

---

[1]**pediatrician**: a doctor who treats children 儿科医生

2 形容词和副词的比较级和最高级

语法讲解

比较级（comparatives）用于表示两种事物或情况的不同之处。最高级（superlatives）用于比较某一事物或情况与其所属群体中的其他事物或情况。比较级和最高级在比较和对比型写作中都十分重要。	In general, Asians are **less relaxed** about time **than** Latinos. The **largest component** of Latino life is the family. In general, sports fans in Latin America follow soccer **more intensely than** baseball. People from traditional U.S. culture communicate **the most directly**.

2.1 形容词和副词的比较级

A 形容词比较级的构成规则如下： 单音节及部分双音节形容词在词尾加 -er，例如 easier，greater，older。 多音节及部分双音节形容词在前面加 more / less，例如 more complex，less efficient。	Mexicans often have **larger** families **than** Chinese. The concept of family is **easier** to define in some cultures **than** in others. The extended family is **more important** in Latino families **than** in some other cultures. The concept of family in the United States is **less rigid than** in other cultures.
B 副词比较级的构成规则如下： 单音节副词在词尾加 -er，例如 harder，faster。 双音节及多音节副词在前面加 more / less，例如 more quickly，less carefully。	Children from traditional U.S. culture usually leave home **earlier than** children in Latino culture. Some people talk **more quickly than** others. In general, the Japanese treat the elderly **more respectfully**.
C 单音节词通常不与 less 连用，可与 not as ... as 连用。	The Asian population is **not as** large **as** the Latino population in the United States. 不说 The Asian population is ~~less large than~~ the Latino population in the United States.
D 在正式学术写作中，than 后要用主格代词 + 助动词（be，have 或 do）。助动词可以省略。 在非正式书面语或口语中，than 后用宾格代词。	正式： My family is more concerned about having dinner together **than I (am)**. 非正式： My family is more concerned about having dinner together **than me**.

2.2 形容词和副词的最高级

A 形容词最高级的构成规则如下：
单音节及部分双音节形容词在词尾加 -est，并在前面加 the，例如 the easiest，the greatest，the oldest。
多音节及部分双音节形容词在前面加 the most / the least，例如 the most common，the least effective。

Latinos are currently one of **the largest** ethnic groups in the United States.

Solidarity is **the most significant** value for people of my culture.

B 副词最高级的构成规则如下：
单音节副词在词尾加 -est，并在前面加 the，例如 the hardest，the fastest。
双音节及多音节副词在前面加 the most / the least，例如 the most quickly，the least significantly。

Researchers often debate about which groups work **the hardest**.
The Latino population in the United States has increased **the most significantly** of all ethnic groups in the country.

2.3 比较级的用法

A 比较级的两个常用用法为：
明确的比较：句中包含被比较的两个部分。

第一部分
Independence is **more valued** in the United States than
第二部分
in other cultures.
第一部分 　　　　　　 第二部分
My sister and I are close, but my brother and I are **closer**.

B 隐含的比较：被比较的另一部分在前文中已出现，或文中没有提及但读者已知。此时，没有必要在比较级后重复"than + 第二部分"。

If people from traditional U.S. culture knew more about other cultures, they perhaps would be **more understanding** (than they are).

📊 实际使用数据分析

在学术写作中，与以 -est 结尾的最高级相比，以 -er 结尾的比较级使用频率更高，这是因为写作者往往要避免作出绝对的论断。常用的形容词比较级和最高级有：
best, better, earlier, easier, greater, greatest, higher, highest, larger, largest, lower, older, smaller, wider
The number of immigrants is **higher** in the United States than in Canada.

练习 2.1 形容词和副词的比较级

A 阅读下列关于美国传统文化的句子。每组中带横线的句子是对前面句子的重述。用括号中形容词或副词的比较级形式将每组中带横线的句子补充完整。在必要的地方添加 than。

1 Children from traditional U.S. culture are very assertive, compared to children from some other cultures.

Children from traditional U.S. culture are ___*more assertive than*___ (assertive) children from some other cultures.

2 Parents from traditional U.S. culture often allow their teenage children to work while they are in school. Parents from some other cultures want their children to focus only on education until they are out of school.

Parents from other cultures are much _____ (likely) parents from traditional U.S. culture to allow their children to work while they are in school.

3 Children from traditional U.S. culture are often permitted to stay out late on weekends. Parents from some other cultures do not allow their children to stay out late.

Parents from traditional U.S. culture behave _____ (strictly) parents from some other cultures.

4 Children from traditional U.S. culture speak informally to their elders. Children in most Asian families speak politely to their elders.

Children in most Asian families speak _____ (politely) to their elders.

5 In traditional U.S. culture, elderly parents don't often live with their grown children like they do in other cultures.

While in many cultures elderly parents often live with their grown children, this is much _____ (common) in traditional U.S. culture.

6 In many cultures, grandparents help to raise their grandchildren. This is not normally the case in traditional U.S. culture.

When it comes to their grandchildren's upbringing, grandparents from other cultures are often _____ (involved) grandparents in traditional U.S. culture.

7 In traditional U.S. culture, the concept of family usually means parents and their children. In other cultures, family can mean parents, their children, the children's grandparents, and sometimes aunts, uncles, and cousins.

In traditional U.S. culture, the concept of family is _____ (complex) in other cultures.

B **结对练习** 和同伴一起，将练习 A 中每个关于美国传统文化的表述与你们所熟悉的另一种文化进行比较。在必要的地方使用"实际使用数据分析"中的单词。完成后，将你们的想法分享给全班同学。

I would say that Japanese children are less assertive than children from traditional U.S. culture because in Japanese culture it is more desirable to be part of a group.

练习 2.2 形容词和副词的最高级

结合你对文化行为的了解，使用括号中形容词和副词的最高级形式将下列句子补充完整。

1 One of ___*the biggest*___ (big) differences between my culture and ___*traditional U.S.*___ culture is ___*the way children speak to their parents*___ .

2 I think _____ (important) thing to know about my culture is _____ .

3 The _____ (strange) thing I ever learned about a different culture is _____ .

4 I think _____ (difficult) thing to understand about _____ culture is _____ .

5 The _____ (significantly) different thing between my culture and _____ culture is _____ .

6 The person in my family who works _____ (hard) is _____ .

7 The person in my family who behaves _____ (patiently) is _____ .

练习 2.3　形容词和副词的比较级和最高级

A 听一段关于文化差异的讲座。根据听到的内容，在表格中正确答案处打√。

	High-Context	Low-Context	Collectivist	Individualist
1 Communication is direct.		√		
2 Communication is indirect.				
3 Tone of voice, gestures, and status are important.				
4 The United States and European countries are examples of this type.				
5 Japan and South Korea are examples of this type.				
6 Africa, Latin America, and Asia are examples of this type.				
7 The group is valued.				
8 Family ties are strong.				
9 Merit and expertise are important.				
10 A person's goals are important.				

B 下列是关于文化行为的句子。根据练习 A 中的表格所提供的信息，用括号中所给形容词或其对应副词的比较级或最高级形式填空。在必要的地方添加 than。

1 There are a lot of important things to consider when working with people of different cultures. However, one of ___*the most important*___ (important) topics to learn about is communication style.

2 In high-context cultures like South Korea and Japan, the communication style is _____ (direct) that of people in low-context cultures.

3 In low-context cultures like the United States and England, people communicate _____ (direct).

4 For people in high-context cultures, words are not the only tool of communication. In low-context cultures, words are _____ (essential) thing.

5 Facial expressions, gestures, and tone of voice are often _____ (important) in low-context cultures.

6 Degree of individualism is one of _____ (big) issues to consider when observing cultural differences.

7 In collectivist cultures, the group is valued _____ (high) it is in individualistic cultures.

8 In individualistic cultures, an individual's goals are _____ (valued) a group's goals.

9 Collectivist cultures consider a person's merit or expertise _____ (important) family ties.

10 Communicating effectively with people from other cultures can be difficult. That's why _____ (critical) important thing to do is to learn about cultural differences beforehand.

3 冠词

语法讲解

冠词（articles）（a/an, the）或零冠词（Ø）置于名词之前。写作者可以用冠词来表示所说的人或物是非特指的、特指的，还是为写作者和读者双方都确知的。冠词的使用在学术写作中非常重要，尤其是在比较和对比型写作中。	In Latin America, Ø families include a mother, a father, Ø sisters, Ø brothers, Ø aunts, Ø uncles, and Ø cousins. I have not met the family that lives across the street from my house.

3.1 定冠词的用法

A 当写作者和读者双方都知道某一名词所涉及的常识或信息时，该名词前用定冠词（definite article）the。	In many cultures, it is important for families to eat meals together in the kitchen. （写作者认为读者也知道一所房子里通常有一间厨房。）
B 当写作者再次提到前文已出现的名词并要介绍更多信息时，该名词前用 the；或当某一名词与前文已出现的名词相关时，该名词前也用 the。	Each person in a <u>family</u> has a moral responsibility to aid other members of the <u>family</u> experiencing financial problems.

C 当某一名词由修饰语限定，指特定的人或事物时，该名词前使用 the。	Mexico is **the** country that is located south of **the** United States.
D 最高级之前用 the。	**The** strictest family I ever met was from **the** United States.
E 以下几类词之前用 the： 缩略语（abbreviations） （但通常不用于首字母缩略词* [acronyms] 之前） 集体名词 表示某个类别的形容词 表示独一无二的事物的名词	**the** CIA, **the** UN, **the** FBI Ø NASA, Ø NATO **the** media, **the** military **the** rich, **the** elderly **the** president, **the** queen, **the** United States, **the** Alps, **the** moon, **the** equator

3.2　不定冠词的用法

A 当某一单数可数名词并不特指某一人或事物时，或当初次提及某一读者不了解的单数可数名词时，用不定冠词（indefinite article）a / an。	**A** young Latino man is **the** new student in class. （没有明确指出这名男子的身份。） The class read **an** article about cultural values. （读者对这篇文章并不了解。）
B 不可数名词或复数名词前不可用 a / an，可用 some 或零冠词。	My cousin borrowed **some money** from me, but he has not paid me back yet. Ø **Large families** can be enjoyable but complicated.
C a / an 可用于引出某一单数可数名词。	**A** young Latina woman is the new student in my class. I found out that she is from Colombia.

*有些首字母组成的缩略语可以像单词一样发音，这类词叫做首字母缩略词。首字母缩略词通常不用冠词。请注意：不是所有首字母组成的缩略语都可以像单词一样发音，例如上面缩略语中所给的例子：the CIA，the UN，the FBI。

3.3 冠词在语篇中的使用

A 在学术写作中，段落和文章常以概括性的陈述开头。当陈述概括性内容时，用零冠词或不定冠词表示泛指：
不可数名词和复数名词之前用零冠词。
单数名词之前用 a / an。

"Ø Advertising is about Ø norms and Ø values, Ø aspirations and Ø prejudices." –Anil Ambani
In some cultures, a teenager is expected to move out of their parents' home and live in a college dormitory.

B 当某一名词的所指之物为读者所知时，该名词前用定冠词。
这一名词可以：
直接给出

在语境中清晰获知

Teens leave their parents' homes to live in a dormitory. **The** parents are often sad to see their children leave. （parents 一词在前文已经提到。）
Although **the** rooms are often very small, most teenagers do not seem to mind. （读者都知道宿舍里是有房间的。）

语法应用

练习 3.1 不定冠词和定冠词

A 这篇文章描述了在美国人口流动如何影响人际关系。阅读文章，在横线上填写最恰当的冠词（a / an，the 或 Ø）。有时正确答案不唯一。

Mobility in the United States

The United States is a very mobile society. People frequently do not live in the same town for their entire lives. Often [1] __Ø__ large corporations require their employees to move if they want to advance in [2] _____ company. Students typically do not go to [3] _____ college near their families. As a result, it is not uncommon for [4] _____ extended families to be separated by hundreds, if not thousands, of miles.

This mobility is probably one of [5] _____ most significant factors influencing [6] _____

relationships in the United States. For example, people tend to be very friendly on a casual basis and open to meeting many new individuals, but these interactions do not always result in ⁷_____ close, lasting relationships. There is ⁸_____ common tendency of people in ⁹_____ United States to say things like, "Let's get together sometime," or "Let's have lunch," and then not follow through with ¹⁰_____ invitation.

People who are not from ¹¹_____ United States sometimes see this informal style as superficial, and it can be confusing. If someone says, "Let's get together," ¹²_____ visitor to the United States might expect the person to make ¹³_____ call and suggest ¹⁴_____ meeting time and place. This doesn't always happen. However, ¹⁵_____ visitor who has this experience shouldn't be offended because ¹⁶_____ expression "Let's get together" has almost ¹⁷_____ same meaning as "hello" to many Americans.

B **小组活动** 与小组成员讨论练习 A 的答案并轮流说明理由。

I chose no article for item 1 because corporations is plural and here the writer is referring to all large corporations, not specific large corporations.

练习 3.2 更多练习：不定冠词和定冠词

A 按照括号中的提示，结合自己的想法，使用正确的冠词写出关于文化差异的句子。

1 (a definition of *family*) ___*A family can consist of parents and children, or it can consist of parents, children, grandparents, and others.*___

2 (a definition of *values*) _____

_____

3 (a generalization about cultural differences – what they are) _____

_____

4 (a description of one cultural difference concerning time, family, relationships, etc.) _____

_____

_____

5 (a detail about your difference in item 4) _____

_____

6 (a statement about a cultural difference that you think is more confusing than any other) _____

_____

7 (a generalization about groups and individuals in your culture) _____

_____

B **结对练习** 与同伴讨论练习 A 中所写的句子。哪些句子是概括性的？哪些句子包含特定的名词？将你们的句子分享给另一组同学，并让对方说明每句话中使用相应冠词或零冠词的原因。

You used "a family" in this sentence because here you are using a singular count noun to make a generalization.

4 描述相似性的常用表达

词汇讲解

在比较和对比型写作中，有些单词和短语常用于表示相似性。	There are many **similarities** between Turkish and Brazilian cultures. Japanese and South Koreans **have something in common**: they tend to avoid directly looking into someone's eyes while speaking.

4.1　similar to，similarities，similarly，likewise，like

A 可以用 be similar to 比较两个名词短语。	Mexican culture **is similar to** Spanish culture in many ways.
B 可以用 "the similarities between ____ and ____" 比较两个名词短语。	Many people believe that **the similarities between** the United States **and** Canada outweigh the differences.
C 可以将 similarly 和 likewise 用作过渡词，连接两个谈论相似性的句子。过渡词后用逗号。	In Nigeria, social recognition is achieved through extended families. **Similarly**, a family's honor is influenced by the action of its members. Chinese children enjoy playing video games. **Likewise**, American children find this an enjoyable activity.

D 可以用 "___ and ___ have + something / one thing / a lot + in common" 引出两个名词具有的共同点。	Germany **and** Spain **have something in common**: their people love coffee.
E 可以在分句之前用 "Like ___," 表示某一名词与分句的主语在某一方面具有相似性。	**Like** bedtime stories in the United States, the stories that Chinese parents tell their children send a strong message about values.

词汇应用

练习 4.1 描述相似性的词

A 从方框中选择恰当的单词或表达，将下列关于文化和网络媒体的句子补充完整。每个单词或表达只可用一次。

in common	like	similarities between
is similar to	~~likewise~~	similarly

1 A person who does business with people from different cultures should be aware of how cultures differ in communication styles. ___*Likewise*___ , website designers should be aware of how people from different cultures will respond to their designs.

2 People from different cultures communicate in different ways, but most have one important thing _____ . People in most cultures use the Internet on a daily basis.

3 Years ago, there were many _____ paper-based media and online media. Both included simple text and images that people read from top to bottom. Now, however, online media is much more interactive.

4 _____ a person engaging in face-to-face communication, a website designer must take into account another person's expectations and assumptions. Some users may expect direct communication, while others may want more indirect messages.

5 In terms of cultural expectations, face-to-face interaction _____ Internet interaction. Some cultures may expect a website to communicate information directly with headlines and clear text. Others may respond better to less text and more images.

6 In some cultures, the relationship between speakers is important in face-to-face communication. _____ , some Internet users may respond better to websites that have animation or interactivity that imitates human interaction.

B **结对练习** 和同伴想一想面对面交流和在线交流的其他相似点。使用练习 A 中的单词或表达，在一张纸上写出 5 个句子。接下来，与另一组同学交换所写的句子，阅读他们的句子，并举一些能说明他们的想法的例子。

5 常见错误提示

1 more 和 -er 都可用于构成比较级，但注意二者不可同时使用。
Middle Eastern families tend to be ~~more~~ closer than families in other cultures.

2 注意不要混淆 best 和 most。
                best
In the 1960s, the ~~most~~-selling child-rearing book in the U.S. was *Raising an Independent Child.*

3 头衔 / 职位 + 名字之前不用定冠词，而用零冠词。
~~The~~ Dr. Benjamin Spock wrote *Baby and Child Care* in 1946.

4 注意不要漏掉固定表达 the same as 中的 the。
                                                    the
Child-rearing beliefs in one culture are rarely ∧same as child-rearing beliefs in another culture.

改错练习

下面是一篇文章的主体段落，文章比较了不同文化中的人庆祝新年的方式。从中找出另外 8 处错误并改正。

                                                           the

The celebration of the New Year in South Korea is not ∧same as in the United States. First of all, South Koreans celebrate the Lunar New Year (the first new moon of the lunar calendar), so the date is not same as in the United States, where the New Year is celebrated on the first day of the Gregorian Calendar

5 (January 1). The New Year is more later in South Korea, usually in February. In addition, the South Korean New Year celebration lasts for three days and involves the entire family. According to the Dr. Sook-Bin Woo, this is because South Korean families tend to be more closer than traditional U.S. families. For example, South Korean families play special games with each other during this holiday. This

10 family closeness may be the reason that many South Koreans report that their most childhood memories are of New Year's celebrations.

    In the United States, the celebration of the New Year begins on the evening of the last day of the year and continues into the following day; it is therefore more shorter than the South Korean celebration. Traditionally, it tends to be

15 primarily an adult celebration for many people. On New Year's Eve, many adults hire a babysitter for their children and go out to a restaurant or to a party to celebrate with other adults. Because U.S. celebrations often do not include children, most Americans are unlikely to say that their most childhood memories are of the celebration of the New Year. Sociologist the Dr. George Lee notes that

20 this tradition is changing in the United States as more adults stay home and celebrate with their children.

比较和对比 4：表示对比和让步的状语从句与过渡词语

Intercultural Communication

1 现实生活中的语法

阅读这篇文章，文章探讨了具有不同文化背景的人共同参加商务会议时可能产生的误解。这是一篇比较和对比型写作的范例。

A 读前准备 在商务会议上，哪些文化差异可能会在来自不同文化的人之间引起误解？阅读文章并思考：在作者看来，哪两种差异可能会引起误解？

B 阅读理解 回答下列问题。

1 According to the essay, what are three main problems that businesspeople might have when they do business with people from different cultures?

2 Why do some cultures perceive the exchange of gifts as inappropriate in a business transaction?

3 According to what you have read in this essay, with whom would businesspeople from your culture possibly have misunderstandings? Explain.

C 语法发现 回答下列问题，注意对比两个事物的句子。

1 在第 2 段中找到表示对比的 in contrast 和 while。这两者中，哪个仅可用于句首，哪个后接逗号？

2 在第 40 行找到表示对比的单词。它的用法与 in contrast 还是 while 相似？

3 比较第 4 段中 even though 和 however 的用法。哪个词的用法与 while 相似？哪个与 in contrast 相似？

4 第 48 行的 even though 表示让步，即其所引出的信息不仅与前文的信息不同，而且也出人意料。解释为什么此处用 even though 比用 while 更合适。

INTERNATIONAL Business Etiquette

Large companies want to remain competitive in today's global markets. To reach their goals, they are often required to take their businesses beyond the boundaries
5 of their home countries. Consequently, they need to interact with individuals from other cultures. Cross-cultural business transactions can be challenging since the rules about what is considered appropriate and acceptable
10 and what might be seen as rude vary across cultures. Some aspects of culture are likely to cause misunderstandings in multicultural business situations.

One aspect of culture that may be
15 problematic during business interactions is the perception of time. People in countries such as the United States or Germany commonly pay close attention to schedules and meeting agendas. In those countries, it is impolite if
20 someone habitually arrives late to meetings. In contrast, in countries such as Mexico and Brazil, people tend to see schedules simply as guidelines. They often see deadlines as being more flexible. A Brazilian businessperson,
25 for example, might find it strange that a U.S. business meeting has an ending time that is nonnegotiable. In Brazil, the length of a meeting is generally dictated by the needs of its participants, while in the United States, a
30 predefined length is often the norm.

The amount of emotion expressed during business interactions can be the cause of other potential cross-cultural problems. This can differ significantly from culture to
35 culture. In some cultures, such as in parts of Italy, people express feelings more openly and argue more passionately about their points of view. For this reason, they may readily show emotion during critical parts of
40 a negotiation, whereas this practice can come across as unprofessional in more emotionally neutral cultures, such as in Sweden. People in these cultures are generally more careful in controlling the feelings they display.
45 Understanding local customs can also be problematic for businesspeople. Some customs may seem inappropriate in some countries even though they are perfectly acceptable in others. For example, exchanging
50 gifts between the parties involved in a business deal is a common practice in many parts of the world. However, this practice could be seen as inappropriate in other places, such as the United States or Britain. In
55 those cultures, it could even be interpreted as being unethical since gift-giving may be seen as improperly influencing the outcome of the negotiation.

Doing business with people from
60 different cultures can be challenging. When someone is conducting business abroad, it is important not to assume that what is considered polite in one culture is universal. Instead, it is essential to understand and
65 respect other traditions and business practices. Being aware of those differences can give business professionals a competitive edge when conducting business abroad. It might make the difference between a deal's
70 success or failure.

2 表示对比和让步的状语从句

语法讲解

状语从句（adverb clauses）可用于表示两个分句之间意思上的关系。表示对比和让步的状语从句常常在学术写作中使用，在比较和对比型写作中尤其实用。	In some cultures punctuality is important, **while** in other cultures, people arrive at events quite late. **Even though** most companies train their executives, cross-cultural problems still arise.

2.1　对比状语从句

A 对比状语从句（adverb clauses of contrast）主要用于对比两种事物或情况。	The official language of Brazil is Portuguese, **while** in Colombia it is Spanish.
B 对比状语从句由从属连词 while 或 whereas 引导。 📊while 的使用频率比 whereas 高。whereas 多用于学术写作中，很少用于口语中。	In Mexico, the length of a meeting varies according to the needs of its participants, **while** in the United States, the time is generally set and unchanging. Women in the United States work an average of 41 hours per week, **whereas** women in Europe work about 30 hours per week.
C 对比状语从句可置于主句之前或之后。如果从句置于主句之前，则后接逗号。但此类状语从句通常置于主句之后。与其他状语从句不同，当对比状语从句置于主句之后来强调对比时，从句之前也可使用逗号。	**While** some countries are open to immigration, other countries have strict policies against it. Some customs may be perceived as inappropriate in some countries, **whereas** they are perfectly acceptable in others.

2.2　让步状语从句

A 让步状语从句（adverb clauses of concession）用于表示一种特殊的对比关系，即主句所描述的内容是令人惊讶或出乎意料的。	让步状语从句 **Although** businesspeople are careful about cultural differences, 出乎意料的结果 misunderstandings sometimes occur during business transactions.

2.2 让步状语从句（续表）

B 引导让步状语从句的从属连词有：although，even though，though，while。 当让步状语从句置于主句之后时，从句前可使用逗号，以强调对比。 注意：while 既可引导对比状语从句，也可引导让步状语从句。	Even though face-to-face communication is preferred, sometimes business has to be conducted virtually. The company is doing more business with South America, though / while in the past, it conducted business more frequently with Europe.

 语法应用

练习 2.1 对比状语从句

 A 听录音中的采访，采访围绕美国和墨西哥商务人士之间可能存在的差异展开。在 Julio Sanchez 博士每个观点所对应的国家处打 √。

		In the U.S.	In Mexico
1	Most people are strict about time.	√	
2	Most people often arrive up to 30 minutes late for business meetings.		
3	It's polite to arrive on time to a dinner party.		
4	Most people share personal information in business meetings.		
5	Most people call each other by their first names as soon as they meet.		
6	Most people have a direct communication style.		
7	Most people may not tell you immediately when they can't attend an event.		

B 利用练习 A 中的表格和采访里的信息，用 while 或 whereas 写出表达对比的句子。有时正确答案不唯一。

1 While *most people in Mexico are flexible about time, most people in the United States are very strict.*

2 Whereas _____

_____

3 _____ , whereas

_____

4 _____ , while

_____

5 While _____

_____

6 _____ , while _____

7 Whereas _____

_____

C **结对练习** 和同伴讨论你们所熟悉的两种文化中存在的行为差异，谈谈你们对这些差异的看法。写出含有对比状语从句的句子来对比这些行为，并将你们的想法分享给全班同学。

    A *In Brazil, people are flexible about time.*

    B *In my opinion, it's different in India. There, it's very important to be on time to meetings. People are flexible about time in Brazil, while it's very important to be on time in India.*

练习 2.2 让步状语从句

A 下列句子是某国际公司对中国商业文化的一些认识。用括号中的从属连词将每对句子组合起来，写出表示让步关系的句子。有时正确答案不唯一。

1 **a** It is not appropriate to treat a Chinese business colleague informally.

    b Doing business in China often involves informal social gatherings where business is not discussed.

    (even though) *It is not appropriate to treat a Chinese business colleague informally even though doing business in China often involves social gatherings where business is not discussed.*

2 **a** Rank is very important.

    b Gender bias is not common.

    (though) _____

_____

3 **a** This lack of gesturing does not mean a lack of responsiveness.

    b The Chinese do not gesture or show much body language.

    (while) _____

_____

4 **a** It is important to send written information about your company well before your arrival in China.

    b Chinese businesspeople like to meet face-to-face rather than over the phone or by email.

    (although) _____

_____

5 a Chinese business meetings are very formal affairs.

   b The meetings may frequently be interrupted by the ringing of cell phones.

(even though) _____

_____

6 a Chinese businesspeople are hardworking and serious.

   b Chinese businesspeople have a great sense of humor.

(though) _____

_____

7 a Some companies may be very successful in their own countries.

   b Their success in China depends on a solid understanding of Chinese culture.

(although) _____

_____

B **小组活动** 用练习 A 中表示让步的从属连词，在一张纸上写出关于另一种文化中的行为习惯的句子。在小组内分享这些句子，并讲述让你感到惊讶的信息。

Even though Brazilian people are not very strict about time, it is necessary to schedule an appointment.

Although most business meetings in Morocco are conducted in French, sometimes English is used. Find out which language will be used before your meeting so that you can hire an interpreter if necessary.

3 表示对比和让步的过渡词语

语法讲解

在比较和对比型写作中，也可以使用过渡词语或介词来表述差异或意想不到的结果。	Nodding means yes in some countries; **however**, this is not universal. U.S. executives prefer time limits for meetings. **In contrast**, Greeks see them as less necessary. **Despite** their significant cultural differences, Mexico and China are strong trade partners.

A 以下过渡词语用于表明差异： conversely，however，in contrast， instead，nevertheless，nonetheless， on the contrary，on the other hand	In some Asian cultures, it is impolite to arrive late at a meeting without an explanation. **In contrast,** in some European cultures, it is more natural to view schedules and start times as guidelines.
B 过渡词语常置于句首，后接逗号和独立分句。 过渡词语前有时用分号，但这种用法并不常见。	People in the United States usually smile when they greet other people. **On the other hand,** they don't always shake hands. Some African cultures do not use the firm handshake common in the United States; **instead,** they prefer a gentle, slightly longer touching of hands.
C 过渡词语也可置于句子的中间。此时，过渡词语的前后均须用逗号。	In some Asian cultures, it is impolite to arrive late at a meeting without an explanation. In some European cultures, **in contrast,** it is more natural to view schedules and start times as guidelines.

A 📊 however 是表示直接对比时最常用的过渡词，含义与 but 相近。	In India, gift-giving is common. **However,** the gifts do not need to be expensive.
B on the contrary 用于驳斥前句所表达的观点，并引出相反的观点。	Adapting to another culture's customs is not a weakness; **on the contrary,** it builds stronger relationships and is simply good business.
C in contrast 用于表示两种情形在某些方面有所不同。	Table manners are informal in Canada. **In contrast,** Moroccan dining usually requires an understanding of a complex set of rules.（两种文化中的餐桌礼仪不同。）
D on the other hand 用于表示一种情形中相对立的方面。 注意：有时 in contrast 和 on the other hand 可互换。	It is not common for people in Türkiye to give gifts in a business relationship. **On the other hand,** they give gifts freely among family members.（在土耳其，向商务伙伴送礼和向家庭成员送礼形成对比。）

3.2 过渡词语：词义差异（续表）

E nevertheless 和 nonetheless 用于引出出乎意料的事实或信息。	Learning about a new culture can be frustrating. **Nevertheless**, a little effort will lead to both personal and professional rewards. Students may be anxious about studying abroad. **Nonetheless**, it is a once-in-a-lifetime chance that should be considered.

3.3 表示对比和让步的介词

A 介词也可用于表示对比或让步。与过渡词语不同，介词后接名词短语。名词短语常以动词 -ing 形式开头。 despite 和 in spite of 用于表示出乎意料的事实或信息。	名词短语 Despite / In spite of <u>their cultural differences</u>, international students usually create close friendships. 名词短语（以动词 -ing 形式开头） Despite / In spite of <u>coming from different cultures</u>, international students usually become very close friends.
instead of 用于表示以一种情形或事物代替另一种情形或事物。 注意：不要混淆 instead 和 instead of。	一种情形 Some African cultures prefer shaking hands gently 被代替的情形 instead of shaking hands firmly like in the United States.

练习 3.1　表示对比和让步的过渡词语和介词

阅读这封电子邮件，其中谈到了不同国家的文化行为。选择正确的过渡词语或介词，将邮件补充完整。

Dear Professor Jones:

　　I am in your Anthropology 101 class. I really enjoyed your lecture today. I was not aware of how different other cultures can be. You asked us to email the most interesting things we learned in Chapter 5. The aspects that really caught my attention were:

1　In many countries, shaking the head from side to side is used to indicate *no*. **Nonetheless, /(However,)** in India, individuals move their head from side to side to acknowledge what another person has said.

2　In many places, people greet by shaking hands. **In contrast, / Despite** people hug and kiss in informal circumstances in Latin America.

3　In Japan, the *OK* hand sign does not mean "fine" or "all right" as it does in the United States. **On the other hand, / Instead,** it means "money."

4　It's fairly common knowledge that bowing is a common practice in some Asian countries. **However, / Despite** this knowledge, not many people are aware that the way people bow depends on the social situation and the reason they are bowing.

5　Many businesses spend millions on cross-cultural training. **On the other hand, / Nonetheless,** embarrassing mistakes continue to occur.

6　Many Canadians can be very direct when sharing their opinions. **On the other hand, / In spite of** they can be vague when making social plans.

7　The tendency for many Canadians to be direct is not a sign of unfriendliness. **Nevertheless, / On the contrary,** they are very friendly people.

8　**In spite of / Instead,** the many opportunities for cultural misunderstandings, people continue to conduct business successfully across cultures.

I am looking forward to reading the next chapter.

Thank you,

Maria Yolanda Tavarez

4 常见错误提示

1 注意 on the other hand 中的正确介词为 on。

In the United States, it is appropriate to send a thank-you letter after an interview. ~~In~~ ^{On} the other hand, a thank-you email is also acceptable in some situations.

In some cultures, it is important to ask co-workers about their families. Asking too many personal questions, ~~at~~ ^{on} the other hand, could seem offensive.

2 注意在 on the other hand 中要用 the other，而不要用 another。

On ~~another~~ ^{the other} hand, many young American businesspeople speak Chinese.

3 on the contrary，in contrast 等过渡词语置于句首时，注意后接逗号。

Business meetings usually begin and end at specific times in the United States. In contrast, meeting times in some cultures are not always exact.

4 在含有 although 引导的让步状语从句的句子中，主句中不能再用 but。

Although many people in the United States speak other languages, ~~but~~ most international business meetings are conducted in English.

改错练习

下面是一篇文章的主体段落，文章比较了同一公司的网站设计在不同文化中的差异。从中找出另外 7 处错误并改正。

　　Although the use of corporate websites is universal, ~~but~~ corporate website design is another aspect of doing business that differs from culture to culture. The different website designs for Good Foods are one example. The company operates globally. It wants to appear as though it sells the same quality products

5　everywhere in the world. On another hand, the company wants to appeal to the consumers in each country where it does business. Therefore, the look of its sites differs from country to country. For example, the website for Good Foods in the United States tends to use a limited number of colors. In contrast the company site in India tends to use a great deal of color. The Indian version uses

10　bright colors, such as pink, red, orange, and purple, while the U.S. version of the site uses only shades of blue and gray. This is because the way people interpret colors is cultural. Bright colors suggest "fun" to people in the United States, while blue and gray suggest "importance." In another example, the Good Foods site in Switzerland shows the company's products; however it rarely shows people

15　using or enjoying them. In the other hand, when it does show people, they are usually alone. In contrast the Good Foods site for Mexico shows families shopping together and large groups of people enjoying the products. This is because people in Mexico tend to prefer being with others. However people in Switzerland value independence and solitude. Although the main purpose of a

20　company's website is to present important information about the business, but the site must also address the cultural values of the people who view it.

叙述 1：过去完成时；情态动词表示过去；常用的时间状语从句

The American Dream

1 现实生活中的语法

The Pact: Three Young Men Make a Promise and Fulfill a Dream (2003) 讲述了三位从小家境贫寒的男士如何取得了成功。阅读这本书的选段和其中一位作者对此的回应。其中，选段是叙述性写作的范例。

A **读前准备** 猜一猜作者笔下的美国梦是什么。阅读文章并思考：在作者看来，现在的人们是否有信心实现美国梦？为什么？

B **阅读理解** 回答下列问题。

  1 Why is the story of the three doctors remarkable?

  2 What are some events that have negatively impacted or affected the American Dream?

  3 According to Rodriguez, why is the American Dream important?

C **语法发现** 按照下列提示回答问题，注意作者是如何描述过去事件的发生顺序的。

  1 再次阅读第 49—53 行的 3 个句子。其中，(a) people had considered the American Dream to be achievable，(b) the idea of the American Dream was damaged，哪一个先发生？什么动词形式表明了这一点？

  2 再次阅读第 53—56 行以 In the late 1980s 开头的句子。其中，(a) less job security for Americans，(b) more job security，哪一个先发生？什么动词形式表明了这一点？

Excerpt from **The Pact: Three Young Men Make a Promise and Fulfill a Dream** (2003)

"We treat them in hospitals every day. They are young brothers, often drug dealers, gang members, or small-time criminals, who show up shot, stabbed, or beaten after a hustle[1] gone
5 bad. To some of our medical colleagues, they are just nameless thugs,[2] perpetuating crime and death in neighborhoods that have seen far too much of these things. But when we look into their faces, we see ourselves as teenagers, we see our friends, we
10 see what we easily could have become as young adults. And we're reminded of the thin line that separates us – three twenty-nine-year-old doctors (an emergency-room physician, an internist, and a dentist) – from those patients whose lives are filled
15 with danger and desperation.

"We grew up in poor, broken homes[3] in New Jersey neighborhoods riddled with crime, drugs, and death, and came of age in the 1980s at the height of a crack epidemic[4] that ravaged
20 communities like ours throughout the nation ... Two of us landed in juvenile-detention centers[5] before our eighteenth birthdays. But inspired early by caring and imaginative role models, one of us in childhood latched on to[6] a dream of becoming a
25 dentist, steered clear of[7] trouble, and in his senior year of high school persuaded his two best friends to apply to a college program for minority students interested in becoming doctors. We knew we'd never survive if we went after it alone. And so we
30 made a pact:[8] we'd help one another through, no matter what" (Davis, Jenkins, & Hunt, 2003, pp. 1–2).

Writer's Response

The excerpt from *The Pact: Three Young Men Make a Promise and Fulfill a Dream* might be
35 described as a contemporary version of the American Dream. Simply stated, the American Dream is the belief that if people work hard and play by the rules, they will have a chance to get ahead. The American Dream is based on the belief that people have the
40 same opportunity regardless of their race, creed, color, national origin, gender, or religion.

For middle-class Americans, the American Dream typically means that each generation will have more material possessions than the last.
45 For some, achieving the American Dream means having a secure job and owning a home. For others, it is the promise that anyone may rise from poverty to wealth with hard work.

For many years, people had considered
50 the American Dream to be achievable. Several decades ago, things changed. A number of events damaged the idea of the American Dream for the American middle class. In the late 1980s and early 1990s, housing costs increased dramatically, and
55 job security, which had been assured for previous generations, became much less certain. As a result, many people believed that they would be worse off than their parents. Global events such as the Great Recession of 2008 further shook people's
60 confidence about the likelihood of reaching the American Dream. More locally, natural disasters such as Hurricane Maria and Superstorm Sandy significantly affected many people's daily lives and, temporarily at least, shattered their hopes.
65 For some, it appears that the dream may have died, but does it really matter? *The LA Times* journalist, Gregory Rodriguez, would say yes. As he states, "The dream is the glue that keeps us all together ... it's the fabled dream
70 that fuses hundreds of millions of separate, even competing individual dreams into one national collective enterprise." Thus, it is the dream that reassures Americans that the factors for success – ability, strong work ethic, and education – will be
75 rewarded. Like the three doctors who had grown up in such poverty before they achieved success, many people rely on the dream for encouragement as they work hard to create their own versions of the American Dream.

---

[1]**hustle:** the act of tricking people to cheat them out of money 欺诈行为

[2]**thug:** a violent person, often a criminal 恶棍，暴徒

[3]**broken home:** a family where one parent has left 破裂的家庭

[4]**crack epidemic:** the widespread drug addiction to crack cocaine in some neighborhoods in the United States during the 1980s 强效可卡因泛滥

[5]**juvenile-detention center:** a form of prison for young people who are not yet considered adults 未成年犯管教所

[6]**latch on to:** become very interested in 对……产生浓厚兴趣

[7]**steer clear of:** avoid 避开

[8]**pact:** a promise or an agreement to do something together in the future 协议

2 过去完成时和过去完成进行时

语法讲解

在学术写作中，可以用过去完成时（past perfect）和过去完成进行时（past perfect progressive）将过去发生的某一事件与在这一事件之前已经发生的另一背景事件进行对比。

By the 1990s, housing costs **had increased** dramatically, and job security **had become** much less certain than for previous generations.

When Bob got his first job, his brother **had** already **been working** for several years.

2.1 过去完成时的用法

A 用一般过去时描述过去发生且已经结束的事件。用过去完成时描述在过去的这个事件之前已经发生的事件。

先发生的事件
By midnight, he **had finished** most of his
后发生的事件
work, so he **decided** to go to bed.

B 过去完成时可用在含有 when, by the time 和 while 引导的时间状语从句的句子中，且常用于主句中。

before 和 after 引导的时间状语从句可以清晰地表明事件的先后顺序。因此，在这类句子中不必使用过去完成时。

注意：when 引导的时间状语从句与其主句中都使用一般过去时也可以体现出时间上的先后顺序。

如果要强调一个动作在另一个动作发生之前已经完成了，则选择过去完成时。

后发生的事件   先发生的事件
<u>When she arrived</u>, the class **had** already **started**.
<u>By the time she registered for classes</u>, the semester **had** already **begun**.
She started college after she **earned / had earned** enough money to pay for the first year.

先发生的事件   后发生的事件
When she <u>arrived</u>, the class <u>started</u>.

C 在叙述或描述中，可以用过去完成时描述更早之前发生的事件。

Nesreen was nervous on her first day of work. She'd never **had** a job before.

D 在叙事性写作及其他类型的学术写作中，可以用过去完成时为过去发生的事件提供背景信息或说明原因。

For years, many people **had considered** the American Dream to be achievable. Then the economy changed.

2.2 过去完成时与时间副词和频度副词连用

过去完成时可以与时间副词和频度副词连用，强调事件发生在更早的过去： after，before，earlier already，not … yet，still … not ever，just，never，recently	No one in her family **had** ever **attended** college <u>before</u>. She'd <u>already</u> **talked** to a few colleges, but she **hadn't applied** <u>yet</u>. She needed to find a way to pay the tuition. They'd <u>recently</u> **applied** for a grant and were waiting for a final response.

2.3 过去完成时和过去完成进行时的用法

A 与过去完成时相似，过去完成进行时可用于给出某一过去事件发生的背景或原因，或描述在更早的过去发生的事件。 注意：be，know，seem 等状态动词不用过去完成进行时，也不用其他进行时形式。	过去完成时 They **had experienced** many challenges, so they **decided** to make a pact. 过去完成进行时 They **had been experiencing** many challenges, so they **decided** to make a pact. She **had known** that she wanted to be in education since she was a young girl. 不说 She ~~had been knowing~~ that she wanted to be in education since she was a young girl.
B 过去完成进行时强调某一动作从过去更早的时间开始，一直延续到过去某个时间点。 当过去的另一个动作发生时，该动作也许仍在持续进行中。 📊 过去完成进行时比过去完成时的使用频率低很多。	He'd **been talking about** applying to medical school for a long time. Finally, last January, he applied. 先发生的事件 They'd **been working** for about an hour 后发生的事件 when the bell rang.

语法应用

练习 2.1 一般过去时和过去完成时

A Naresh 移民到了美国，用括号中动词的一般过去时或过去完成时形式及副词把下列关于他的句子补充完整。

1 Naresh ___*had studied*___ (study) English for three years in his native country, India, before he ___*came*___ (come) to the United States.

2 Naresh _____ (arrive) in the United States six months ago to study.
   He _____ (never / be) here before.

3 At first, he _____ (stay) in a motel because he _____ (neglect) to look for a place to live before arriving.

4 Naresh's parents _____ (be) worried about him because after a month, he still _____ (not find) an apartment.

5 They _____ (contact) their friend Sam who was living in the United States. Naresh's parents _____ (help) Sam 25 years earlier to adjust to living in India.

6 Sam and his wife, Lea, _____ (be) good friends with Naresh's parents. They _____ (go) to visit Naresh's family several times.

7 Naresh _____ (hope) to live on his own, but after struggling so much, he _____ (be) happy to accept Sam and Lea's offer to stay with them.

8 Sam and Lea _____ (give) Naresh as much help as they could, just like Naresh's parents _____ (assist) Sam 25 years earlier.

B **结对练习** 向同伴解释练习 A 中所给答案的理由。你同意对方的解释吗？

First, Naresh studied English and second, he came to the United States. So we need to use the past perfect form had studied *and the simple past form* came.

练习 2.2 过去完成时和过去完成进行时

A 下面是关于一位移居美国的韩国女士的句子。圈出正确的动词形式。有时两种形式都正确。

1 Mi Young's mother **had planned /(had been planning)** to visit her daughter in the United States for several years, but by Mi Young's fifth year in New York, her mother still **(hadn't visited)/ hadn't been visiting** her.

2 Mi Young's mother **had gone / had been going** to Los Angeles once before to visit her sister when she was much younger, and she **had wanted / had been wanting** to return ever since then.

3 At one point, it seemed as if Mi Young might come home because she **had lost / had been losing** her job and she **had looked / had been looking** for a new job for several months.

4 Mi Young **had thought / had been thinking** about moving back to South Korea when she got a job offer in Los Angeles. It was a company that a friend of hers **had just started / had been starting** to work for.

5 Mi Young's mom **had worried / had been worrying** about traveling all the way to New York, so she was happy when Mi Young moved to Los Angeles. The flight was a lot shorter!

6 Also, her mother **had had / had been having** a nice time in Los Angeles on her first trip, so she **had hoped / had been hoping** since then that Mi Young might get a job there.

B 结对练习 想想你自己或你熟悉的人在生活中经历过的重大变化，比如搬家、结婚、找到新工作等。在必要的地方使用过去完成时或过去完成进行时，描述引起这种变化的事件。

My boyfriend and I had been talking about getting married for over a year when he proposed to me. We'd been together for three years by that time. I'd known soon after we met that I was going to marry him, but I was still nervous about making the commitment. When I told my parents, they weren't surprised at all, but they thought I was too young. I was 21 at the time ...

3 情态动词和类似情态动词的表达表示过去

语法讲解

情态动词（modals）和类似情态动词的表达可以表达说话者或写作者对某一事件的看法，例如认为某事是可能的、必要的、值得做的等等。	I **should have studied** French when I was in high school. Joanna **could not finish** college in four years because she **had to work** full-time.

3.1 情态动词和类似情态动词的表达表示过去

A 可以用以下类似情态动词的表达表示过去必须或不必做某事： had to 表示过去必须做某事 did not have to 表示过去不必做某事	The three friends came from poor families, so they **had to find** a way to pay for their education. They **did not have to pay** for their college education because they got scholarships.
B 可以用以下情态动词表示过去允许或禁止做某事： could 表示过去允许做某事 could not 表示过去不允许做某事	In the past, minority students **could apply** for special college grants. Nonminority students **could not apply** for these special college grants.
C 可以用以下"情态动词 + have + 过去分词"的形式表达对过去已发生或未发生动作的不赞成或后悔： should have，should not have，could have	I **should have applied** for a work-study job.（我本来可以申请，但是我没有，因而现在感到后悔。） She **shouldn't have missed** so many classes.（她本来可以不缺课，但是她缺了很多，因而现在要不及格了。） We **could have asked** for help.（我们本来可以请求帮助，但我们没有，因而现在感到遗憾。）

D 可以用以下"情态动词 + have + 过去分词"的形式表示过去某一动作可能或不可能发生：

could / might have 表达可能发生

He **could / might have found out** about the job opening through the school's career center.
（这是有可能的，因为我知道他去过那儿。）

could not have 表达不可能发生

We **could not have predicted** that the number of college applications would increase so much this year.（这不可能被预测到。）

3.2　would 和 used to 表示过去的习惯

A "would / used to + 动词原形"用于描述过去经常发生但现在不再发生的习惯或惯例。
使用 would 时，必须表明其所述之事发生在过去，例如可以用表示过去的时间状语从句来体现。
在学术写作中，would 比 used to 的使用频率更高。

While I was living in my country, I **would go** for long walks.

I **used to study** on the bus to school every day. Now I drive my car to school, so I can't study then.

B used to 可以和状态动词（例如 have, be 等）连用来描述过去的状态或情况，而 would 不用于描述过去的状态或情况。

I **used to be** a manager at a hotel, but now I work at a bank.
My brother **used to have** a bike. Now he has a car.
I **used to like** long walks in the country.
不说 I ~~would~~ like long walks in the country.

3.3　was / were supposed to 和 was / were going to 表示过去的期待

was / were supposed to 和 was / were going to 后接动词原形，表示在过去依照规定或安排本应发生但却没有发生的动作。这些表达通常后接由 but 引导的分句，以解释该动作没有发生的原因。

The foundation **was supposed to provide** full funding for 30 students.
The students **were going to get** part-time jobs, **but there were none available**.
She **was supposed to start** classes this fall, **but she didn't have enough money for tuition**.

语法应用

练习 3.1　情态动词和类似情态动词的表达表示过去

下列句子讲述了一位女士通过努力工作获得成功的故事。根据每个句子前的提示选择 could，could have，had to，might have，should have 或它们的否定形式，然后用括号中动词的适当形式填空。

1 [necessary] Sarah ___*had to work*___ (work) when she was young because her father's salary wasn't enough for the family.

2 [not necessary] Every day, Sarah went to school and then went to work at a pizza shop. Her school and the pizza shop were close to home, so she _____ (drive) or take the bus.

3 [possible] When Sarah finished high school, she wanted to go to college, but she didn't have enough money. She _____ (win) a scholarship because she had high grades, but she never applied for one.

4 [regret] Later she realized that she _____ (apply) for every possible scholarship.

5 [not necessary] Sarah decided that she could be a success even without a college education. Because she _____ (go) to school anymore, she began working full time.

6 [possible] She worked 60 hours a week at the pizza shop and made a lot of money, yet she hardly spent any. Her thriftiness _____ (be) the result of growing up in a poor household.

7 [not permitted] After a few years, the owner of the pizza shop decided he wanted to sell the shop. Sarah wanted to buy it. She didn't have enough money, so she tried to take out a loan at the bank, but she _____ (get) a loan.

8 [allowed] The pizza shop owner really liked Sarah because she was such a hard worker. He told her that she _____ (buy) the shop from him and pay him over five years.

9 [disapproval] The owner's friends thought it was a bad idea. They told him he _____ (loan) her the money, but he knew he had made the right decision.

10 [possibility] Once Sarah had bought the shop, she made it more successful than it had ever been. No one _____ (predict) how successful Sarah would be.

11 [impossibility] Sarah continued to work hard, and after 10 years, she bought five more shops. She herself _____ (guess) that she would one day become such a successful businesswoman.

练习 3.2 used to 和 would

A Rita 和 Edwin 是一对来自多米尼加共和国的夫妻，听一段关于他们的故事。如果下列句子表达的意思与听到的内容一致，标记 T；如果不一致，标记 F。

1 __F__ Rita and Edwin used to live in New York.

2 _____ Every semester, they would enroll in the free English classes offered at schools.

3 _____ In his English classes, Edwin would always sit next to Spanish-speaking students.

4 _____ When she started classes, Rita wouldn't speak when the teacher called on her.

5 _____ She used to always start crying when she got nervous in class.

6 _____ Rita would often talk to her classmates.

7 _____ When he got a job at a hotel, Edwin would sometimes take a bus to get there.

8 _____ Rita and Edwin used to dream of a better life.

B **结对练习** 向同伴讲述你过去经常做的事情，并与现在的生活进行对比，再解释这些习惯发生变化的原因。

I used to work as a waiter in a restaurant, but now I'm a full-time student.
I realized that it was difficult to work and study at the same time, so I quit my job.

练习 3.3 was / were supposed to 和 was / were going to

A 下面的表格展示了 John 自己和熟悉他的人对他生活的期望和计划，以及这些期望和计划未能实现的原因。结合表格中的信息，使用 was / were supposed to 或 was / were going to 写出关于 John 的句子。

Expectations	Reasons Why the Plans Did Not Come True
1 Everyone expected John to become a doctor.	Nobody knew that he couldn't stand the sight of blood.
2 John planned to major in biology.	He changed his mind and decided to major in business instead.
3 John and his friends planned to go into business together after college.	They didn't have enough money.
4 John planned to move to California to find a job.	He was offered a job in Japan.
5 Everyone thought John would marry his high school sweetheart.	He fell in love with a girl in Japan.
6 John's parents planned to visit him this month.	His father broke his leg, so they postponed the trip.

1 *John was going to be a doctor, but nobody knew he couldn't stand the sight of blood.*

2 _____

3 _____

4 _____

5 _____

6 _____

B 结对练习 向同伴讲述你自己以及你熟悉的人曾经有过但又改变了的计划，并解释计划发生改变的原因。

I was going to major in computer science, but I decided I was more interested in history. My brother has always loved animals. We always thought he was going to be a veterinarian, but he ended up majoring in business. He said that he changed his mind when he started working at a bank. He really wants to own his own business some day.

4 常用的时间状语从句

语法讲解

时间状语从句（time clauses）可以表示时间或事件的发生顺序。在叙述性写作中，这类从句常见于较长、较复杂的句子中。

After I finished high school, I had to find a job. I started practicing interview skills **when** I heard that I had a job interview.

4.1 常用的时间状语从句

A 表示时间关系的从属分句由 after，as，before，while 等从属连词引导。这样的从句有时被称为时间状语从句。

Life in the U.S. was difficult at first. I did my English homework **while** my baby was sleeping.

B 可以用以下从属连词来表示不同的时间关系和事件发生的顺序：

after 表示从句中的事件先发生。

先发生　　　　　　　后发生

After he started working on campus, it was very difficult to keep up with his classes.

后发生　　　　　　　先发生

before 表示从句中的事件后发生。

Before I moved to this country, I did not know how to cook.

every time 表示现在或过去重复发生的事件。

Every time they moved, the children had to adjust to a new school.

since（与之连用的主句常用现在完成时或过去完成时）表示某个动作或状态开始于什么时候。

He's worked here **since** he left high school.

once，when 和 as soon as 表示一个事件紧接着另一个事件发生。

Once I finished college, I started looking for a job.

when，while 和 as 表示两个事件同时发生。

He worked full-time at a grocery store **while** he was going to college.

until 表示某种情况一直持续到某个时间点或某个事件为止。

I had to work night shifts **until** I found a better job.

📊 before，when，until 和 after 是学术写作中最常用的从属连词。

💻 **语法应用**

练习 4.1 常用的时间状语从句

用括号中的从属连词，将下列每组关于作家 Stephen King 的句子组合起来。

1 Stephen King struggled a lot in his life. Then he became a famous author.

(before) ___*Stephen King struggled a lot in life before he became a famous author.*___

2 He was two years old. His father left.

(when) _____

_____

3 His father left. Then his mother struggled to take care of him and his brother.

(after) _____

_____

4 He was 12. He became interested in writing horror stories.

(when) _____

5 He was in school. He wrote many stories.

(while) _____

6 He sold stories to his classmates. Then the teachers asked him to stop.

(until) _____

7 His first short story was published. Then he graduated college.

(before) _____

8 His mother died. Then his first novel, *Carrie*, was published.

(after) _____

练习 4.2　更多练习：常用的时间状语从句

A 结合下面表格中关于 Martin Luther King, Jr. 博士生平事迹的时间线信息，圈出正确的从属连词，完成后面的短文。

1955 – Rosa Parks arrested on December 1 for refusing to give up her seat on a bus to a white passenger in Montgomery, Alabama; started a boycott on December 5 to stop segregation on Montgomery buses
1956 – In June, segregation law declared unconstitutional; in December, bus segregation stopped
1963 – King delivered "I Have a Dream" speech at the Lincoln Memorial in Washington, D.C.
1968 – King assassinated at the Lorraine Motel in Memphis, Tennessee
1986 – The third Monday in January declared a national holiday in honor of the birthday of Dr. Martin Luther King, Jr.
2011 – Memorial statue of King put up in Washington, D.C.

August, 1963, at the March on Washington

Dr. Martin Luther King, Jr. was an influential leader in the 1950s and 1960s in the Civil Rights movement, a movement that ended segregation and discrimination of African Americans in American society. [1] **After /(While)** other leaders were considering violence as the way to bring about social changes in the early 1950s, King was urging people to use nonviolent means, such as boycotts and demonstrations. The movement did not become energized [2] **until / as soon as** Rosa Parks, a social activist, refused to give her seat on a bus to a white man. On December 5, 1955, black residents in Montgomery, Alabama, boycotted the buses and elected King as their leader. [3] **Once / As** the boycott continued into 1956, King's reputation as a courageous leader grew, and his outstanding speaking skills inspired many to join the movement. [4] **Before / After** the U.S. Supreme Court declared Alabama's segregation laws unconstitutional in June, segregation on

Montgomery buses finally ended that following December. [5] __Once / Since__ the Supreme Court made its decision, King ended the boycott. In 1963, King delivered his famous "I Have a Dream" speech. Just five years [6] __since / after__ he delivered that speech, King was assassinated in Memphis, Tennessee. [7] __Since / Until__ the Civil Rights Act of 1964 was passed, many people have benefited from it. Among other provisions, the act made it illegal to discriminate against someone based on race, religion, and gender. Dr. Martin Luther King, Jr. continues to be an icon for the civil rights movement. [8] __As / Until__ more and more people recognized King's significant contribution to civil rights and equality over time, political figures began to ask for a day of remembrance. The first Martin Luther King Day of Service was observed in 1986. In 2011, a memorial was dedicated to King on the National Mall in Washington, D.C.

B 想一想你自己或你崇拜的人生命中所经历过的重要事件，在一张纸上列出与练习 A 中类似的时间线，并用时间状语从句向同伴讲述这些事件。

Since I was young, I've wanted to go to college to study math. Before I started college, I spent two years in the army. As soon as I got out of the army, I sent out applications for college.

5 常见错误提示 ⚠

1 注意过去完成时的构成形式，had 后要用过去分词。

gone
He had ~~went~~ to college, so he already had a degree.

come
Blanca's family had ~~came~~ to the United States when she was still a child.

2 强调发生在 when 引导的时间状语从句所述动作之前的另一个动作已持续一段时间时，注意在主句中用过去完成进行时，而不用过去进行时。

had been taking
She ~~was taking~~ care of children for many years when she realized she needed an A.A. degree.

had been working
Ahmet ~~was working~~ in a restaurant for a long time when he decided to go to college.

3 描述一个已经结束的动作或状态时，注意用一般过去时，而非过去完成时。过去完成时常用于表示在过去某一时间之前发生的事件。

graduated
I ~~had graduated~~ from college last year.

改错练习

下面是关于改变职业道路的叙述性短文，从中找出关于过去完成时和过去完成进行时使用的另外 9 处错误并改正。

Changing Careers

had been asking

Jessica had always loved photography, even as a child. She ~~was asking~~ for a camera for a long time when her father had gave her one on her tenth birthday. She would take her camera everywhere and record the small moments of everyday life that caught her eye: a cluster of leaves on the sidewalk, or a spider web on a garden fence. Jessica had
5 always see photography as a hobby. Moreover, since she had came from a family that had endured economic hardships when she was growing up, she had always know that she had to choose a career that paid well and was secure. Therefore, after high school, she got a degree in landscape design. She was considering a job with the city during her last year of college, but when her uncle, the owner of a landscape company, asked her to
10 work for him, she changed her mind. She had joined his landscaping business right after graduation. However, Jessica never lost her love of photography. She eventually bought herself a higher quality camera and continued to take pictures whenever she had the opportunity.

Jessica was working at the landscaping company for about two years when her uncle
15 decided to build a website to advertise the business. He needed images of the company's best work to publish on the site and immediately thought of Jessica. She was taking photos of the company's projects the entire time that she had worked there. The website had been a success. More importantly, other companies saw it and wanted to know who the great photographer was. Soon, Jessica was working full time as a photographer. Her
20 uncle missed Jessica's presence, but everyone was pleased that she was now earning a living doing something that she truly loved.

叙述 2：指示词；常用的时间标志词

Immigration

1 现实生活中的语法

阅读这篇关于美国移民史的文章。这是一篇历史叙事的范例。

A **读前准备** 人们移民的原因有哪些？移民通常会遇到什么问题？阅读文章并思考：多年来美国是如何因移民而受益的？

B **阅读理解** 回答下列问题。

1 Describe the immigrants who traveled to the United States in the seventeenth century.

2 When and why did the U.S. government start to restrict entrance into the United States?

3 Why does the writer say that the United States will continue to be built with the help of immigrants?

C **语法发现** 按照下列提示找出指示词和时间标志词，并试着理解它们的用法。

1 在第 20—24 行以 Even though some of these immigrants 开头的句子中，注意 these 的用法。these 指什么？

2 在第 28—30 行以 During that period 开头的句子中，注意 that 的用法。that 指什么？

3 第 2 段中提到了两段时间，在作者用以标示时间段的介词下面画线。

Immigration
and the United States

SINCE THE SEVENTEENTH CENTURY, immigrants from all over the world have come to the United States in search of safety, freedom, and economic opportunities. Immigration patterns
5 have varied over time, with distinct periods of immigration from different countries. In each of these periods, immigrants helped shape U.S. society and the economy. However, the flow of immigrants has also brought challenges
10 that continue into the present.

The period from the seventeenth century through the early nineteenth century is the first and longest U.S. immigration wave. During this time, most immigrants came from Europe,
15 including France and the Netherlands. The number of immigrants was small, and most of the newcomers became farmers. By the 1820s, this pattern started to change. From the 1820s to 1880s, approximately 15 million immigrants
20 settled in the United States. Even though some of these immigrants decided to work in agriculture in the Midwest and Northeast, many more moved to big cities, such as New York City and Boston.

25 The immigration wave that took place between the 1890s and the beginning of the twentieth century is often referred to as the flood of immigrants. During that period, nearly 25 million immigrants arrived in the United
30 States. They were mainly young Europeans from countries such as Italy, Greece, Hungary, and Poland.

Each group of immigrants presented distinct characteristics. Some groups were
35 less formally educated and some were mostly young, for example. However, they all contributed to the growth of many industries, including steel, automobile, and textile. Because of them, the United States turned into
40 one of the world's most powerful countries.

Over the course of the late nineteenth and early twentieth centuries, protests over immigrants grew. Many people were troubled by the new religions and customs that
45 immigrants brought to the United States. As a result, in 1921 the government passed laws limiting the number of immigrants allowed to enter each year. Even though immigrants contributed to the economic growth of the
50 United States, the country made it difficult for them to enter.

In the early 2000s, the immigration debate was reignited due to high numbers of immigrants, documented and undocumented.
55 Opponents argued that immigrants took jobs away from people and that the cost of maintaining their welfare was a drain on the education and health care systems. Although the arguments continue to this day, it is
60 important to remember that the country was and will continue to be built with the help of immigrants.

2 指示词

语法讲解

指示词（demonstratives）包括 this，that，these 和 those。指示词用在各种类型的写作中，以连接信息或使行文连贯。	In my neighborhood, there are people from all over the world. Most of **these** people have good jobs. The article is about recent immigration. **That** topic always generates interesting conversation.

2.1　指示词

指示词 this，that，these 和 those 可用于表示某人或某事物与说话者在空间或时间上的距离。 this / these 指时空上距离说话者较近的人或事物。 that / those 指时空上距离说话者较远的人或事物。	**This** unit is about immigration. Let's look at the first page. I remember **those** days when I'd been in this new country for only three weeks and didn't speak any English.

2.2　连接信息的指示词

A 指示词可与名词连用，以连接邻近的信息，使文章衔接紧密。这类指示词也被称为指示形容词（demonstrative adjectives）。	Immigrants came from all over Europe. Most of **these** <u>immigrants</u> opted for farming.（这些移民指来自欧洲各地的移民。） The flood of immigrants occurred between the 1890s and the beginning of the twentieth century. During **that** <u>period</u>, nearly 25 million immigrants arrived in the United States.
B 指示词也可不与名词连用。单独使用时，也被称为指示代词（demonstrative pronouns）。 it 也有相同的用法。	Climate change affects everyone. Indeed, **this** is the most important environmental issue of our time.（this 指代气候变化。） Climate change affects everyone. Indeed, **it** is the most important environmental issue of our time.（it 指代气候变化。）
C 指示代词可用于总结或指代在同一段落中已提及的信息。	Economic disparity is widespread and increasing. **This** is an especially significant problem for developing countries.（this 指代经济差距正在扩大这一事实。）

2.2　连接信息的指示词（续表）

D 指示词可以与一些能概括或阐明其所指的名词连用，例如：approach，aspect，development，experience，factor，reason，phenomenon，topic	Nearly 25 million Europeans traveled to the United States at the end of the nineteenth century and early twentieth century. **That development** changed the demographics of the country.（That development 指前一句中的信息。）
E 指示词与一些总结性的单词或短语连用，可以表达作者对于已述话题的看法，例如：controversial argument，indisputable fact，questionable claim，undisputed fact	Some people believe immigration leads to increases in crime. **This controversial argument** has been challenged by many. Millions of people have immigrated to the United States. **This undisputed fact** constitutes one of the central elements in the country's development.

语法应用

练习 2.1　指示词

A　阅读下列关于欧洲移民的句子，用正确的指示词填空。有时正确答案不唯一。

1　The European Union has expanded in recent years to include over two dozen countries. ___*This*___ has contributed to increased immigration all over Europe.

2　In 2004, ten countries joined the European Union. _____ countries included Hungary, Poland, Lithuania, and Slovakia.

3　Citizens of European Union member nations have permission to live in any EU country where they work. _____ makes it fairly easy for people to move from one EU country to another.

4　About 4.7 million people immigrated to one of the EU Member States in 2015 alone. _____ figure includes not only people from outside the EU but also people moving between EU countries.

5　There are about five million immigrants living in Italy. _____ people make up just over 8 percent of the population.

6　In 2017, 25,600 people wanted to immigrate to Sweden for asylum.[1] _____ was 11.72 percent less than in 2016.

[1]**asylum:** protection or safety（政治）避难，（政治）庇护

B 结对练习 与同伴轮流说一说练习 A 中每个句子里的指示词所指的内容。

In sentence 1, This refers to the expansion of the European Union.

A 某位作者就移民所带来的挑战发表了看法。阅读下文，圈出正确的选项。

Millions of people move to new countries every year. This ¹ (phenomenon)/ reason can cause challenges for both the residents of the host country and for the immigrants. Often, the people from the host country and the immigrants have difficulty relating to each other and understanding each other's customs. Also, the language of the host country and the immigrants' language are sometimes very different. If people cannot speak to each other, they cannot begin to understand each other. This ² fact / argument may be the underlying cause of most misunderstandings between residents and immigrant groups. People often fear what they do not understand.

However, people disagree about which language immigrants should speak. This ³ development / controversial issue can produce very different responses. Some people believe that immigrants should stop speaking their native language and speak the host country's language, even in their homes. They feel that immigrants will be able to assimilate better if they adopt the host country's language. This ⁴ questionable claim / aspect is directly opposed to the opinion of those who believe that it is important for immigrants to continue to speak their own language while they learn the host country's language. Many believe that this second ⁵ aspect / approach is the best one for young children. These ⁶ people / factors argue that individuals who have a strong command of their own language are better able to learn a new language. This ⁷ argument / topic seems to have some validity since research shows that immigrant children who cannot read and write in their parent's language have trouble learning to read and write their adopted country's language.

B 结对练习 与同伴讨论练习 A 的答案。你认为作者对于移民及语言问题的看法是什么？你是如何得知的？你同意作者的看法吗？用指示词和练习 A 中的词语写出 4—5 个句子来回应作者的观点，再将这些句子分享给另一组同学或全班同学。

The writer believes that immigration can cause problems for countries and immigrants. We understand that there are sometimes issues that need to be resolved, but we strongly feel that this phenomenon is actually, in the long run, good for both the countries and the immigrants because …

3 常用的时间标志词

词汇讲解

时间标志词（time signals）的使用在叙述性写作中相当重要，用上它们能够帮助写作者更清晰地呈现事件或信息的顺序。	**Over the past twenty years,** immigration has become a controversial issue in many European countries. This is not **the first time** in U.S. history that immigrants have been criticized.

3.1 常用的时间标志词

A 最常使用的时间标志词是介词短语，例如： by + 具体时间 from + 具体时间 + through / to + 具体时间 after / since + 具体时间 over / during the course of + 时间段 over the past / next / last + 时间段 in the past / next / last + 时间段 for + 时间段	The immigration situation changed **by** <u>the mid 1800s</u>. The first and longest immigration era stretched **from** <u>the seventeenth century</u> **to** <u>the early nineteenth century</u>. **After** <u>the end of World War I (from 1914 to 1918)</u>, Congress changed the nation's basic policy about immigration. **Over the course of** <u>the late nineteenth and early twentieth centuries</u>, the government took measures to slow down immigration. **Over the last / past** <u>20 years</u>, immigration has increased. **In the next** <u>10 years</u>, immigration is likely to decrease. The high rate of immigration continued **for** <u>almost one hundred years</u>.
B 下列时间副词也被视为时间标志词： already，always，ever，just，lately，never，now，recently，since，yet，the first / last time 注意：this is the first time 与现在完成时连用。	We've **always** lived in this neighborhood. I will **never** again feel so helpless. I **now** work in a clinic that serves immigrants. It felt great **the first time** I realized I could make my own choice. The debate over immigration has heated up **recently**. 错误用法： **This is the first time** I ~~read / am reading~~ about immigration issues. 修正： **This is the first time** I<u>'ve read</u> about immigration issues.

C every day，once (once more / once again / once or twice) 和 twice 表示频率。	**Every day**, I'm amazed by how far I've gone. By 2000, the United States had **once again** become a nation of immigrants.
D "时间 + later / earlier" 表示与另一个事件有关的某个事件的发生时间。	I left my neighborhood when I was just 11. <u>Years</u> **later**, I returned to Boston to go to medical school.

 词汇应用

练习 3.1 时间标志词

听一篇由一位移民美国的越南人所写的文章。录音共播放两遍。听第一遍时，填入所缺词语；听第二遍时，核对答案。

I was born in Vietnam. My family moved to the United States ¹ ___***when I was eight***___.
² _____, I lived in San Jose, California. All our neighbors were immigrants.
³ _____ a new immigrant family arrived, we helped them settle. We lived there
⁴ _____.

Vietnamese American Tet Festival in San Jose, California

⁵ _____,
I studied very hard in school. My parents taught me to value education even though they were poorly educated. Then ⁶_____, I went to college and ⁷_____ to medical school. I ⁸_____ work in a hospital in the same neighborhood that I grew up in, and ⁹_____ I feel happy that I can give back to my community.

I am very grateful for the life I have now. Even though it is ¹⁰_____ that I arrived, sometimes that first day here seems like yesterday. ¹¹_____ I still remember how terrified I felt ¹²_____ I took the bus to school. ¹³_____ I wait for my young son's school bus to arrive and watch him get on the bus. ¹⁴_____ I intend to teach my son about the values of hard work and the sacrifices that his grandparents made so that he can enjoy the world he lives in.

练习 3.2　更多练习：时间标志词

A　结合你自己生活中发生过或正在发生的重要事件，以及你对未来生活的期望，完成下列句子。

1　I _____ for the first time in

_____

2　By the time I was _____

I _____

3　Years later, I _____

4　After I _____

I _____

5　Over the past few years, I _____

6　I recently _____

7　Every day, I _____

8　In the next few years, I hope to _____

B　**结对练习**　将句子分享给同伴，并描述更多细节。

I flew in a plane for the first time in 2002. I was 16 years old. I flew from Beijing to Australia to see my aunt who had immigrated there. We spent a few days at a beach. It was so beautiful. We also went to a national park, and I saw koalas and kangaroos.

4 常见错误提示 ⚠

1 注意 this / that 与单数名词连用，these / those 与复数名词连用。

These
~~This~~ ideas about immigrants are common.

2 注意不要漏掉 over the past year，in the next five years 等时间标志词中的 the。

   the
In∧last five years, our neighborhood has become less diverse.

3 注意频度副词通常置于主要动词之前，动词 be 之后。

     never
He ~~never~~ has∧seen so much traffic.

     always
The traffic ~~always~~ is∧bad.

He usually
~~Usually he~~ arrives late.

改错练习

下文介绍了一种在发展中国家应用的新型器具，从中找出另外 8 处错误并改正。

The lack of clean drinking water is a problem in many parts of the world, but even when people have a source of water, collecting it can be arduous.

5 Every morning, Isha gets water for her
    It always
family. ~~Always it~~ takes her 30 minutes to get to the well and about an hour to walk back with a heavy clay container of water balanced on top

10 of her head. By time she returns, her body is aching from the weight of the water. She has been bringing water home like this for last 20 years. Isha lives in Niger, a country in West Africa. In Africa, women, and sometimes children, often are the ones responsible for collecting their family's water, and these responsibility takes a toll on their bodies. For some women, the journey to a water source is very long.

15 This women have to walk up to 18 miles (29 kilometers) a day for water. Hans Hendrikse, a native South African, wanted to do something about this problem.

Working with his engineer brother, Pieter, he created a new way of transporting water. It is called the Q-Drum. The Q-Drum is lightweight, durable, and affordable, and it can hold 50 liters of water. While this features alone make the product appealing, the most

20 groundbreaking feature is its doughnut shape. When a rope is looped through the hole in the Q-Drum, the container can be rolled along the ground like a wheel. The Q-Drum's unique design allows even a young child to pull water for several miles, so the women never will have to carry the water solely on their heads. Over next decade this invention will have a major impact on the lives of the people of Africa, especially the women.

11

分类和定义 1：被动语态；表示分类的常用单词和短语

Job Interviews

1 现实生活中的语法

阅读这篇关于求职面试的类型的文章。文章对信息进行了分类，是一篇分类写作的范例。

A **读前准备** 你参加过求职面试吗？你的经历是怎样的？阅读文章并思考：作者是如何对求职面试进行分类的？

B **阅读理解** 回答下列问题。

1 According to the writer, what are the main differences between remote and face-to-face interviews?

2 Why is an audition considered a less conventional type of interview?

3 Do you agree with the writer's conclusions in the final paragraph? Why or why not?

C **语法发现** 在文章中找到与下列句子意思相同的句子，并在横线上填写该句子的行数，再比较下列句子中标有下划线的动词与文章中对应句子里的动词。作者使用了什么动词形式？你认为作者为什么使用这种动词形式？

1 It is possible <u>to divide</u> interviews <u>into</u> two types. _____

2 You can <u>classify</u> face-to-face interviews <u>as</u> either collective or sequential. _____

3 A single interviewer <u>screens</u> multiple candidates in a group interview. _____

4 Interviewers <u>might ask</u> a candidate for a marketing job to persuade them to buy a fictitious product. _____

Interviews

[1] **remote:** not near, at a distance, far away 远程的
[2] **screening:** the process of sorting something into different groups 甄别，审查

Interviews are a familiar process for anyone entering the job market. They are by far the most common method used by companies to recruit new employees. All job interviews have the same goals – getting to know the job candidate better and giving
5 the candidate a chance to learn about the job. However, they can take several different forms depending on geographic location and format.

Depending on the geographic location of the candidates, interviews can be divided into two types: remote[1] and face-to-face.
10 In remote interviews, candidates are geographically separated from the interviewers. This type of interview is usually the preferred method for initial screening,[2] as it eliminates traveling expenses. These interviews can be conducted over a teleconferencing system or over the phone. Face-to-face interviews, in contrast, require the
15 physical presence of the candidate. They are normally reserved for candidates who have already gone through a first round of remote screening.

Face-to-face interviews can be classified as either collective or sequential, depending on the number of people interacting
20 with the candidate. Collective interviews can have two possible structures: team interviews and group interviews. In a team interview, multiple interviewers interact with the candidate. In a group interview, multiple candidates are screened by a single interviewer. Sequential interviews, on the other hand, involve
25 private, one-on-one conversations between the candidate and several interviewers, one after another.

As far as the format is concerned, interviews can be divided into two categories: structured and unstructured. In a structured interview, the same list of questions is rigidly followed with
30 all candidates. Companies sometimes use this format to ensure equal treatment among interviewees. It also makes it easy for recruiters to directly compare how two candidates responded to the same question. Conversely, unstructured interviews have a less strict format. Candidates might be asked more open-ended questions that encourage them to lead the discussion. For example, the interviewer could start by asking candidates to talk about
35 themselves. Interviewers could also ask them to describe their professional experience.

Finally, there are a few less conventional types of interview formats. One example is an audition. In this type of interview, recruiters might ask candidates to perform a task that simulates the actual duties of that job. For example, a candidate for a computer programming position could be required to write a small piece of computer code. Candidates for a marketing
40 job might be asked to persuade their interviewers to buy a fictitious product, and interviewees applying for a teaching job may be invited to prepare and deliver a mini-lesson.

Despite their possible variations, interviews should be seen as almost always having two main objectives. First, they are a way for the employer to test the potential employee. Second, but equally important, they are an opportunity for candidates to learn more about
45 the company and to evaluate their interest in the job. Being aware of the different types of interviews will help job seekers to be more prepared to accomplish those goals.

2 被动语态

语法讲解

被动语态（passive）强调的是动作，而非承受这一动作的人或事物。在学术写作中，被动语态也可用于建立句子间的联系，使语义衔接更加紧密。

Candidates **are asked** several <u>questions</u> during the interview. The interview <u>questions</u> **are created** by a hiring committee.

2.1 被动语态的构成

<u>The committee</u>（施动者）presented <u>the results of the survey</u>（受动者）at the meeting.（主动句）

<u>The results of the survey</u> were presented <u>by the committee</u> at the meeting.（被动句）

2.2 被动语态

A 被动句与主动句的意思相近，但强调的重点不同。
在主动句中，主语为施动者，即实施动词所表示的动作的人或物。
在被动句中，主语为受动者，即承受动词所表示的动作的人或物。

主动句：<u>HR</u>（施动者）**screens** <u>the candidates</u>（受动者）.

被动句：<u>Candidates</u>（受动者）**are screened** <u>by HR</u>（施动者）.

B 被动句由"be 的适当形式 + 动词的过去分词"构成。

一般现在时：Remote interviews **are considered** to be effective.
现在进行时：The candidate **is being interviewed**.
现在完成时：The final candidates **have** already **been selected**.
一般过去时：Candidates **were expected** to send a thank-you note after the interview.
过去进行时：The candidate **was being interviewed** when his cell phone rang.
过去完成时：Several candidates **had** already **been interviewed** when I arrived for my interview.

2.2 被动语态（续表）

C 情态动词也可用于被动结构中。	By Friday, several candidates will have been chosen. Candidates may be asked difficult questions. The candidates should have been asked more questions about their problem-solving skills.
D 有些动词常以被动形式出现，并后接介词，例如： associated with，based on，compared to / with，involved in，linked to，related to	Interview questions should be based on job requirements.
E 有些表示说话和思考的动词的被动形式常后接不定式。 常用的此类动词有： 📊ask，believe，expect，find，know，say，think，understand	Approximately 100 people are expected to apply for the job. Auditions are known to be effective job interview tools.

📊 实际使用数据分析

在学术写作中，下列动词常用被动形式： analyze, argue, carry out, conduct, consider, discuss, estimate, examine, explain, find, illustrate, include, note, observe, perform, present, study, suggest	Personal questions about age and marital status are never included in the interview process. Job responsibilities are discussed with the candidates at the interview.

2.3 被动语态的用法

A 当某一行为的施动者未知、不明显或不重要时，可以使用被动语态。	Many types of interview formats have been used at the research lab. Some candidates are required to perform a task.
B 被动语态可用于增强句子间信息的衔接。	In the group interview, multiple candidates are screened by a single interviewer. The interviewer asks a set of questions on standard topics. These questions have been chosen by the managers.

C 被动语态可用于描述过程。常用的此类动词有：classify，compare，develop，examine，measure，study，test	In many community colleges, interview questions **are** carefully **developed** and **tested** before they are used. Face-to-face interviews **can be classified into** several different types.
D 被动语态也可用于新闻事件的报道中。	According to a government report, fewer people **were hired** by companies in June than in May.

语法应用

练习 2.1 被动语态

下列句子描述了求职面试的相关建议和信息。将句中的黑体部分从主动形式变为被动形式，改写下列句子。当施动者不重要、未知或不明显时，可省略。

1 Occasionally **a member of the human resources staff will observe an interview**.

   Occasionally an interview will be observed by a member of the human resources staff.

2 **A company may not even consider you** for the job if you arrive late to the interview.

3 During the interview, **the interviewer will ask you questions** about your résumé.

4 **Interviewers may conduct interviews** over the phone.

5 One question you could ask is "What **training programs does the company offer?**"

6 **Employers often base the decision to employ someone on** a person's behavior during an interview.

7 **Federal and state laws prohibit employers** from asking certain questions about race, religion, and age.

8 **People have known some employers** to give tests during interviews.

9 If you do well, **an interviewer might ask you** to come in for a second interview.

10 Interviewers often see more than one candidate in a day, so **they will probably compare you** with other candidates.

练习 2.2 **更多练习：被动语态**

A 下面的电子邮件描述了一家软件公司最近的面试情况。用括号中动词的正确被动形式填空，并在恰当的地方使用括号中的情态动词。

> To chen_kim@cup.org
> From campbell_peter@cup.org
> Subject The search for project managers
>
> Hi Kim,
>   Our search for new project managers is going very well so far. Ten interviews
> [1] _have been conducted_ (conduct) this week so far. The following procedures
> [2] _____ (follow) each time. First, the interviewees all had individual interviews
> during which they [3] _____ (ask) about their previous work experience.
> Then the interviewees [4] _____ (divide) into two groups: those with project
> management experience and those without that experience. After that, each interviewee
> [5] _____ (give) a problem-solving test. The test items [6] _____ (base) on
> the kinds of problems that project managers might encounter. My experience has shown
> me that a lot [7] _____ (can / learn) about a candidate through a problem-solving
> test.
>   Then the interviewees [8] _____ (give) a short writing test. They
> [9] _____ (tell) when they applied that they might have to do some writing.
> After the writing test, the interviewees went home. The tests [10] _____
> (should / evaluate) by Friday, and three interviewees [11] _____ (will / choose) to
> come in for second interviews.
>   Let me know if you have any questions.
>   Peter

B 结对练习　与同伴讨论你自己或你熟悉的人的求职面试经历或大学申请面试经历。如有可能，请使用被动语态。

When I went to the interview for my current job, I was interviewed by my manager first. Then I was asked to take a test. After that, they told me they would call me if they were interested. They called, and I went in, and I talked to someone in the personnel department.

3 分类写作中的常用单词和短语

词汇讲解

在分类写作中，有些单词和短语常用于整理信息或对信息进行分类。	Colleges **can be classified** into different types. Most colleges offer the most popular majors, which **include** business administration and psychology.

3.1　表示分类的单词和短语

A 下面的动词和短语（按使用频率从高到低排序）常用于对事物进行分类：

involves _____ involves not only _____ but also _____ can be classified into _____ is a combination of _____ , _____ , and _____ consists of _____ is made up of _____ can be / is / are divided into _____ is composed of _____	The job **involves** a lot of traveling. Preparing for an interview **involves not only** physical preparation **but also** mental preparation. Interviews **can be classified into** two types. A strong cover letter is **a combination of** confidence, preparation, **and** curiosity. A typical job application **consists of** a cover letter and a résumé. A résumé **is divided into** several key sections.

B 下面的名词常用于表示类别或种类：

categories, classifications, divisions, factions, groups, kinds, parts, sections, sets, types, units	Job interviews can be divided into two **categories**. Interviews can be divided into two **kinds**: remote and face-to-face. There are two main **types** of interviews.

3.1 表示分类的单词和短语（续表）

C 下面的英文表达常用于展开话题：

话题, which are A and B.

话题，which include A and B.

话题，such as A and B.

话题: A, B, and C.

话题，including A, B, and C.

话题．These are A, B, and C.

注意这些结构中逗号的使用。

There are two main <u>types of interviews</u>, _{话题}

which are remote and face-to-face. _A _和 _B

The field of health care provides many <u>opportunities</u>: _{话题}

therapy, outpatient care, and home health care. _A _B _和 _C

D 下面的短语常用于介绍分类的标准（或方法）：

according to, based on, depending on, on the basis of

<u>Job interviews</u> can be classified **according to** _{话题} _{短语}

<u>their structure</u>. _{标准}

Depending on <u>the number of participants</u>, _{短语} _{标准}

<u>job interviews</u> can be divided into two categories. _{话题}

词汇应用

练习 3.1 表示分类的单词和短语

选出正确的选项，将下列关于工作的句子补充完整。

1 A successful job search _____ determination, networking, and luck.

   a can be divided into   (b involves)   c can be classified

2 Job descriptions on websites often _____ job titles, salaries, and benefits.

   a are divided into   b can be classified into   c consist of

3 Succeeding in an interview _____ both preparation and an ability to adapt quickly to a situation.

   a involves   b is composed of   c is made up of

4 Some companies prefer interviewing people in _____ .

   a types   b parts   c groups

5 Most people want a job that ____ interesting opportunities, challenging tasks, and nice co-workers.

   a is a combination of   b can be divided into   c can be classified into

6 Most businesses ____ several divisions.

   a can be classified into   b are composed of   c involve

7 There are three ____ of a small business owner's job: managing employees, handling the finances, and marketing the business.

   a kinds   b sets   c parts

8 Data Technician and Social Worker I are two ____ of government jobs listed online.

   a classifications   b sections   c sets

练习 3.2 更多练习：表示分类的单词和短语

阅读下列问题后，听一段关于美国高等教育的讲座，边听边做笔记，再用括号中表示分类的词语写出完整的回答。

1 How many categories can higher education in the United States be divided into? (can be divided into) _Higher education in the United States can be divided into five categories, which are universities, community colleges, liberal arts colleges, vocational-technical and career colleges, and special interest colleges._

2 What are the main criteria for determining whether an institution of higher education is a community college or a university?

   (classified / according to) _____

   _____

3 What are the three degree programs in a university?

   (is composed of / generally) _____

   _____

4 What is another way that schools can be divided?

   (can be divided by) _____

   _____

5 How many funding classifications of schools are there?

   (which are) _____

   _____

6 What are the types of publicly supported schools?

(can be subdivided into) _____

_____

7 What are the advantages of attending a community college?

(including) _____

_____

练习 3.3 更多练习：表示分类的单词和短语

A 结合自己的想法，使用下列表达写出关于求职面试的句子。

1 a job interview involves

I think a job interview involves not only talking about your experience but also making a good impression on the interviewers.

2 interviews can be classified into

_____

3 a successful job search is a combination of

_____

4 the perfect job involves

_____

5 a good résumé consists of

_____

6 I answer job advertisements on the basis of

_____

B **结对练习** 将写好的句子分享给同伴，共同选出最佳回答，并分享给全班同学。

I said that a job interview involves talking about your experience and making a good impression. My partner said that it involves finding out about job requirements. We agreed that my answer was probably the better answer because it's very competitive, so people need to sell themselves very well.

4 常见错误提示 ⚠

1 在被动句中注意副词要位于情态动词之后。

often

Leadership skills can‸be ~~often~~ determined in group interviews.

2 注意在 based on 中使用正确的介词 on。

on

The company's hiring decisions are based ~~in~~ candidates' interview behavior.

3 注意在 involved in 中使用正确的介词 in。

in

The company vice presidents are rarely involved ~~on~~ hiring decisions.

改错练习

下面是一篇文章的引入段和主体段，文章介绍了一些可以支付大学学费的方式。从中找出另外 7 处错误并改正。

Funding Options for Higher Education

in

There are many issues involved ~~on~~ choosing an institution of higher education. A prospective student's choice might be based in the location of the institution, or it might be based in the reputation of the academic programs and the faculty. However, for many students, the process of choosing a university
5 may be often determined by economics. A college education may be one of the greatest expenditures an individual will make in his or her lifetime. If money is an issue in a student's choice, there are several funding options.

One funding option available to low-income college students is a grant. A grant is a sum of money that does not have to be paid back. Government programs are the
10 primary source of education grants. In addition to government sources, grants may be sometimes awarded by private organizations and companies. The main factor involved on the awarding of government grants is income level. Private grants may often be based in additional factors, such as ethnicity, grades, or other academic achievements. As reporting one's income is always involved on the process of applying for a grant, a good
15 place to begin is with the U.S. Department of Education's Free Application for Federal Student Aid (FAFSA). The FAFSA application simplifies the income-reporting process and matches the applicant's income with several grant opportunities. Grants are often the first and best choice for students who cannot afford a college education on their own.

FAFSA®

FREE APPLICATION for FEDERAL STU...

Step One (Student): For questions 1-3

Your full name (exactly as it appears on your Social Se...
1. Last name

Your permanent mailing address
4. Number and street (include apt. number)

. City (and country if not U.S.)

Your Social Security Number   See Notes page 9.   9. Your ...

1040   Department of the Treasury—In...
Form   **U.S. Individual I...**

For the year Jan. 1–Dec. 31, 2016, or other tax year be...
Your first name and initial

If a joint return, spouse's first name and initial

Home address (number and street). If you have

City, town or post office, state, and ZIP code. If yo...

Foreign country name

Filing Status   1   ☐ Single
2   ☐ Married f
Check only one box.   3   ☐ Married f
and full ...

Exemptions   6a   ☐ Yours
b   ☐ Spou
c   Depende
(1) First name

If more than four dependents, see

分类和定义 2：表示定义的语言；同位语

Your Ideal Job

1 现实生活中的语法

阅读这篇文章，文章探讨了职业心理学家 John Holland 的理论，介绍了他如何根据性格对人群进行分类，并给出了每种性格的定义。

A 读前准备 你会如何描述自己的性格？你认为你的性格对你的职业选择有影响吗？阅读文章并思考：文中描述的 6 种性格类型分别是什么？

B 阅读理解 回答下列问题。

1 Why are people's career choices so important for success?

2 According to the essay, how will understanding one's vocational personality type be helpful?

3 Based on this essay, what is your personality type? Why?

C 语法发现 找到定义性格类型的句子，注意作者在介绍定义时使用的语法，并在用于给出定义的动词短语下面画线。

1 Artistic personality type on lines 12–15.

2 Investigative personality type on lines 15–17.

3 Realistic personality type on lines 18–20.

4 Social personality type on lines 22–23.

Matching **Personality Type** and **Work Environment**

Most people spend over a third of their waking hours at work. Because work is such an enormous part of people's lives, their career choices are critical for personal and professional success. Vocational¹ counselors, who are trained to help with these choices, use many tools to help people find
5 the best jobs. One tool is the use of personality tests to suggest job choices that could lead to greater job satisfaction. The most popular of these tests was created by John Holland, a leading researcher in vocational psychology. He developed six categories of personality type – *Artistic, Investigative, Realistic, Social, Enterprising, and Conventional* – which are used to help
10 identify the best job choices. Understanding these personality types can help identify an appropriate job for one's personality.

Each personality type has defining characteristics. An Artistic personality type refers to a person who enjoys creative activities like art, dance, or creative writing, and who generally avoids highly structured or
15 repetitive activities. A person with an Investigative personality type, on the other hand, is defined as someone who likes to study and solve math or science problems. People who fall into the Investigative personality type generally see themselves as scientific and intellectual. Having a Realistic personality type means valuing practical work, such as jobs that require
20 technical or manual skills and are productive. A person with a Realistic personality type particularly values environments where they produce goods or use machines. Other people have good skills at teaching, counseling, nursing, or giving information. They are referred to as Social personalities. People with Enterprising personalities are good at leading people and
25 selling things or ideas. Many entrepreneurs fall into the Enterprising category. Finally, people who have a Conventional personality type are able to work with written records and numbers in a systematic way. These people are usually very detail-oriented and value structure and planning.

Holland's personality types can provide insights into compatible
30 jobs and work environments where people can best use their abilities. For example, Realistic personality types would look for environments that allow them to use tools or machines and generally avoid those that require a lot of interaction with people. Artistic people are more likely to find satisfaction and success in an artistic environment, such as an arts center or theater.
35 Someone with an Investigative personality type would be best suited for a job in an investigative field, such as medicine or mathematics. Figure 1 provides examples of jobs that match each personality type. Holland believed that people who look for jobs that suit their abilities are more likely to find environments in which they can succeed and be satisfied.

Figure 1. Holland Personality Types and Career Examples

ARTISTIC	INVESTIGATIVE	REALISTIC	SOCIAL	ENTERPRISING	CONVENTIONAL
Architect	Mathematician	Auto Mechanic	Nurse	Flight Attendant	Accountant
Dancer	Professor	Cook	Teacher	Lawyer	Cashier
Musician	Scientist	Electrician	Therapist	Salesperson	Secretary

40 Matching someone's personality type with a work environment is actually a more complicated process because people are often a combination of two or three personality types. This means that the range of suitable jobs can actually be quite diverse. For example, a person may have a Realistic personality type but also have characteristics of an Enterprising
45 personality type and a Social personality type. This person would likely be suitable for a job as an electrician, a salesperson, or a nurse. Discovering one's major personality types involves using assessment tools that identify skills and strengths.

For many people, it is often a difficult
50 task to decide on a career. Realizing that much of one's life will be spent doing a certain kind of work can make the decision stressful. Many people use tools like Holland's personality types to help make their decisions.
55 Information about personality types can be interesting and useful. Holland's theory is a valuable guide for people in choosing satisfying jobs and careers.

2 表示定义的语言

语法讲解

定义在学术写作中非常常见。作者通过对文中的关键术语进行定义，让读者理解该概念的准确含义。定义中通常使用 be 的一般现在时形式、动词 mean 或某些动词的被动形式。

Having a Conventional personality type **means** being good at working with written records and numbers in a systematic way.

A person with an Investigative personality type **is defined as** someone who likes to study and solve math or science problems.

2.1 定义

A 定义通常遵循以下结构： 术语 + be + 泛指词 + 关键细节	术语 is / are 泛指词 <u>Realistic personality types</u> **are** people 关键细节 who value practical work.
泛指词比被定义的术语所指的范畴更大，比术语更具概括性。	术语 泛指词 <u>A Realistic person</u> is a **person** with practical skills. <u>Visual learning</u> means **learning** by seeing.
常用限制性关系从句或介词短语给出关键细节。	限制性关系从句 A headhunter is a person **whose job is to find qualified people to take high-paying jobs.** 介词短语 A chief executive officer is the person **with the most important position in a company.**
B 也可以使用动词 mean 给出定义。	Conventional **means** standard, predictable, or normal.
C 注意避免在定义中使用表示特定性别的单数代词。 可以将名词变为复数形式，并使用 their。 或 保留名词的单数形式，并使用 his or her 或 his / her。	单数名词：特定性别的 A general practitioner is a doctor who provides basic medical services to **his** patients. （这句话假设医生是男性，而非女性。） 复数名词：性别中立的 General practitioners are doctors who provide basic medical services to **their** patients. 单数名词：性别中立的 A general practitioner is a doctor who provides basic medical services to **his / her** patients.

2.2 被动语态用于表示定义

给某个术语下定义时，可以使用动词 call，define，know 或 refer 的被动形式。
使用 is / are defined as 时，定义位于术语之后。
使用 is / are known as，is / are called 或 is / are referred to as 时，定义位于术语之前。

术语
A certified public accountant (CPA) **is defined as**
定义
a person who has passed a state accounting exam.
定义
A person who has passed a state accounting exam
术语
is known as a certified public accountant (CPA)
定义
A person who instructs or trains others, especially
术语
in a school, **is called** a teacher.

2.3 定义的用法

A 可以将被定义的术语置于句尾，以增强其与下个句子主语的联系。

People who are skillful at occupations such as nursing, teaching, and counseling are known as Social types.

The types of people in this group like to work in social environments. （术语 Social types 与下一句之间的联系更紧密。）

B 较复杂的定义可分为两个句子来表达。在第二个句子中使用代词来与前一个句子衔接。

Some people are good at jobs that require working with numbers and following strict procedures. **They are called** Conventional personality types. （Conventional personality types 的定义在前一个句子中。）

语法应用

练习 2.1　识别定义的不同部分

A　将下列词语重新排序，写出定义不同类型的职业的句子。

1　who repairs / water pipes, baths, / is / a person / a plumber / and toilets
   A plumber is a person who repairs water pipes, baths, and toilets.

2　who designs / is a person / certain that they / new buildings and makes / an architect / are built correctly

3 sell merchandise / who work / are sometimes referred to / people / as sales associates / in stores and

_____

4 is called / a musician / who / someone / is skilled / in playing music

_____

5 out of materials / sculptors / make art / are artists / like clay, marble, and metal / who

_____

6 as stylists / fashionable clothing, / who / hairstyles, and makeup / are known / people / help their clients choose

_____

B 用括号中的词改写练习 A 中的句子。

1 (is called) _**A person who repairs water pipes, baths, and toilets is called a plumber.**_

2 (is referred to as) _____

_____

3 (are people who) _____

_____

4 (is defined as) _____

_____

5 (are known as) _____

_____

6 (are people who) _____

_____

C **结对练习** 想想其他职业的定义，向同伴提问，看她 / 他能否猜出来。在提问时使用不同的表示定义的语言。

A _What do you call someone who flies an airplane?_

B _A person who flies an airplane is called a pilot._

练习 2.2 写定义

A 两个学生正在准备刑事司法考试。听录音，将术语与正确的定义对应起来。

Field	Noun	Noun	Verb	Verb	Adjective + Noun
law	testimony	bankruptcy	to appeal	to sentence	~~admissible evidence~~

1 _**admissible evidence**_ : the kind of evidence that juries or judges can consider in civil and criminal cases

2 _____ : a system of rules that a community recognizes as regulators of behaviors and actions of people

3 _____ : evidence presented orally by witnesses during trials or before grand juries

4 _____ : to ask a higher court to review a decision after a trial to determine if it was correct

5 _____ : to announce a punishment to someone convicted of a crime

6 _____ : a legal procedure for dealing with debt problems of individuals and businesses

B 用括号中的动词写出练习 A 中术语的定义。

1 (define) *Evidence that juries or judges can consider in civil and criminal cases is defined as admissible evidence.*

2 (be) _____

_____

3 (know) _____

_____

4 (mean) _____

_____

5 (call) _____

_____

6 (refer) _____

_____

3 同位语

语法讲解

在学术写作中，可以使用同位语（appositives）来提供关于某个名词或名词短语的额外信息。同位语是一种跟在名词或名词短语之后，对其进行定义或重述，或补充关于其重要信息的名词短语。	John Zappa, president of Sylvania Community College, believes that instructors should always be aware of different learning styles. People with Enterprising personalities, personalities that have leadership traits, are good at leading people and selling things or ideas.

A 当一个名词短语和它前面的名词指的是同一个人或事物时，这个名词短语就叫同位语。

使用同位语的句子与使用非限制性关系从句的句子可以表示相同的意思。唯一的区别是前者省略了关系代词和动词 be。

主要名词　　　　　　　同位语
John Holland, **a leading researcher in vocational psychology**, developed a theory about career choices.
（John Holland 和 a leading researcher 指同一个人。）

非限制性关系从句
John Holland, **who is a leading researcher in vocational psychology**, developed a theory about career choices.

B 通常使用逗号来凸显同位语。

也可用破折号或括号来凸显同位语。

主要名词　　　　　　　　　同位语
Enterprising personalities, **personalities that have leadership traits,** are good at leading people and selling things or ideas.

主要名词　　　　　　　　　同位语
Kinesthetic learners – **people who learn through moving, doing, and touching** – prefer actively exploring the physical world around them.

主要名词
Workers with the Enterprising personality type
同位语
(people who are energetic, ambitious, and sociable) often work in real estate agencies and law firms.

C 同位语也可置于其所解释的名词之前。

同位语
A leading vocational psychologist, John Holland developed a well-known list of personality types.

A 可以用同位语来对专有名词进行补充说明或为其提供定义。

用于补充说明的同位语
Ben Cohen, **co-founder of Ben & Jerry's,** is a good
用于提供定义的同位语
example of a "Healer," **a business leader who provides nurturing harmony to a business.**

B 可以用同位语来标示表格、图表或引文。首字母缩略词或缩略语也可以作为同位语使用。其中，表格名称和首字母缩略词常置于括号中。

这些用法在学术写作中很常见。

To illustrate his theory, Holland created a model of
同位语
personality types **(Figure 1)**.
Federal data are now collected using the North
同位语
American Industrial Classification System **(NAICS)**.

语法应用

练习 3.1 同位语

下列句子描述了 8 位卓越的人物与 1 个著名的组织。将每题中的一个或两个句子改写为一个含有同位语的句子。

Michael Pollan   Bono   Howard Gardner

1 Michael Pollan is the author of *Food Rules* and *The Omnivore's Dilemma*. Michael Pollan believes we should all examine our eating habits.

   *Michael Pollan, the author of **Food Rules** and **The Omnivore's Dilemma**, believes we should all examine our eating habits.*

2 Steve Jobs, who was a driving force in technology, had an enormous impact on the way we use technology on a daily basis.

3 One supporter of the nonprofit housing organization Habitat for Humanity is Jimmy Carter. Jimmy Carter is a former U.S. president.

4 Desmond Tutu is a Nobel Peace Prize laureate and retired South African archbishop. Desmond Tutu has promoted peaceful conflict resolution for many years.

5 Dr. Douglas Schwartzentruber and Dr. Larry Kwak are cancer researchers. Dr. Douglas Schwartzentruber and Dr. Larry Kwak are both working separately to find a vaccine against cancer.

6 Bono is a famous singer with the band U2. Bono works to improve health and nutrition throughout the world.

_____

7 Howard Gardner proposed nine types of intelligences. The nine types of intelligences are in Table 1.

_____

8 The Ronald McDonald House Charities helps families of children who are receiving medical treatment for serious diseases. The abbreviation for the organization is RMHC.

_____

练习 3.2　更多练习：同位语

在一张纸上写出 5 个含有同位语的句子，描述你了解的人、地点或组织。尝试在句子中使用不同的标点符号：逗号、破折号和括号。

Jules Yakakao, an expert in English language learning, works at a major university in Côte d'Ivoire.

4　常见错误提示 ⚠

1　在给出定义时，注意正确使用单数名词和复数名词。

           people   enjoy
Artistic types are ~~a person~~ who ~~enjoys~~ creative activities.

2　在给出定义时，注意正确使用动词的被动形式。

                      referred
Sometimes, emergency medical technicians are ~~refer~~ to as paramedics.

3　在关系从句中注意使用正确的关系代词。注意 who 只用于指代表示有生命事物的名词。

       that
A résumé ~~who~~ does not include dates is called a functional résumé.

     who
People ~~which~~ are energetic and sociable often work in sales.

4　使用代词时，确保其可以清楚地指代前文出现的名词。若指代不明，则不使用代词，而使用更准确的词来说明。

Julio and Luis are creative people. They work in an art studio making large murals.

                               the artists   their work
The murals are very expensive. Many people come to see ~~them~~ to learn about ~~them~~.

改错练习

下面是一篇关于性格测试的文章的引入段和主体段，从中找出另外 5 处错误并改正。

The Myers-Briggs Personality Type Indicator

The Myers-Briggs Type Indicator, MBTI, is a
personality assessment tool ~~who~~ *that* has increasingly
gained popularity in the workplace. It is based on
a psychological theory developed by Carl Jung.

5 Jung proposed that there are two basic categories
of thinking styles: rational and irrational. Rational
functions involve thinking and feeling. Irrational
functions involve sensing and intuition. Jung
further proposed that there are two basic types
10 of people, introverts and extroverts. While there are several personality qualities who
psychologists associate with each type, introverts are usually define as people who
are more interested in ideas and thinking. In contrast, extroverts are define as people
who are more action-oriented. The MBTI has taken these four basic Jungian personality
categories and types and established four sets of opposing pairs: extrovert / introvert,
15 sensing / intuition, thinking / feeling, and judgment / perception. While individuals use all
of these thinking styles, their MBTI results indicate their thinking-style preferences. They
can help match individuals to careers and help managers understand how to best work
with these employees.

One of the MBTI personality types, ISTJ (Introvert, Sensing, Thinking, Judgment),
20 illustrates the way in which the MBTI assessment tool can match individuals to
appropriate working environments. ISTJ personality types are a person who tends to be
quiet. They prefer to be alone. They attend to details rather than to the Big Picture. They
prefer thinking to feeling. This means that they use logic when making decisions. ISTJ
personality types like controlled, organized environments. They are concrete, ordered,
25 and predictable. They are more in tune with facts than with other people's feelings. ISTJs
do well as accountants and in law enforcement. Managers of ISTJ types who are having
difficulty getting along with others need to take action. They can be placed in situations
where they can work alone, for example. Other remedies for unhappy ISTJs might include
moving them to a more organized work group.

问题和解决方法 1：现在完成时与现在完成进行时；名词短语结构

Food and Technology

1 现实生活中的语法

阅读这篇讨论转基因食物的文章。作者在文中提出了一个问题，并给出了一些可能的解决方法。这是一篇问题解决型写作的范例。

A **读前准备** 你担心从超市购买的食物的安全吗？你认为包装食品的标签上应包含什么信息？阅读文章并思考：作者想在食品标签上看到什么信息？

B **阅读理解** 回答下列问题。

1 According to the writer, what is the problem with GM foods?

2 Give two reasons why food is genetically modified, according to the essay.

3 In the third paragraph, the word "enhanced" is in quotation marks. Why do you think the writer used quotation marks around this word?

C **语法发现** 按照下列提示，找出并试着理解作者在文中说明问题时用到的语法。

1 再次阅读第 2 段。

   a 动词形式 have entered 和 has been done 涉及的是到现在为止的一段时间还是过去的某个特定时间？

   b 动词形式 has been warning 的含义与 a 中动词的含义有何不同？哪种动词形式强调动作可能仍在进行，现在完成时还是现在完成进行时？

2 再次阅读第 33 行以 Statistics have revealed 开头的句子。你认为作者为什么使用了动词的现在完成时形式（have revealed），而不是动词的过去时形式（revealed）？

Genetically Modified Foods

Any time humans make technological advances, they have the potential to do great harm and great good. Genetically modified (GM) foods, which are foods that
5 have had changes made to their DNA, are no exception. Many people believe that there are possible advantages to genetically modifying plants, for example, to improve their nutritional value or protect them
10 from pests as they grow. So far, scientists have added a cattle growth hormone to fish for faster growth and high starch to potatoes so that they absorb less oil when fried. Despite these alleged[1] benefits, there
15 are some scientists and consumer groups that fiercely question the safety of these foods for human consumption and the environment. Peter Katel, a writer for CQ Researcher (a publication that reports on
20 congressional news), has claimed that more independent tests are needed in order to conclude whether GM foods are suitable for consumption by the general public. Researchers must continue to thoroughly
25 test GM foods to verify their safety, and consumers need to educate themselves and demand that food companies be more open in their identification of food sources.

According to the Center for Food Safety,
30 GM foods have entered nearly every sector of the food market. This shift means that a majority of the public is consuming GM foods as part of their regular diet. Statistics have revealed a little known fact: Up to 92 percent
35 of U.S. corn has been genetically engineered, along with 94 percent of cotton. Current estimates are that 75 percent or more of

prepared foods in a typical supermarket in the United States contain GM ingredients.
40 However, not enough research has been done concerning the existence of any short- or long-term side effects. Larry Trivieri, author of several books on alternative medicine, has pointed out that the U.S. Food and Drug
45 Administration does not require independent safety tests on GM food. Because of the lack of conclusive research, Neal Barnard, a well-known physician and promoter of plant-based diets, as well as other researchers, has
50 been warning us that potential health risks may be associated with the consumption of these foods.

As consumers, we must make informed choices in the food we buy for the sake of
55 our health. To do that, we need to educate ourselves on the issues surrounding GM foods so that we can choose whether to buy this "enhanced" food or not. Even though research has been inconclusive as to the
60 effects of eating GM foods, there is some evidence that it may result in increased food allergies. Currently, foods with genetically modified ingredients are not always labeled as such. One way to address the problem is
65 by systematically labeling all foods. Almost two decades ago, Eli Kintisch, a writer for The New Republic (a well-known magazine of politics and arts), suggested that the few remaining products should be simply
70 labeled "GM-free." Currently, confusion arises from the number of different labels given to GM foods. These include the term bioengineered, often abbreviated to "BE," which few people fully understand. Likewise,
75 legislation in the U.S. allows for symbols instead of words, which causes further confusion and misunderstanding.

---

[1]alleged: said to be true, but without proof that it is true（未经证实而）声称的

2 现在完成时与现在完成进行时

语法讲解

在问题解决型写作中，现在完成时（present perfect）用于描述对问题有影响的情况、最新研究或趋势。现在完成时强调从过去到现在的一段时间。这段时间可能结束了，也可能没有结束，但无论哪种情况，都与现在相关联。现在完成进行时（present perfect progressive）用于描述开始于过去的动作，并强调该动作至今仍在进行中。	Genetically modified food **has been** available in grocery stores for many years. Researchers **have been studying** the impact of GM foods on our health.

2.1 现在完成时的用法

A 现在完成时用于描述开始于过去某一未知时间或不确定时间的事件。该事件也许已经完成，也许将持续至将来。 注意：现在完成时不用于描述发生在过去某一具体时间的事件。	Some researchers **demonstrated** that genetically modified foods may cause damage to humans.（完成了的事件） The consumption of GM foods **has increased** significantly in the last ten years.（这个事件可能会持续下去。） 一般过去时 Sales of GM foods **increased** dramatically between 2001 and 2011.
B 现在完成时用于表明过去的事件与现在有联系，并且现在仍有重要意义。这些事件往往是近期发生的。 这些事件可包括到目前为止的普遍情况。	Researchers **have discovered** recently that some GM foods may cause health problems.（这个发现很重要，而且与现在紧密相关。） It is true that most people **have not noticed** any difference after eating GM foods. The research team **has received** several grants for GM food research.
C 用现在完成时来介绍关于某一问题的概况并提供背景信息。 之后，用一般过去时来描述引起该问题的详细情况。	The farming of GM foods **has increased** in recent years. In 2010, Brazil dramatically **increased** the use of land for farming GM crops.

2.1 现在完成时的用法（续表）

D 现在完成时常与副词 already，ever，never 和 yet 连用。	Many farmers **have** <u>already</u> **seen** enormous gains in productivity using GM crops. **Has** any technological advance <u>ever</u> **been accepted** immediately? They **haven't finished** the research <u>yet</u>.
E 在学术写作中，提及前文内容时使用现在完成时。 介绍其他研究时也可使用现在完成时。	**As we have seen**, there is no easy answer to the problem of our nation's food shortage. **Swanson has argued that** labeling foods may be the only short-term solution to the problem of GM foods. **Critics have examined** the situation carefully but have not proposed any definitive solution to the problem.

2.2 现在完成进行时的用法

A 现在完成进行时用于描述开始于过去的动作，同时强调该动作持续到现在，并可能持续至将来。 注意：状态动词不用现在完成进行时，也不用其他进行时形式。	Researchers **have been warning** us for many years that GM foods have potential health risks. This group **has been studying** the effects of GM foods since 2001.（他们至今仍在研究。） Some scientists **have believed** for years that GM foods are unsafe. 不说 Some scientists ~~have been believing~~ for years that GM foods are unsafe.
B 现在完成进行时可与某些表示时间的短语连用，强调动作持续了多长时间。 all (semester)，for (years)，in (months)，not ... in (a long time) 用于说明某一动作或事件持续的时间长度。 since (2010) 用于说明某一动作或事件开始的时间点。	He's **been collecting** data <u>all semester</u>. They've **been interviewing** consumers <u>for three months</u>. Stores **have not been carrying** that product <u>since 2010</u>.
C 在现在完成进行时的句子中，往往不用表示时间的短语。	What **has** your research group **been working on**? We've **been studying** GM crops.

2.2 现在完成进行时的用法（续表）

D 现在完成时与现在完成进行时经常可表示相同的意思，可以互相替换。	The number of farms that grow GM foods **has increased** <u>since 2005</u>. The number of farms that grow GM foods **has been increasing** <u>since 2005</u>.

语法应用

练习 2.1 现在完成时还是一般过去时？

A 下面的段落叙述了一位农民将转用有机耕种方式的故事。用括号中所给词的正确形式填空。在恰当的地方使用被动形式。有时正确答案不唯一。

Since 1990, [1] ***I've been farming*** (farm) using conventional methods and [2] _____ (get) good results. However, after my first daughter [3] _____ (be) born, I [4] _____ (start) to think of the world that she would live in and to consider organic farming. It means making a lot of changes, though. I [5] _____ (always / apply) chemical fertilizers to promote plant growth, but that will change. For years, I [6] _____ (spray) insecticides to reduce pests and disease, but that will change, too. Starting next year, I will use birds, insects, and traps to do that. For the entire time I [7] _____ (live) on the farm, chemical herbicides [8] _____ (use) to kill weeds. Once in 2006, I [9] _____ (use) natural herbicides, but they [10] _____ (not work) well, so I [11] _____ (stop) using them, and I [12] _____ (go) back to using chemical herbicides. However, starting next year, I will rotate crops to manage weeds.

B **结对练习** 与同伴分别扮演对转基因食物持不同意见的两个人，展开一场讨论。在适当的地方使用现在完成时和现在完成进行时。

Student A You are skeptical about the farming of GM foods and think that not enough research has been done. You do not trust food companies and you wish that more information about GM foods were available. You believe that the use of the foods may harm the ecosystem. Your solution: There should be more research done on GM foods.

Student B You are enthusiastic about GM foods. You have read some research on the foods and are convinced that they are not harmful and that our bodies will adapt to eating them. You think that the use of technology to create new foods will allow people to be healthier and potentially reduce starvation worldwide. Your solution: There should be more GM foods.

A *The farming of GM foods is a problem. The research on GM foods has suggested that they could be harmful, so I don't feel confident that the foods are good for society.*

B *I disagree. We've been eating these foods for years now with no ill effects, and it seems the advantages outweigh the disadvantages ...*

练习 2.2 **更多练习：现在完成时还是一般过去时？**

使用括号中动词的现在完成时、现在完成进行时或一般过去时形式填空。在必要的地方使用被动形式。圈出有助于判断时态的时间标志语。有时正确答案不唯一。

1 (From 2000 to 2007), the value of GM crops ___*increased*___ (increase) considerably.

2 For the past 20 years, researchers _____ (track) the areas used to grow GM crops in the world.

3 Over the past 15 years, the number of GM crops _____ (grow) significantly.

4 Over 457 million acres of land _____ (use) for GM crops in 2016 compared to 444 million in 2015.

5 Many people are not even aware that farmers _____ (begin) growing GM crops in the mid-nineties.

6 Statistics show that the global area of GM crops _____ (increase) steadily since the mid-nineties.

7 In 2017, 18 million farmers from 24 countries, including the U.S., Brazil, and China, _____ (plant) GM crops.

8 The effects of GM foods on people _____ (not / determine), and scientists continue to do research.

9 Research _____ (not / show) yet that GM foods have a negative effect on our health and environment.

10 Until there is definite proof that GM foods are not harmful, some people _____ (decide) to avoid them.

先阅读下列句子，再听一段关于城市园艺广播节目的录音。根据听到的内容，判断下列说法是否正确。如果正确，圈选 T；如果错误，圈选 F。

T /(F) **1** Residents of urban areas such as Los Angeles grow vegetables in their apartments.

T / F **2** Mark Johnson started a rooftop garden five years ago.

T / F **3** Mark Johnson no longer has a rooftop garden.

T / F **4** The neighborhood swap in Mark's neighborhood started four years ago.

T / F **5** Emily Ling regularly brought cooked food to the neighborhood swap.

T / F **6** Emily Ling goes every week to the neighborhood swap.

T / F **7** Emily and her neighbors haven't bought vegetables from stores for a long time.

T / F **8** Neighborhood gardens have been popular for a while in Emily's city.

T / F **9** Annie Suarez started to grow food in her local neighborhood garden in 2010.

T / F **10** Annie Suarez currently writes a gardening blog.

3 常用的名词短语结构

词汇讲解

在学术写作中，某些名词短语结构用于指称和重述较复杂的意思。它们有时被称为"外壳名词"（shell nouns），一般用于指前文已经提到或后文将要出现的信息。在问题解决型写作中，这类结构可用于阐明某个问题并解释其重要性。

It is important to identify **the causes of** famine.

Research needs to be done because of **the fact that** more and more people are consuming GM foods.

3.1 名词短语与 of 连用

A 有些名词短语与 of 连用，可以解释、标记或定义一个概念，例如：
the basis of，the concept(s) of，the definition of，the essence of，the idea of，the meaning(s) of，the notion of

It is important that the public understands **the concept of** genetic engineering and its implications.
The definition of organic farming is agriculture that relies on natural methods and limits the use of chemical fertilizers and pesticides.

B 有些名词短语与 of 连用，可以说明影响或结果，例如：
the cause(s) of，the consequence(s) of，the effect(s) of，the result(s) of

Consumers need to be aware of **the potential consequences of** GM foods on their health.
No one has studied **the effects of** GM foods on babies.

C 有些名词短语与 of 连用，可以说明目标，例如：
the aim of，the benefit(s) of，the goal(s) of，the purpose(s) of

The aim of the program is to reduce reliance on pesticides.
The purpose of food labeling is to help consumers make more informed decisions.

D 有些名词短语与 of 连用，可以表示某一概念的重要性，例如：
the core of，the heart of，the importance of

Sustainability is **the heart of** organic farming.
The importance of organic farming is sustainability – not harming the environment and managing it well.

E 有些名词短语与 of 连用，可以表示数量，例如：
the amount of，the frequency of，the majority of，a number of，the number of，the rest of
注意：a number of 的意思为"一些；许多"，与复数动词连用。the number of 指某个具体的数字，与单数动词连用。

Consumers need to be aware of **the amount of** GM foods that they eat.
The majority of GM products come from crops such as soybeans, corn, and cotton.
A number of people **have asked** about the benefits of organic farming.
The number of consumers who buy GM foods **is increasing**.

A 有些名词短语后接 that 从句，用于表达结论或事实：conclusion，fact

The fact that the population continues to increase makes efficient food production essential.

表达想法：claim，idea，notion

New research may support **the notion that** modifying food has a negative impact on health.

表达观点：belief，doubt，sense，view

Many governments hold **the view that** genetically modified food has successfully fed many hungry people.

表达未被证实的说法：assumption，hope，hypothesis，impression，observation，possibility，suggestion

Many people are concerned about **the possibility that** GM foods can be dangerous.

B "名词短语 + that 从句" 结构与名词短语一样，可用于主语、宾语等位置。

主语
The claim that GM foods can be beneficial is true.

主语
The fact that conventional agricultural products can have an "organic" label has created skepticism in consumers.

宾语
I support **the idea that GM foods should be labeled**.

C the fact that 与 the idea that 是学术写作中特别常用的表达。

the fact that 常用于引出人们普遍接受的事实而非个人观点，可用于说服读者。读者一般不会质疑其后所述内容。

The writer cites **the fact that** no long-term studies have been done on the effects of GM foods.

Not all consumers agree with **the idea that** it is necessary to label foods.

词汇应用

练习 3.1　名词短语与 of 连用

A　用方框中的名词短语结构填空，将下列谈论转基因食物的句子补充完整。有时正确答案不唯一。

a number of	the basis of	~~the concept of~~	the heart of	the number of
the aims of	the benefits of	the effects of	the majority of	

1　__*The concept of*__　genetic modification is not new.

2　One of _____ modifying food genetically is to produce enough food, especially corn, rice, and soybeans, for people all over the world.

3　However, _____ genetic modification of food are still not completely understood.

4　In a recent study, _____ people surveyed were uncomfortable with the idea of GM foods. In fact, _____ them avoided the foods.

5　At _____ their concern is the fact that researchers don't really know whether GM foods are completely safe.

6　_____ GM foods produced every year is steadily growing.

7　Proponents of this technology talk about what _____ this technology will be; however, only time will tell if they are correct to be so optimistic.

8　Opponents of GM foods do not think that the government should allow more GM foods on _____ inconclusive findings.

B　**小组活动**　以小组为单位，回答下列关于转基因食物的问题。在回答中使用练习 A 方框中的名词短语结构。将小组的答案分享给全班同学。

1　What are some reasons why scientists created GM foods?

2　What are some advantages and disadvantages of GM foods?

3　What do you think the majority of people know about GM foods? What do they base their understandings on? What are some of their concerns?

A 下文介绍了食用本地自产食物的好处。阅读短文，圈出正确的选项。

Among the many current food trends, one is based on ¹ (the belief that)/ the fact that it is better to eat locally grown food than food exported from far away.

² The doubt that / The notion that local food is better for you is based on a few facts.

First, ³ the idea that / the fact that food has only traveled a few miles to get to your supermarket means that the food is probably fresher than meat or produce that has been shipped from the other side of the world. There is ⁴ a conclusion that / a possibility that produce that has traveled a long way may have lost some of its nutrients or begun to deteriorate during the trip.

Second, people who prefer local food might hold ⁵ the view that / the conclusion that eating locally grown food is good for the community. For example, buying this food supports local farmers and other food producers, like cheese manufacturers and bread bakers.

Third, ⁶ the doubt that / the hope that eating locally grown food will help protect the environment – because less fuel is required to transport the food – might motivate some people to follow this trend.

Ironically, locally grown food can sometimes be more expensive than exported food even though it doesn't have to travel very far. This is often due to ⁷ the impression that / the fact that local food producers usually consist of small businesses with high overhead costs and low levels of production.

B **结对练习** 你对食用本地自产食物的看法是什么？它有哪些好处？可能有哪些弊端？与同伴就此展开讨论，阐述你的观点。注意在讨论过程中使用"名词短语 + that 从句"结构。

The possibility that exported food may be less nutritious is surprising to me. I didn't realize that food could lose nutritional value like that. I think the fact that locally grown food might be more nutritious is a strong argument for eating food that is produced near my home.

4 常见错误提示

1 注意 advice，equipment，evidence，information，knowledge，research 等不可数名词无复数形式。

information
We do not have enough ~~informations~~ on the health effects of GM foods.

2 注意要用 the fact that，而不要用 this fact that。

the
Many people are not aware of ~~this~~ fact that many snack foods contain GM ingredients.

3 注意 a number of 要与复数可数名词和复数动词连用。

experts agree
A number of ~~expert agrees~~ that GM foods may help solve world hunger.

改错练习

下面是一篇文章的主体段落，文章讲述了与食物生产相关的环境问题。从中找出另外 8 处错误并改正。

Engineered Food and the Environment

activists think
A number of animal rights ~~activist thinks~~ that laboratory-generated meat, also known as cultured meat, provides a solution to the negative environmental effects of food production. Cultured meat is grown in a laboratory from animal tissue cells. There are many benefits of cultured meat. First, animals do not have
5 to be killed for food. According to Compassion in World Farming, 70 billion farm animals are farmed and killed for food worldwide each year. This fact that cultured meat would virtually eliminate animal suffering is not in dispute. Additionally, most people are aware that raising animals for food is harmful to the environment. This is because processing meat requires large amounts of resources
10 such as land and water. There is also a great deal of informations on this fact that raising animals for meat contributes to greenhouse gases and pollutes water, air, and land. Recent researches on the environmental impact of cultured meat is very promising. A number of environmentalist agrees that cultured meat would greatly reduce greenhouse gas emissions. There is also
15 evidences that cultured meat might be healthier and safer. A number of scientist is continuing to do researches on cultured meat. Many of these experts predict that we will see cultured meat in supermarkets within five to ten years. It seems clear
20 that relying more on engineered food products may someday help to solve some of the environmental problems that we face today.

问题和解决方法 2：转述动词；含有 as 的状语；描述图表信息的词汇

Children and Health

1 现实生活中的语法

阅读这篇关注儿童肥胖问题的文章。作者在文中描述了问题，分析了该问题存在的原因，并在结尾呼吁寻找问题的解决方法。这是一篇问题解决型写作的范例。

A **读前准备** 在过去 20 年间，儿童的生活方式发生了哪些变化？这些变化如何影响着他们的健康？阅读文章并思考：在作者看来，造成儿童肥胖的主要原因是什么？

B **阅读理解** 回答下列问题。

1 According to the essay, what are some health issues that result from children being overweight or obese?

2 What are the social concerns for children who are overweight or obese?

3 Why does the author say, "It is clear that the reasons for the rise in childhood obesity are complex"?

C **语法发现** 在文中找到作者用来转述观点和信息的动词，并填写在横线上。

1 The Centers for Disease Control and Prevention
_____*state that*_____ ...

2 Former President Bill Clinton _____ ...

3 Finally, other studies of obese children and teens
_____ ...

4 Researchers _____ ...

5 Parents, doctors, scientists, and policy makers all
_____ ...

Fighting Childhood OBESITY

CHILDHOOD OBESITY IS A MAJOR CONCERN in the United States and in many other countries around the world. Obesity in U.S. children has more than tripled since the late 1970s. The
5 Centers for Disease Control and Prevention state that an overweight child has a Body Mass Index (BMI, a measure of weight in relation to the child's age, sex, and height) above the 85th percentile and less than the 95th percentile for
10 his or her age and sex. As an example of this, a second grader whose weight is above the 85th percentile would weigh 95 pounds or more. An obese child has a BMI at or above the 95th percentile. While it appears that the rates of
15 obesity are falling for younger children, this trend is still likely to persist and perhaps worsen in the future for older children.

Many high-profile people are concerned about this epidemic. Among those people is
20 former President Bill Clinton, a supporter of stronger policy on childhood obesity. Clinton asserts that the causes of this health crisis range from overworked parents, with no time to prepare healthy food, to a lack of sidewalks
25 and safe outside play areas for children. Another contributing factor is the marketing of inexpensive large-portion meals at fast-food restaurants. Companies make these meals for children even more attractive by giving away
30 small toys and prizes with each meal.

Doctors are concerned about increased childhood obesity because of its health-related consequences. One consequence of obesity is cardiovascular disease.[1] Certain risk factors,
35 such as high blood pressure, high cholesterol, and high blood sugar, are present in people who develop this disease. Several studies of obese children and adolescents has shown that obesity in childhood is associated with a higher
40 chance of disability and dying prematurely.

There are additional health risks associated with being overweight or obese. Though less common, they are serious health issues. They include asthma, sleep apnea (when breathing
45 stops during sleep for at least 10 seconds), and Type 2 diabetes. While Type 2 diabetes has been a common health consequence of adult obesity, in recent years it has become a problem among children and adolescents. Finally, other studies
50 of obese children and teens have indicated that these young people are more likely to develop certain cancers in later life.

Apart from physical issues, childhood obesity can also generate social problems.
55 Researchers note that overweight and obese children are often discriminated against socially, and that this can cause stress and low self-esteem. These feelings are likely to have an impact on children's academic and social lives.

60 Parents, doctors, scientists, and policy makers all believe that childhood obesity is a critical issue. It is clear that the reasons for the rise in childhood obesity are complex. Therefore, the solution must involve everyone – parents,
65 doctors, the media, as well as the community. A committed response now will ensure that the obese child of today will not grow up to be an obese adult.

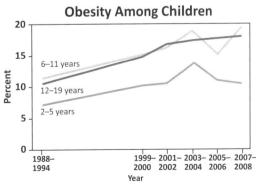

Obesity Among Children

NOTE: Obesity is body mass index (BMI) for age and sex at or above the 95th percentile of the CDC growth charts.
SOURCE: CDC/NCHS *Health, United States, 2010*, Figure 13. Data from the National Health and Nutrition Examination Survey.

---

[1]**cardiovascular disease:** heart disease 心血管疾病

Children and Health **157**

2 转述动词

语法讲解

在学术写作中，写作者使用转述动词（reporting verbs）来转述他人的观点或研究结果。	Bill Clinton **provides** several reasons for the increase in childhood obesity. The study **illustrates** several possible consequences of childhood obesity.

2.1 转述动词

A 转述动词的使用遵循下面的结构：
信息来源 + 转述动词 + that + 描述转述信息的从句

信息来源　　　转述动词
Researchers **point out that**
　　　　　描述转述信息的从句
obese children are targets of social discrimination.

B 在不太正式的写作中，转述动词后的 that 可省略。
在学术写作中，that 最好保留。

非正式：　Many parents **believe** children should avoid junk food.
正式：　　Doctors **believe that** children should avoid junk food.

C 许多转述动词后也可接名词短语，例如下面这些动词：
illustrate，point out，show，suggest

名词短语
Figure 1 **illustrates** <u>the three levels of influence on children's health</u>.

D 有些转述动词后只可接名词短语，不可接 that 从句，例如下面这些动词：
describe，display，evaluate，give，investigate，present，summarize

Chart 1 **describes** seven parental influences on children's health.
不说 Chart 1 describes ~~that there are~~ seven parental influences on children's health.
Figure 1 **gives** eight community influences on children's health.

实际使用数据分析

下面为后接 that 从句的常见转述动词（按使用频率从高到低排序）：
say, show, assume, suggest, complain, announce, argue, add, declare, explain, imply, mention, point out, propose, recommend, remark, report, state, write, warn

A recent government report **suggests that** obesity is a problem for all ages, but it is most significant among children.

2.2 转述动词的用法

A 大多数转述动词的语气都是中性的，用于转述事实。	Research **demonstrates that** the consumption of fast food has increased in the last 10 years. The authors of the study **conclude that** childhood obesity can be very harmful.
B 有些转述动词用于转述观点，例如：believe, emphasize, predict, recognize, recommend, suggest	The U.S. Department of Health and Human Services **believes that** people should read food labels carefully when shopping. Doctors **recommend that** people get 30 minutes of exercise daily.
C 有些转述动词用于转述结果，例如：conclude, demonstrate, estimate 注意：动词 demonstrate 和 estimate 后也可接名词短语，但与后接 that 从句时表示的意思不同。	The U. S. Department of Health and Human Services **concluded that** consumers should read ingredient lists carefully. The workshop **demonstrated** <u>ways for children to improve their health</u>.
D 当你怀疑或不确定原作者的说法是否真实时，用动词 allege 和 claim。	Ramirez **claims that** the number of fast-food restaurants in the world has increased. The attorney general **alleges that** the problem started with a complaint from parents in the public schools.
E 动词 propose 和 suggest 用于转述可能真实但仍不确定的信息。	Davidson **suggests that** the consumption of fast food has increased.

语法应用

练习 2.1 转述动词

下面是一封写给报社的信，信中讨论了儿童肥胖问题。在其中的转述动词下面画线。

> Dear Editor,
>   I want to bring your readers' attention to the issue of childhood obesity in the United States. Recent studies <u>show</u> that 37 percent of children and adolescents in the United States are overweight. Doctors claim that unhealthy childhood weight can affect adult weight. Some reports estimate that children who are overweight
> 5 before the age of 15 are 80 percent more likely to be obese at 25 than children with healthy weights.

Experts suggest that some of the main causes of childhood obesity are a lack of parental influences, a lack of nutritious foods available in the home, and availability of fast-food restaurants. However, we should also consider the role that school plays in
10 influencing a child's diet and weight. Because students spend a large part of their day at school, that is where they do much of their eating. Research indicates that children get as much as 50 percent of their daily calories while they are at school. This statistic suggests a link between school lunches and childhood obesity. In addition, most students these days have to do a lot of homework. Some parents estimate that their
15 children have to do more than three hours of homework a night. This keeps them from spending their after-school time engaging in physical activities. I don't want to blame schools for childhood obesity, but I do think we should all work together to help our children be healthy.

Sincerely,

A concerned parent

练习 2.2　更多练习：转述动词

A 选择恰当的转述动词补全下列句子，记得在转述动词后添加 that。

1 A report from the Dietary Guidelines for Americans
__suggests that__ people should "eat fewer calories, be more active, and make wiser food choices."

a suggests　　b complains　　c demonstrates

2 The Centers for Disease Control and Prevention (CDC) _____ one way to fight childhood obesity is to remove high-calorie, low-nutrition snacks.

a emphasizes　　b illustrates　　c warns

3 Former President Bill Clinton _____ many parents are overworked and don't have time to prepare healthy food for their children.

a describes　　b believes　　c estimates

4 A report by the Centers for Disease Control and Prevention _____ a child whose body mass index is above the 85th percentile is overweight.

a states　　b recommends　　c warns

5 The Dietary Guidelines for Americans _____ people can reduce the risk of many chronic diseases, including cancer, through better nutrition.

a assume　　b predict　　c point out

6 A spokesperson from the American Academy of Pediatrics _____ it is unhealthy to allow children age two or younger to watch television.

a recommends　　b mentions　　c claims

7 The results of various studies _____ overweight children are often bullied and teased by their peers.

    a evaluate   **b** demonstrate   **c** believe

8 Several states have had court cases in which the state _____ childhood obesity is a form of child abuse.

    a has emphasized   **b** has alleged   **c** has recommended

B 结对练习 与同伴讨论练习 A 的答案，并说明选择的理由。

I think suggest *is the best answer for item 1 because the Dietary Guidelines for Americans are not forcing people to do anything, but telling people what might be a good thing for them to do. The guidelines are certainly not complaining about anything or demonstrating something.*

练习 2.3 转述动词的用法

结对练习 与同伴讨论下面的一个话题或老师认可的其他话题。在讨论时记下同伴的回答，并使用转述动词向全班同学讲述同伴的想法。

- At what age should children have cell phones?
- At what age should children be allowed to join social networks?
- At what age should children have their own computers?
- At what age should children have TVs in their rooms?

Monica argues that children under 10 should not have cell phones. She points out that cell phones are expensive and young children could easily break them. She also believes that children under 10 should always have an adult present, so they wouldn't need their own phones.

3 含有 as 的状语

语法讲解

含有 as 的状语从句和短语可用于指出消息的来源。	**As seen in Figure 1**, the number of fast-food restaurants in the country has increased significantly. **As researchers point out**, there is a variety of reasons related to the increase in childhood obesity.

A as 引导的状语从句可用于指出信息来自图表或其他来源。 as 引导的状语从句中常用的动词及短语动词有： demonstrate, illustrate, point out, show	As **Figure 1** illustrates, eating habits have changed recently. As **a recent study** points out, a key issue is the stigma of obesity.
这类从句后使用逗号。	As **Dr. Jarolimova** illustrates, there are many things that children can do every day to become healthier.
B 含有 as 的短语也可用被动形式，例如： as demonstrated in / by _____ , as illustrated in _____ , as seen in _____ , as shown in / by _____	As demonstrated in **Table 1**, there is a positive trend in the results. As shown by **Professor Green**, there are actions that can effectively address the problem.
C 这类被动形式的短语中可用情态动词，例如： as can / may be seen in _____	As can be seen in **Graph 1**, a higher percentage of boys has become overweight in the past two decades.

🖳 语法应用

練習 3.1　as 引导的状语从句的用法

A　下面的图表呈现了弗吉尼亚州儿童肥胖问题的调查结果。根据图表信息，用 as 引导的状语从句和括号中动词的正确形式，回答下列问题。在恰当的地方使用情态动词＋动词的被动形式。

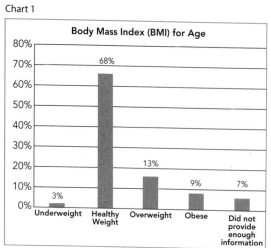

Chart 1

Body Mass Index (BMI) for Age

- Underweight 3%
- Healthy Weight 68%
- Overweight 13%
- Obese 9%
- Did not provide enough information 7%

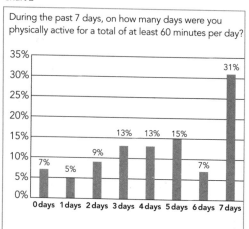

Chart 2

During the past 7 days, on how many days were you physically active for a total of at least 60 minutes per day?

- 0 days 7%
- 1 days 5%
- 2 days 9%
- 3 days 13%
- 4 days 13%
- 5 days 15%
- 6 days 7%
- 7 days 31%

1 What percentage of Virginia children are physically active at least twice a week?

   (demonstrate) _As demonstrated in Chart 2, / As Chart 2 demonstrates, 88 percent_
   of Virginia children are physically active at least twice a week.

2 What percentage of Virginia children are obese?

   (show) _____

3 Are the majority of Virginia children overweight?

   (illustrate) _____

4 Are most Virginia children active at least four days a week?

   (point out) _____

5 What percentage of Virginia children are not at a healthy weight?

   (demonstrate) _____

6 What percentage of Virginia children are physically active less than two days per week?

   (see) _____

B 结对练习 与同伴对比答案，再根据图表信息另提出两个问题并进行回答。

练习 3.2 含有 as 的短语的用法

下面的图表呈现了关于弗吉尼亚州儿童肥胖问题的调查信息。根据提示，用含有 as 的短语
写出完整的句子。

Chart 3

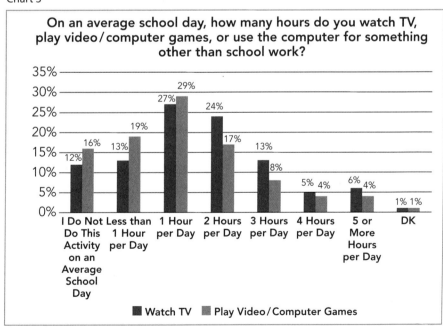

1 Compare the percentage of Virginia children who watch TV for two or more hours per day with those who spend two or more hours playing video games. *As Chart 3 shows, Virginia children spend more time watching TV than playing video and computer games.*

2 Compare the percentage of Virginia children who don't watch TV with those who don't play video / computer games.

_____

3 Compare the percentage of Virginia children who spend one hour or less watching TV per day with those who spend one hour or less playing video / computer games.

_____

4 Compare the percentage of Virginia children who spend three hours per day playing video games with those who spend one hour playing video games.

_____

5 Compare the percentage of Virginia children who don't watch TV or play video / computer games with those who spend five or more hours watching TV and playing video / computer games.

_____

4 描述图表信息的常用词汇

词汇讲解

| 图表（表格、条形图、曲线图等）有助于为文章中的观点提供可视化的数据支持。有些单词和短语常用于介绍图表，将读者的注意力引向其中的某一具体信息。 | It can be seen from Figure 1 that the number of girls and young women in sports has increased dramatically in recent decades. Chart 2 shows that overall participation in physical education has declined. |

4.1 描述图表信息的常用词汇

A 谈到图表时首先指明是哪一个图表，再强调希望读者关注的具体信息。

Chart 1 shows _____ .

The graph shows (that) _____ .

指明图表　　　强调具体信息

Chart 1 shows that most students watched one hour or less of TV per average school day.

The graph shows how many hours a day individuals from certain countries spend watching television.

The graph shows that there is a relationship between weight and amount of exercise.

B 可以使用被动形式引出图表所提供的信息。

From _____ , it can be concluded / estimated / inferred / seen that _____ .

From the chart, **it can be concluded that** individuals in the United States are getting much less exercise than a few decades ago.

From the chart, **it can be inferred that** individuals in Switzerland maintain active lifestyles and healthy weights.

C 下面的名词可用于描述变化：

↑increase，rise

↑↓fluctuation

↓decline，decrease，drop，fall

There was **an increase** in girls' participation in team sports from 2016 to 2018.

Figure 1 shows **the fluctuation** in funding for physical education in the last three decades.

There was **a decrease** in students' participation in physical education between ninth and tenth grades.

D 下面的形容词可用于描述变化的强度：

slight，slow

gradual，steady

dramatic，rapid，sharp，steep，sudden

There was a **slight** rise in physical activity among ninth graders between 2015 and 2018.

There was a **gradual** decline in physical education participation during high school.

There was a **sharp** drop in physical education participation between ninth and tenth grades.

E 下面的动词也可用于描述变化：

decline，drop，fall，increase，reduce，rise

Participation in sports **fell** in three grades in the last few years.

Participation has **increased** only for ninth graders.

F 下面的动词可用于表示没有变化：

remain，stay，maintain

The hours students spent in physical activity each week has **remained** steady for the past few years.

练习 4.1　描述图表信息的词汇

A　去年，Cascades High School 的校长发起了一个旨在解决学生精力不足问题的行动项目。听一听校长对该项目及其结果的介绍，补出折线图中缺失的信息。

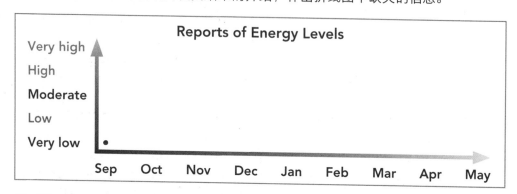

B　结对练习　用描述图表信息的常用词汇，描述练习 A 中折线图的信息。

练习 4.2　更多练习：描述图表信息的词汇

结对练习　在一张纸上，仿照上面练习 4.1 中的图画一个类似的折线图，表示你想象的一年中学生患流感或感冒的情况，然后用描述图表信息的常用词汇向同伴描述你的图表。

As shown in the chart, the number of colds remained low from September through October. Then in November there was a sharp rise. This was probably a result of the fluctuation in temperature during the day and cold winds ...

5 常见错误提示

> **1** 当情态动词用于被动结构中时，注意情态动词后接动词 be 的原形。
>
> From the chart, it can_∧inferred that simple lifestyle changes result in major health gains. *(be)*
>
> **2** demonstrate, illustrate, show 等转述动词后可接 that 从句或名词短语。注意正确使用这两种形式。
>
> Table C shows that_∧an increase in weight loss. *(there is)*
>
> Figure 8 illustrates ~~that~~ the results of increased exercise over a three-week period.
>
> **3** 用 As ... 说明有编号的图表或其他信息来源时，通常不使用冠词。
>
> As ~~the~~ Chart 1 shows, the number of hours participants engaged in physical activity per week had a direct effect on their body weight.

改错练习

下面是一篇谈论肥胖问题的文章的主体段落，从中找出另外 8 处错误并改正。

Genetics and Obesity

Several studies have shown ~~that~~ a connection between genetics and obesity. As the Smith's study shows, people who have access to exactly the same foods will use those calories differently. Figure A demonstrates that the differences. It shows how a controlled diet and exercise program affected a group of 50
5 participants: some people in the group gained weight, others maintained their weight, and a small percentage even lost weight. From this study, it can inferred that these different responses to the same situation are primarily genetic. Wu's research provides further support for the genetic connection to obesity. Her long-range study on body weight and family history clearly demonstrates that a
10 genetic link to obesity. As the Figure B illustrates, there was very little variation in body weight among three generations of ten families. Finally, several studies have shown that a connection between a gene called FTO and obesity. These studies also demonstrate that a relationship between FTO and diabetes and other diseases. From these and other studies, it can argued that genetics plays a
15 role in body weight.

问题和解决方法 3：表示目的的状语从句和不定式；简化的状语从句；描述问题和解决方法的表达

Health and Technology

1 现实生活中的语法

阅读这篇关于人们利用互联网进行自我诊断和查找疾病信息的文章。这是一篇问题解决型写作的范例。

A **读前准备** 你或你熟悉的人是否经常用互联网来诊断病症？阅读文章并思考：在作者看来，医生对此有哪些担心？

B **阅读理解** 回答下列问题。

1 What is cyberchondria?

2 What concerns doctors most when patients use the Internet to self-diagnose?

3 What is the solution suggested in the essay?

C **语法发现** 按照下列提示回答问题，注意作者如何使用状语从句或短语来表示目的或原因。

1 在第 1 段的最后一句中，哪个短语说明了所提及的某些解决方法的目的？

2 在第 2 段中找到以 while 开头的句子。while 后接的动词是什么形式？ while 引导的短语的逻辑主语是什么？

3 在第 68—70 行找到以 When searching 开头的句子，并在第 80—83 行找到以 However, when health-care website providers 开头的句子。when 在这两个句子中的用法在结构上有何不同？

Doctor–Patient Relationships in the 21st Century

There was a time when a person with a medical problem would ask a family member, friend, or neighbor about their symptoms before visiting a doctor. Now, many people gather a great deal of information before their first visit. Their first source for this information is now the Internet. In fact, a survey by Pew Research Center's Internet & American Life Project (2011) found that 80 percent of American adults use the Internet for health-related information. This increased use of the Internet for health purposes has led to a new phenomenon, *cyberchondria*. Cyberchondria is a situation in which people with no medical background diagnose themselves by reviewing symptoms and other information online and determine that their situation is worse than it really is. Educating patients about using online information, identifying changes doctors could make, and using online medical information more effectively are all necessary in order to solve this problem of cyberchondria.

The term *cyberchondria* is based on the term *hypochondria*, a belief that one has a serious disease even though there is no medical confirmation. After gathering information online, cyberchondriacs often conclude that they have a disease or health issue that is worse than the one that their doctor diagnoses. While not being a real physical condition, cyberchondria can lead to problems. For example, patients often find it difficult to accept their doctor's diagnosis, causing friction[1] between patients and doctors.

With patients self-diagnosing more often, a shift has occurred in the patient–doctor relationship. For example, patients may challenge doctors more aggressively and spend more time discussing topics that they had researched online. Another concern is that patients do not always use credible websites. As a result, they may find information that is based on out-of-date research. Most importantly, doctors are concerned that patients will scare themselves when reading symptoms online. As Brazilian cardiologist Dr. Fernando Botelho explains, "Patients read non-contextualized information and do not know how to process it. This situation can bring anxiety."

45 While acknowledging these concerns, many doctors also see the benefit of having more actively engaged patients. Dr. Igor Barrios, a surgeon in Venezuela, believes that these changes will lead to better care. He feels that doctors will have to become 50 more effective communicators. Doctors should become more sensitive to patients' more active role and learn to accept that they will have to be able to provide explanations for patients' questions about information they find on the Internet.

55 Using medical information available on the Internet wisely can also address the problem of cyberchondria. Health-care websites must state clearly that their information should be in addition to, rather than a replacement of, a consultation with 60 a doctor and medical treatment. For doctors, while it may be difficult, they need to acknowledge that the old rules have changed – they are no longer the only source of information. They should educate their patients on how to evaluate the health 65 information they find on the Internet so that the process of diagnosing becomes collaborative rather than adversarial.[2] Finally, the last part of the solution involves patients. When searching for information on the Internet, patients should remember that no 70 website can replace a doctor's physical exam. Before approaching their doctor, they should check that the information they have is up-to-date and credible. In this way, they can avoid wasting time during appointments.

75 This cooperation will not be easy to implement. It will be difficult to persuade health-care website providers to change information online. It will also be challenging for doctors and patients to change their roles, especially without additional training 80 about these new relationships. However, when health-care website providers, doctors, and patients all realize that these changes will benefit health care, they will be more likely to collaborate. This cooperation will help create a stronger twenty-first-85 century model for patient–doctor relationships.

---

[1]**friction:** unpleasant feelings caused by differences of opinion 不合，冲突
[2]**adversarial:** opposing each other, like enemies 对抗性的

2 表示目的的状语从句和不定式

语法讲解

状语从句和不定式（infinitives）可用于表示某一动作或想法的目的或原因，通常置于主句之后。这类从句和不定式常用于问题解决型写作中，以解释提出某种解决方法的原因。	Some clinics have computer stations **so that** patients can go online in the waiting room. She researched the disease on the Internet **in order to** learn more about it.

2.1 目的状语从句

A 目的状语从句属于从属分句，可用于回答由 why 引导的疑问句。	Doctors should educate their patients about how to evaluate medical information on the Internet **so that the process of diagnosing becomes collaborative rather than adversarial.**
B so that 是最常用于引导目的状语从句的表达，有时可简化为 so。	He cut down on fatty food **so that** he could lose weight. He cut down on fatty food **so** he could lose weight.
C 目的状语从句通常位于主句之后。	常见用法： The clinic provided training for using online medical reference information **so that patients would feel less anxious**. 不常见用法： **So that patients would feel less anxious**, the doctors provided training for using online medical reference information.

2.2 表示目的的不定式

A 当主句的主语与目的状语从句的主语相同时，可将 in order 或 so as 与表示目的的不定式（to + 动词原形）连用。形式如下：
in order to + 动词原形
当句意清晰时，可省略 in order。

so as to + 动词原形

Doctors place brochures on medical conditions in their waiting rooms (in order) to provide patients with valuable information.
Doctors should discuss treatment options with patients so as to address any concerns.

B 也可使用上面两种结构的否定形式。not 置于不定式之前：
in order not to + 动词原形
so as not to + 动词原形

A patient might not say anything about what he or she reads on the Internet in order not to make the doctor angry.
Patients should avoid the use of unqualified medical websites so as not to make false assumptions about their medical issues.

C 当不定式后接表示目的的不定式时，为确保句意清晰，应使用 in order to 或 so as to 代替表示目的的不定式。

句意不清：Some patients write a list of questions <u>to ask</u> to use time efficiently during medical appointments.
句意清晰：Some patients write a list of questions <u>to ask</u> in order to use time efficiently during medical appointments.

📊 实际使用数据分析

下面是 10 个最常用于 in order to 之后的动词（按使用频率从高到低排序）：
be, make, get, obtain, keep, determine, avoid, see, protect, provide
Why can't we email our doctor **in order to make** an appointment?

下面是 10 个最常用于 so as to 之后的动词（按使用频率从高到低排序）：
avoid, be, make, provide, have, create, form, maintain, preserve, give
Ari made his next appointment before he left the doctor's office so as to avoid having to do it later.

练习 2.1 表示目的的状语从句和不定式

下面这篇杂志文章讲述了一位母亲如何利用互联网来诊断她儿子的疾病。阅读文章，用下划线标出另外 7 个表示目的的状语从句和不定式。

Before the invention of the Internet, people would visit their doctors <u>in order to find out what was wrong with them</u>. These days, when people begin to feel ill, they often turn to the Internet to diagnose themselves. Many medical professionals agree that self-diagnosis by the Internet can often cause unnecessary and unwarranted fears. However, once in a while, the patient's hunches are correct.

Take the case of Alison Chambers. Alison has a 10-year-old son named Miles. When Miles was about two years old, he began getting fevers on a regular basis. She took him to a doctor to get help, and her doctor told her that children often get fevers and it was nothing to worry about. The doctor told Alison that Miles should stay home from day care when other children were ill so as not to get sick. He also said that Miles should wash his hands often so that he would not pick up other children's germs as readily. Although Alison was very careful to follow the doctor's advice, Miles continued to get a fever about once a month. She took Miles to three more doctors so that she could get other opinions, but they all agreed with her doctor's diagnosis.

Alison began to get very frustrated and started researching Miles's symptoms online so as to find out some information for herself. She read about a rare disease whose symptoms sounded like Miles's symptoms. She visited Miles's doctor to ask his opinion. He thought it was unlikely that Miles had the disease, but he agreed to test him for it. The test showed that Miles did have the rare disease. Alison was scared but relieved to know what was wrong with her son. Miles received treatment and stopped getting fevers soon after. It can be dangerous to rely on the Internet for medical information, but in Alison and Miles's case, it paid off.

练习 2.2　更多练习：表示目的的状语从句和不定式

A 听一段讨论用数字工具助力健康管理的播客访谈，并用表示目的的状语从句和不定式回答下列问题。

1 Why did Cindy interview people?

Cindy interviewed people to understand how they used digital tools to monitor and improve their health.

2 Why did a writer for *The New York Times* use Twitter?

_____

_____

3 Why does Pam use an app to take pictures of her food?

_____

4 Why does Pam use a running app?

_____

5 Why do people need to commit to using digital resources?

_____

6 Why do we need to arrive at the doctor's office armed with knowledge?

_____

7 Why might doctors have to change their relationships with patients?

_____

8 Why does Jeff want Cindy to tell one more piece of advice?

_____

B **结对练习**　与同伴讨论上面访谈中人们使用的应用软件。这些应用软件会对你有所帮助吗？理由是什么？哪一款应用软件对你来说最有用？原因是什么？你还了解其他可用于改善健康或改掉坏习惯的应用软件吗？你想发明一款什么样的软件来改善健康、提高生活水平？

I liked the app that calculated calories based on pictures. I'd use it with my boyfriend so that I could persuade him to make better choices too. I don't run, but I'd like an app to motivate me and to remind me of my goals. I'd love someone to invent an app that I could easily use to describe symptoms and conditions in English so as to make it easier to communicate with doctors.

3 状语从句简化为短语

语法讲解

状语从句可简化为短语。简化后的短语作状语，用于修饰主句的主语，可描述问题和解决方法。	Sometimes patients become frightened when they read symptoms online. → Sometimes patients become frightened when reading symptoms online.

3.1 状语从句简化为短语

A 当状语从句由 when，while，before 和 after 引导，并且其主语与主句的主语相同时，状语从句可以简化为短语。	状语从句 Joanna tried various home remedies before she saw the doctor. 简化后的短语作状语 Joanna tried various home remedies before seeing the doctor.
B 当状语从句中的动词为现在进行时或过去进行时形式时，可通过省略主语和动词 be 来简化从句。	When I am dieting, I never eat sugar or red meat. When dieting, I never eat sugar or red meat. While Tran was searching the Internet, he found positive reviews about his doctor. While searching the Internet, Tran found positive reviews about his doctor.
C 当状语从句中的动词为一般现在时或一般过去时形式时，可通过省略主语，并将动词形式变为 -ing 形式来简化从句。	Before they see a doctor, many patients use the Internet to find information about their symptoms. Before seeing a doctor for an appointment, many patients use the Internet to find information about their symptoms. In the past before they saw a doctor, people would ask for advice from family and friends. In the past before seeing a doctor, people would ask for advice from family and friends.
D 当状语从句中的动词为现在完成时或过去完成时形式时，可通过省略主语，并将 have/had 变为 having 来简化从句。	After you've read multiple articles online, you'll have a better understanding of your doctor's diagnosis. After having read multiple articles online, you'll have a better understanding of your doctor's diagnosis. After he'd read multiple articles online, he had a better understanding of his doctor's diagnosis. After having read multiple articles online, he had a better understanding of his doctor's diagnosis.

语法应用

练习 3.1　简化状语从句

A 以下内容摘自一篇博客文章，文章讲述了如何甄别与健康相关的网站上的信息。将其中的每个状语从句简化为短语，记得使用逗号。

A few months back, I was plagued with headaches and fatigue.

[1] **Before going to the doctor,** I decided to read up on possible diagnoses.
(before I went to the doctor)

[2] _____ I was frantic. My long list of ailments included
(after I'd visited a few sites)

migraines, Lyme disease, and one deadly disease. [3] _____
(while she was looking at the list)

my wife kept shaking her head and frowning. She asked me where I found the

information. I didn't remember. Then she emailed a friend of hers who is a nurse

practitioner and we got the following advice on how to use the Web wisely for

research:

- [4] _____ look for websites with the domains .gov and
  (when you do research)
  .edu, which tend to be more credible.

- Also, [5] _____ look for websites that are
  (when you consider which websites to go to)
  operated by hospitals, universities, and recognized medical institutions.

- [6] _____ search for the name of the author (if
  (after you've read an article that interests you)
  there is one) to find out his / her credentials.

- Be extra critical [7] _____ . A lot of advertising
  (when you visit websites that try to sell you products)
  might mean that the objective of the website is really to sell merchandise.

- [8] _____ make a list of questions about it to ask
  (after you collect all the information)
  your doctor.

- [9] _____ if something doesn't feel right, you should
  (after you've been diagnosed)
  tell your doctor and continue your research because you never know when

  you'll come across important new therapies and medicines for you and your

  doctor to discuss.

B　结对练习 向同伴讲述你或你熟悉的人为了达到治疗疾病或保持健康的目的是如何使用互联网的。注意用短语来作状语。

After hearing or reading about some new research on health that I'm interested in, I'll look it up on the Internet and find out more about it. While searching, I try to go to a variety of sites so that I can find out a few opinions of the information.

下面的句子描述了线上互助小组的情况。根据动作的先后顺序，恰当使用含 when，while，before 或 after 的短语，将每对句子合并为一个句子。

	FIRST ACTION	SECOND ACTION	SIMULTANEOUS ACTIONS
1	Some people discover they have a serious illness.	Some people find help through online support groups.	
2			■ People go through treatment. ■ People find it comforting to communicate with others diagnosed with their disease.
3	People talk with others about their illness.	People don't feel so alone.	
4	People should read the messages that members post to make sure the group is supportive.	People choose a group to join.	
5			■ Leaders monitor members' messages. ■ Leaders should encourage positive participation.
6	Members notice that a member is going through a difficult time.	The members of good groups offer encouragement and advice.	
7	Members of good groups receive the support they asked for.	Members of good groups stay with the group and give others support.	

1 *After discovering they have a serious illness, some people find help through online support groups.*

2 _____

_____

3 _____

_____

4 _____

_____

5 _____

_____

6 _____

_____

7 _____

_____

描述问题和解决方法的常用表达

词汇讲解

在问题解决型写作中，有些表达很实用。	**The most important problem is** finding the right doctor to treat your illness. **There are several ways to address the problem of** cyberchondria. **One solution for** cyberchondria **would be to** avoid unreliable websites.

4.1 用于提出问题的表达

可以用下列表达来提出问题：
The key / main / primary / most important problem is _____ .
A / The secondary issue / problem is _____ .
While _____ are issues / problems / factors, the most important / urgent / pressing / critical issue / problem is _____ .

For doctors, **the main problem is** the extra time they spend arguing with ill-informed patients.
A secondary issue is the patients' increased stress.
While wasted time and patient stress **are factors, the most urgent issue is** misinformation on the Internet.

4.2 用于提出解决方法的表达

A 可以用下列表达来提出解决方法：
The solution to the problem lies in _____ .
There are several ways to address the problem of _____ .
One solution to / for _____ would be to _____ .
The problem of _____ can be solved by _____ .

_____ is a possible solution to the problem of _____ .

The solution to the problem lies in medical websites, doctors, and patients.
There are several ways to address the problem of cyberchondria.
One solution to cyberchondria **would be to** educate patients.
The problem of cyberchondria **can be solved by** reorganizing information on medical websites.
Educating patients **is a possible solution to the problem of** cyberchondria.

B 可以用下列表达来建议可能的解决方法：
is needed

is necessary

should be / may be / might be / must be considered

A definite decision by the government **is needed**.
Based on the results, it **will be necessary** to make changes to the treatment.
An individual's caloric needs **should be considered** before starting any diet.

练习 4.1 用于提出问题和解决方法的表达

下文讲述了医患关系。用方框中所给的描述问题和解决方法的表达填空。

a secondary issue	one solution for the first problem	the problem of
can be solved by	~~the most important problem~~	

^{1} *The most important problem* when communicating with doctors is that sometimes they don't understand exactly what a patient is feeling. ^{2}_____ is the fact that patients don't always ask the right questions. ^{3}_____ would be to require doctors to use checklists when discussing symptoms so that there is more discussion of feelings. ^{4}_____ asking the right questions ^{5}_____ providing patients with frequently asked questions about their illness to help them come up with questions.

are issues	there are several ways to address the problem of
is necessary	while
the most urgent issue is	

The patient–doctor relationship has changed in recent years and new issues have arisen. Patients come to appointments with a great deal of information and strong opinions. Doctors can feel uncomfortable with their patients' new assertiveness, and patients can feel mistrustful and even skeptical of their doctor's opinions. ^{6}_____ patients' mistrust and skepticism ^{7}_____ , ^{8}_____ the antagonistic relationship that can develop. ^{9}_____ antagonism. One way is for doctors to help their patients use the Internet more discerningly and discuss findings. In sum, a change in the patient–doctor relationship ^{10}_____ in order to adapt to the current information age.

练习 4.2 更多练习：用于提出问题和解决方法的表达

A **结对练习** 与同伴一起，将下列医患间存在的 3 个问题从 1（最严重）到 3（最不严重）进行排序。

- Some patients believe inaccurate information.

- Some patients don't follow advice.

- Some patients are unwilling to admit the seriousness of their health issues.

接下来，针对每个问题为医生想出可能的解决方法，用下面方框中的或第 177 页 4.2 中的表达进行描述，再将你们的想法分享给另一组同学。

The primary issue with patients is …	One solution to the problem might be …
The secondary issue with patients is …	… is a possible solution to the problem of …
The last issue with patients is …	The problem of … can be solved by …

In my opinion, the primary issue with patients is that they don't follow their doctor's advice. I think that one solution to the problem might be for doctors to ask the patient to follow up and call after a week or two to report how he or she is doing. This will motivate the patient to follow the advice and avoid getting sicker.

B **小组活动** 以小组为单位，从下面涉及身体健康的问题中选择一个并集思广益，讨论这一问题可能的解决方法。用提出问题和解决方法的常用表达，写出 1 个句子描述该问题，再写出 3—4 个句子描述该问题可能的解决方法，再将你们小组写好的句子分享给全班同学。

- You are sick and you disagree with your doctor's diagnosis.

- You have insomnia.

- You have a friend who is a cyberchondriac.

- Present a different problem that your teacher approves.

There are many things you can do if you feel sick and you disagree with your doctor's diagnosis. One solution would be to …

1 注意 for example 中的 example 总是用单数形式，即使后面跟了多个例子也是如此。

There are many solutions to the problem of cyberchondria. For ~~examples~~, (example)
using credible websites or avoiding the Internet altogether are ways to solve
cyberchondria.

2 描述某个普遍问题时，注意 the problem of 之后的名词短语前不加 the。

The problem of ~~the~~ Internet addiction can be solved by limiting time spent
online.

3 注意不要将 so that（表示目的）与 so（表示结果）混淆。so that 之前不用逗号。

The physician provided her patients with a list of credible medical ~~websites, so~~ (websites so that)
they would stop arguing with her about their symptoms.（目的）

The patient stopped consulting medical ~~websites so that~~ (websites, so) he argued much less
with his physician.（结果）

改错练习

下面是一篇关于网络疑病症的文章的主体段落，从中找出另外 8 处错误并改正。

Cyberchondria

A solution to the problem of ~~the~~ cyberchondria is to help individuals become informed Internet users. The Internet can be a useful source of information, but only if people use It wisely. Individuals need to know how to evaluate search results, so they can avoid misleading information. For examples, a website may
5 be out of date, or it may not be published by a credible medical source. Users should look for a date somewhere on the site, so they know that content is updated regularly. The solution to the problem of the unreliable medical websites is to establish the validity of sites. For examples, users should avoid sites with URLs ending in ".com" and sites that do not have scientific or medical sponsors. A
10 commercial website that looks like a medical source may actually be a business selling products. However, medical sites with URLs ending in ".gov" or ".edu" tend to have credible content so that users can be more confident of the information they contain. Physicians can also help solve the problem of the cyberchondria by directing their patients to their own preferred sites. This will reduce patient
15 anxiety and frustration, so physicians can use their consultation time more productively.

16

问题和解决方法 4：it 结构；说明问题解决步骤的过渡词语

Leading a Healthy Life

1 现实生活中的语法

阅读这篇文章。文章讨论了生活中人们为拥有更健康的生活方式可以作出的改变。在这篇问题解决型文章中，作者描述了实施改进方案的步骤。

A 读前准备 为了享有健康的生活，人们可以做哪些事情？在现代社会中，为什么有些为实现健康生活而必须做的事有时却很难做到？阅读文章并思考：作者对此提出了什么样的解决方法？

B 阅读理解 回答下列问题。

1 According to the essay, what is the main reason that people are prevented from leading a healthy life?

2 What are some of the beliefs that people have when it comes to healthy eating and exercising?

3 Do you think the writer would think that you have a healthy lifestyle? Why or why not?

C 语法发现 按照下列提示回答问题，注意作者是如何使用 it 结构的。

1 再次阅读第 8—10 行和第 22—25 行中含有 it 的句子。其中一个 it 指代前文提到过的事情，另一个 it 则不是。哪一个 it 不用于指代前文提到过的事情？

2 再次阅读第 35—36 行中含有 it 的句子。这句话使用了被动语态。被动语态和 it 的使用使句子更主观还是更客观？

3 再次阅读第 60—62 行中以 On the contrary 开头的句子，注意作者如何用 it 来引出自己的提议。作者在 it 之后使用了哪个形容词来使提议的语气更强？

Leading a
HEALTHY *Life*

In the last few decades, the average person's life has become increasingly unhealthy. The rules of modern society seem to have forced many into a stressful lifestyle. As individuals strive to meet the demands of their lives, they often overlook the multiple sources of stress and unhealthiness in their lives. Even though the task is challenging, it is not impossible to make some changes that can lead to a healthier lifestyle.

Many factors can contribute to creating tension in everyday life. For most people, a busy work schedule usually prevents them from dedicating time to other stress-relieving activities. Lack of exercise and not enough sleep are only two of the consequences of such a lifestyle. Also, as time is consumed by work-related responsibilities, individuals tend to have less time to eat well. Many people end up eating fast food as a strategy to save time, which adds to unhealthy practices.

Contrary to what many people may think, living a healthy life does not have to be difficult; nor does it have to be time-consuming. In terms of eating habits, a few changes can go a long way. First, individuals need to be committed to the challenge. Next, in order to have a healthier diet, they should buy low-calorie and low-fat foods that are easy to cook, such as broccoli, cauliflower, carrots, chicken, and fish. Then they can cook more quantities of food over the weekend and freeze the leftovers in small containers so that the food can be consumed throughout the week. It has been argued that freezing the food destroys some of the nutrients. This may be true. However, this solution is certainly better than the fast-food option.

40 Just as with eating habits, it is a common belief that exercising takes away many hours of an average person's week. However, first, it is important to find an activity that is enjoyable, such as playing a sport or hiking. Even simple activities, like taking the stairs, 45 raking leaves, or sweeping the floor, contribute to keeping someone active. Next, after finding an enjoyable activity, people need to commit to it. This means that people need to exercise regularly and make it part of their routine, just 50 like brushing their teeth or combing their hair. Many people will agree that their level of stress tends to decrease once exercising becomes part of their daily lives.

Maintaining a healthy lifestyle does 55 not have to be challenging but can be accomplished with a series of small steps. Setting a few reachable goals can make a huge difference. Drastic diets, fasting,[1] or very demanding exercise routines are not that likely 60 to generate permanent improvements. On the contrary, it is essential to take a holistic approach[2] to good health. Such an approach starts with healthy food and regular exercise. When these items are part of someone's life, 65 lack of time becomes just an excuse for not adopting a healthier lifestyle.

---

[1]**fasting:** intentionally eating no food for a long period of time 禁食
[2]**holistic approach:** a way of solving a health problem by looking at the social, psychological, and physical aspects of the problem 全面的方法

Leading a Healthy Life **183**

2 it 结构

语法讲解

it 结构常用于学术写作中，可以使文章更加客观且不带个人感情色彩。在问题解决型写作中，当提出某一问题的解决方法并对其进行评价时，常用 it 结构。	**It is important to** find an exercise that is enjoyable, such as playing a sport or hiking. **It has been argued that** freezing the food destroys some of the nutrients.

2.1　it 结构

A it 结构的构成： it + be + 形容词 + that 从句 it + be + 形容词 + 不定式 it 不是真正的主语。可通过在不定式之前加 "for + 名词短语" 的方式为句子添加具体的主语。	**It is true that** people who exercise usually have more energy than people who do not. **It is difficult to find** time to exercise every day. **It is difficult** <u>for many adults</u> **to find time** to exercise every day.
B 系动词 appear 和 seem 常用于 it 结构中，后接 that 从句： it + appears / seems + that 从句 it + appears / seems + 形容词 + that 从句 当作者对其某一说法的真实性几乎确定但并不完全确定时，使用 appear 和 seem 进行表达。	**It appears that** researchers have made the connection between exercise and mental health. **It seems that** people who eat healthier are frequently in a good mood. **It appears unlikely that** the government will issue new guidelines for healthy eating within the year.
C it 结构中可使用情态动词： may，might，could 这些情态动词用于削弱作者对于其说法的真实性的确定程度。	**It may be true that** people who eat healthier are always in a good mood. **It might seem that** people are not losing weight when they start a new diet program. **It could be that** genetics plays the main role in obesity.

📊 实际使用数据分析

下面这些形容词常用于 it is 之后，表示对后面所述内容的评价（按使用频率排序）： important to, clear that, difficult to, possible that, possible to, necessary to, better to, impossible that, likely that, true that, essential to, common to, doubtful that, easy to, evident that, unlikely that	It is important to eat a healthy diet and exercise every day.
it seems 的使用频率是 it appears 的两倍。 it seems 之后常接下面这些形容词： likely, unlikely, clear, possible, reasonable, obvious, certain, impossible, logical, probable	It seems reasonable that many people would make the connection between nutrition and physical health.
it appears 之后常接下面这些形容词： possible, unlikely, plausible	It appears possible that health insurance companies will provide more guidance on nutrition issues.

2.2　it 结构的被动形式

可以在 it 结构的被动形式中使用转述动词。这样作者就无需说明（或重述）所述内容的来源，同时也强调了所述内容。	It has generally been accepted that people who exercise frequently have more energy. It was found that certain fruits and vegetables can help with weight loss.

📊 实际使用数据分析

常用于"it + 现在完成时的被动形式"中的动词有： shown, suggested, reported, proposed, demonstrated, determined, linked, observed, documented, called, estimated, used, recognized, known, found, argued, applied, approved, associated	It has been shown that drastic diets are less likely to generate permanent health improvements.
在 it 结构的被动形式中，常出现以下情态动词： can, should, could, must 注意：will，would 和 shall 不常用于 it 结构的被动形式中。	It can be argued that schools should be more involved in teaching about healthy living.

A 在问题解决型写作中，某些形容词可用于 it 结构中，以强调某个问题的重要性及其解决方法的有效性。

这类形容词包括：

accepted, certain, clear, evident, important, indisputable, obvious

It is clear that exercising is good for children.

From the results of the study, **it is obvious** that children are healthier if they watch only one hour of TV a day.

B 下面这些形容词可用于表达对某一观点或说法的确定程度：

accepted，certain，indisputable 和 true 用于表达某事是确定无疑的。

likely 和 possible 用于表达某事是可能的。

unlikely 和 unusual 用于表达某事是不大可能的。

impossible 用于表达某事是不可能的。

It is true that children are heavier, but the causes are not clear.

It is likely that genes also play a big role in health.

It appears unlikely that cell phone use will decrease.

It is impossible to address health without including exercise.

下面这些形容词用于表达困难程度：

difficult, easy, hard

It is difficult to imagine restaurants eliminating desserts.

下面这些形容词用于表达作者的态度或观点：

clear, curious, evident, important, obvious, strange

It seems curious that fruit and vegetables are not emphasized.

It is evident that people's lifestyles contribute to their stress.

2.4　it 结构的用法

it 结构可用于代替直接说明信息来源的陈述。

陈述

Doctors and health officials agree that people should exercise at least three times a week.

it 结构

It is important to exercise at least three times a week.

it 结构是一种更加正式地提供信息的方式。

非正式：　**She argued that** exercising is very time consuming.

更加正式：**It has been argued** that exercising is very time consuming.

语法应用

练习 2.1 it 结构

A 选择恰当的形容词来描述下列句子中关于健康生活的观点，再用含有所选形容词的 it 结构改写这些句子。注意在 it 结构中使用 that 从句或不定式，在必要的地方添加 for。

1 People need to find time to prepare a healthy dinner every night.

　　a difficult　　(b important)　　c unusual

　　It is important for people to find time to prepare
　　a healthy dinner every night.

2 Everyone can eat good food by planning meals ahead of time.

　　a accepted　　b likely　　c easy

3 Young people don't usually pay attention to their dietary habits.

　　a possible　　b impossible　　c unusual

4 There is a good chance that meditation or yoga can reduce stress.

　　a possible　　b unlikely　　c obvious

5 Doctors agree that people should focus on their exercise and eating habits.

　　a clear　　b unlikely　　c strange

6 There is no doubt that moderate exercise results in fewer diseases such as diabetes.

　　a unlikely　　b indisputable　　c strange

7 There is a good chance that working out regularly improves mood.

　　a may be impossible　　b could be obvious　　c might be true

8 We can't really say why some people like to exercise and some don't.

　　a evident　　b impossible　　c reasonable

9 There is little evidence that regular exercise can cause physical harm.
   a unlikely   **b** impossible   **c** important

10 Everyone knows that good support systems have a positive impact on one's health.
   a curious   **b** likely   **c** evident

B **结对练习** 与同伴想出 4 种对健康有益或有害的事物或行为并展开讨论，说一说你们的看法。使用 it 结构来表达某事物是确定的、可能的、不可能的或困难的，与另一组同学分享你们的观点。

From what we have read, it is accepted that vitamins can be beneficial for one's health. I personally don't think that people need vitamins if they eat well. I have also read that it appears unlikely that cell phone use is harmful to one's health. No one's really sure about this, though.

练习 2.2 it 结构的被动形式

A 将下列词语重新排序，写出比较美国现在与过去的医学观念的句子。

1 **a** your health / accepted / cigarettes / bad for / it is / that / are
   __It is accepted that cigarettes are bad for your health.__

   b the body / that tobacco / believed / was / it was / good for / in the 60s,

   c thought / a person's life / and were good for / that cigarettes / might lengthen / years ago, / it was / his or her teeth

2 **a** been recently / that sugar / one's health / it has / is bad for / shown

   b a good source / argued / of energy for children / it was / that sugar was / years ago,

3 **a** generally been / is bad for children / accepted / it has / that watching / too much television / now,

   b suggested / that too much / it / from doing physical activities / has been / television keeps children

   c children's grades / that watching television / could improve / it was / believed / in the 60s,

B　**小组活动**　以小组为单位比较现在与过去的医学观念。用 it 结构的被动形式将你的想法分享给小组成员。

It was once accepted that eggs were one of the causes of high cholesterol, but I think that it is evident from current research that they are not a primary cause.

3 说明问题解决步骤的常用过渡词语

词汇讲解

向读者阐明某一解决方法或过程的步骤时，常用过渡词语。	**First**, it is important for people to find an activity that is enjoyable, such as playing a sport or hiking. **Next**, they need to commit to doing it.

3.1　说明问题解决步骤的过渡词语的用法

A 可以用 first，to begin 等过渡词语引出所述解决方法的第一步。当其位于句首时，后用逗号。	**First,** one needs to acknowledge that a problem exists. **To begin,** put the problem into words.
B 可以用 after that，following that，next，second，third，subsequently 和 then 引出接下来的步骤。 用 at the same time 引出同时进行或需要同时进行的步骤。	**Following that,** ways to address specific aspects of the problem should be developed. **Next,** key terms should be clearly defined. **At the same time,** the scope and effects of the problem need to be identified.
C 可以用 finally，in the end，last 和 lastly 总结前文所述的步骤。	**Finally,** the set of strategies should be implemented.
D 也可以在句子中间用 next，then 等，置于动词之前。 next 也可置于句尾。	The scope and effects of the problem **then** need to be identified. The people associated with the problem need to be contacted **next**.

E the first step，the second step，the third step 等短语也可用于表述解决步骤。这些短语之后常接 "be + 不定式" 结构。	**First**, one needs to acknowledge that a problem exists. **The first step is to acknowledge** that a problem exists.

3.2 在问题解决型写作中使用过渡词语

在问题解决型写作中，可以用过渡词语来连接解决方法的步骤，使句子间的衔接更加紧密。	**First**, one needs to acknowledge that a problem exists. The scope and effects of the problem **then** need to be identified. **Next**, key terms and ideas should be clearly defined. **Following that,** ways to address specific aspects of the problem should be developed. **Finally**, the set of strategies should be implemented.

 词汇应用

练习 3.1 说明问题解决步骤的过渡词语

A 听一段讲座，这段讲座谈论了公司如何处理工作中出现的特定健康问题。用听到的词填空，补全下面解决方法的步骤，注意用于说明步骤先后顺序的过渡词语。

Notes:

Problem: For data-entry workers, sitting at a computer for hours every day leads to weight gain, back pain, neck pain, and wrist pain.

Solution: Set up a plan to address the specific problems that workers have.

Steps:

1 _____*The first step is to*_____ identify _____*the health issues*_____ .

2 _____ determine _____ .

3 _____ implement _____ .

4 _____ evaluate _____ .

B **结对练习** 从下列话题中选择一个，与同伴展开讨论。仿照练习 A 中的示例，写出问题和解决方法，并使用至少 3 个过渡词语描述可能的解决步骤。完成后，向全班同学汇报。

- Smokers who want to give up smoking
- Students who don't study enough
- People who worry too much

下列句子描述了在生活中关注健康的方法，将其按照正确的步骤排序。

_____ Next, keep a journal for a week and write down what you eat every day and how you spend your time.

_____ At the same time, substitute at least one hour of the time that you spent watching TV or doing some other unnecessary activity with one hour of exercise. Do this for 21 days because some experts claim that it takes 21 days to make or break a habit.

___1___ To begin, acknowledge that you need to focus on your health.

_____ Subsequently, look at your journal and circle the unhealthy foods that you ate during the week.

_____ At the same time, circle the things that you did during the week that were unnecessary or could be cut down. For example, did you spend your lunch break surfing online, or did you watch three hours of TV after dinner?

_____ Finally, evaluate how you feel after three weeks of eating better and exercising one hour a day. You should feel great and have more energy.

_____ Also, hopefully you'll have created a new, healthy habit for yourself!

_____ After you examine your journal, substitute each unhealthy food with a healthy food like fruit, vegetables, or lean proteins.

4 常见错误提示

1 注意使用 it is important to，而不是 it is import to 或 it is importand to。

>   important
> It is ~~import~~ to admit that the problem exists.
>
>   important
> It is ~~importand~~ to find an exercise routine that is convenient.

2 注意 impossible 后接 to 或 for。

>   to
> For many people, it is impossible ∧find the time for exercise.
>
>   for
> It is impossible ∧some people to slow down and relax.

3 注意用 then，而非 than，来引出接下来的步骤。

>   Then
> First, one needs to identify the sources of the stress. ~~Than~~, ways to eliminate them should be considered.

改错练习

下面是一篇文章的主体段落，文章讨论了改善健康的方法。从中找出另外 6 处错误并改正。

important
It is ~~importand~~ to get an adequate amount of sleep in order to maintain a healthy lifestyle. For many people, it is almost impossible get a good night's sleep. Stress and the demands of work have a tremendous effect on one's ability to sleep. Lack of sleep can also result from certain lifestyle habits. However, it is virtually impossible people to
5 function well without adequate sleep. Studies have shown that lack of sleep can lead to a variety of physical and emotional problems. Therefore, it is import to get at least seven to eight hours of sleep at night because getting the recommended amount of sleep means optimal health and energy, more acute mental faculties, and a better memory. It also means getting sick less and being better able to deal with the stresses and strains
10 of everyday life. Although at times it may seem impossible get enough sleep, there are a few simple strategies for improving one's chances. First, one needs to determine the causes of sleeplessness, such as lack of exercise or consuming too much caffeine. Than, one needs to commit to making a few small lifestyle changes. People who have difficulty sleeping should increase their daily exercise, but not exercise too late in the day.
15 They should avoid consuming too much caffeine and eating close to bedtime. It is also importand to have a regular bedtime and to get the same number of hours of sleep each night. These small changes to one's daily routine can lead to a better night's sleep and improved health.

UNIT 17

总结和回应：表示过去的非真实条件句；用于总结和回应型写作中的表达

Privacy in the Digital Age

1 现实生活中的语法

阅读这篇讨论计算机与隐私的文章，再阅读随后的一篇对此进行总结与回应的文章。

A 读前准备 使用互联网时，存有哪些潜在危险？面对这些危险，人们可以如何保护自己？阅读这两篇文章并思考：互联网用户可以采用哪些方法来保护自己？

B 阅读理解 回答下列问题。

1 What two suggestions does the writer of "Privacy and Computers" make for being safe on the Internet?

2 What important issues does the summary–response writer believe are missing from the original article?

3 What other privacy concerns do you have concerning the use of your personal information? What do you do to keep your information safe?

C 语法发现 按照下列提示，看 "Privacy and Computers" 的作者是如何使用非真实条件句的。

1 再次阅读文章的第 2 段。去度假的人们经历了什么？在第 25—27 行的非真实条件句下面画线。非真实条件句的使用帮助作者达到了什么目的？

2 再次阅读文章的第 3 段。那位在不安全的网站上购买商品的男士经历了什么？在第 43—45 行的非真实条件句下面画线。非真实条件句的使用帮助作者达到了什么目的？

3 再次阅读文章的最后一段，找到含有 if 从句的句子，将其与第 3 段中画出的句子进行比较。哪个句子描述了想象的过去的结果？哪个句子描述了想象的现在的结果？这两个句子中的动词形式有何不同？

194

Privacy and Computers

by Robert Erani

In an era of online social media, people can announce any event to their virtual network of friends, family, and acquaintances within moments. From birthday celebrations
5 to baby pictures, friends get news about each other from texts, tweets, or social networks. In addition, many people use credit cards to purchase products and complete numerous online forms with personal information for
10 a variety of purposes. As a result, personal information is ending up in the hands of other people. There are critics who are concerned by the lack of privacy. Despite such concerns, by following a few common-sense measures,
15 people can use the Internet enjoyably and safely.

In our fast-paced world, social networking sites are, for many people, an important way to keep up with friends and family. The issue
20 now is how open one should be with sharing private information since the information could be stolen by criminals. For example, some people have had their homes broken into because they had posted the details of
25 their vacation online. If they had not posted those details, the thieves would not have known that they had gone away. One way to reduce the risk of this happening is to activate the privacy controls on social networking sites
30 and smartphones. In other words, think about who will see your information and consider how they might use it.

Another important step is to shop only on secure websites so that one's accounts,
35 passwords, and financial records are protected. Some experts recommend that people should treat their online information like they would treat the contents of their wallets. For example, a man bought
40 merchandise on a website that did not have a security padlock, and as a result of this transaction, his bank accounts were emptied. If he had paid attention to the security on the site, he would not have lost his
45 money. However, it appears that people are becoming more aware of the risks of fraud and taking steps to avoid them since the total percentage of incidences of fraud have remained steady. It may be that people who
50 have grown up using the Internet understand its risks as well as its strengths.

The ease of sharing information provides opportunities for crimes and abuses. While it may be impossible to entirely eliminate the
55 risks, if people followed reasonable guidelines to protect important data, they could greatly reduce these risks. The benefits of being able to do such things as bank online, keep medical records updated almost instantly,
60 and share the thrills both big and small of everyday life with friends outweigh these concerns.

Summary–Response Essay on "Privacy and Computers"

Robert Erani, in the article "Privacy and Computers," explains the issues concerning the sharing of personal information online. According to Erani, one area of concern is that people may sometime share details of their lives online without thinking about the consequences. As the author points out, "The issue now is how open one should be with sharing private information since the information could be stolen by criminals" (para. 2). The author describes a situation in which people were robbed after revealing their vacation plans online. The author further states how important it is for consumers to protect their personal information when they purchase products online. Erani concludes the article by stating that, despite the concerns about privacy, one can still use online services safely by using common sense and privacy controls.

In sum, the author provides a general introduction to the issues of privacy online and offers some advice on how to avoid problems. I agree that insecure websites are a problem, but I disagree with the author's contention that people who have grown up using the Internet are more savvy about using it. Hackers and scammers continue to come up with more sophisticated and convincing schemes. The consumer needs to constantly be wary of them. In addition, the article fails to address the more controversial issues concerning the consequences of posting information regarding health issues, job dissatisfaction, or even political views. This is an oversight because these issues impact individuals every day. It is becoming increasingly common for employers, for instance, to view the online profiles of potential employees as part of their selection process. Despite these shortcomings, the author rightly states that the concern around privacy issues seems to be an acceptable exchange for many people for the benefits of sharing their lives with others.

2 表示过去的非真实条件句

语法讲解

表示过去的非真实条件句（past unreal conditionals）可用于讨论假设的（即想象中的、与过去事实不符的）情况及其结果。在学术写作中，写作者可以用这类句子来对比过去可能发生、但没有发生的事件（即非真实的事件）与过去实际发生的事件（即真实的事件）。	If the author **had discussed** education in his article, the text **would have been** stronger. If this information **had been taught** years ago, we **would not have had** so many problems.

2.1 表示过去的非真实条件句

表示过去的非真实条件句的构成：
if 从句（过去完成时）+ 主句（would /
could / might + have + 过去分词）
if 从句可置于主句之前或之后。当 if
从句位于主句之前时，用逗号将其与
主句分隔开。

if 从句（过去完成时）
If I **had read** the privacy policy on the company's
website carefully,
主句（would / could / might + have + 过去分词）
I **would have avoided** the problem.
主句   if 从句
I would have avoided the problem if I **had read**
the website's privacy policy carefully.

2.2 表示过去的非真实条件句的用法

A 用 if 从句给出与过去事实不符的某
个假设的情况，用主句描述这一情
况所对应的结果。

if 从句：表示过去的非真实的条件
If she **had used** separate accounts for work and
personal email,
主句：想象的过去的结果
she **would have avoided** trouble.（真实情况：她
的个人邮箱和工作邮箱是同一个账户，所以惹上了
麻烦。）
表示过去的非真实的条件
If he **hadn't made** his passwords difficult,
想象的过去的结果
the thieves **would have been able to access** his
accounts.（真实情况：他的密码很复杂，所以窃贼
没法盗取他的账户。）

B 与其他情态动词相比，用 would
have 描述想象的过去的结果时，
表示较为确定。
could have 和 might have 表示较
为不确定。

If I had noticed the lack of security on that
website, I **wouldn't have ordered** merchandise
from it.
If I had ordered merchandise from that website,
I **might have had** my information stolen.

C 表示过去的非真实条件句可用于表
达对过去发生过的情况或动作感到
后悔。

If I **had insured** my laptop, the insurance company
would have reimbursed me when it was stolen.
（我后悔没有为笔记本电脑买保险。）

D 表示过去的非真实条件句也可用于
描述想象的现在的结果。此时，主
句中使用"would / could / might +
动词原形"这一结构。

表示过去的非真实的条件
If the author **had mentioned** his sources,
想象的现在的结果
the article **would be** more compelling.

练习 2.1　表示过去的非真实条件句

阅读这个关于身份盗窃的故事，用括号中动词的正确形式以及恰当的情态动词填空。有时正确答案不唯一。

I know that thieves have ways to steal people's identities online, so I'm always careful about the emails I read and the links that I click on. However, I didn't realize that thieves sometimes go through people's garbage to look for personal information. I [1] **_'d have been_** (be) more careful if I [1] **_'d known_** (know) that.

Last year, I put a letter that had my Social Security number on it in the garbage. Normally, I shred important documents, but I was in a hurry that day. If I [2]_____ (not be) in a hurry, I definitely [2]_____ (shred) it. A few days later, there was no money in my checking account. I realized that if someone [3]_____ (take) the letter out of the garbage, he or she [3]_____ (have) my Social Security number now. I knew that if someone [4]_____ (find) my Social Security number, they [4]_____ (have) the ability to access my bank accounts, use my credit cards, and get new credit cards in my name.

By the time I realized that my identity had been stolen, the thief had taken all my money and applied for 10 new credit cards. If I [5]_____ (realize) sooner that a thief had found my Social Security number, I [5]_____ (be) able to stop him or her from using it. The identity theft has caused all kinds of problems for me. I can't get a loan to buy a car, and I can't get a new credit card. If someone [6]_____ (not steal) my identity, I [6]_____ (not have) all these problems now.

I shred all my important documents now before I throw them away. Last week, I told my neighbor what had happened to me. She was going to put some important mail in her garbage without shredding it. She immediately shredded the mail. If I [7]_____ (not warn) her, she [7]_____ (have) the same problems that I do now.

练习 2.2　更多练习：表示过去的非真实条件句

A　下列每组句子描述了一件不幸的事情。用表示过去的非真实条件句来表述每组句子的意思。有时正确答案不唯一。

1　I visited my friend Eric for the weekend. I lost all my credit cards and my cell phone.

   If I hadn't visited my friend Eric for the weekend,
   I wouldn't have lost all my credit cards and my cell
   phone.

2　Eric wasn't ready to go swimming on Saturday morning. I went to the beach alone.

   _____

   _____

3　Eric wasn't with me. I left my wallet and phone on the beach while I went swimming.

   _____

4　I went swimming. Someone stole my credit cards and my phone.

   _____

5　I forgot the address of Eric's house. I couldn't find the house.

   _____

6　I didn't have my cell phone. I couldn't call Eric.

   _____

7　My cell phone wasn't password-protected. The thief was able to use my phone.

   _____

8　I had personal information on my cell phone. The thief got my bank account numbers.

   _____

9　I also forgot to wear sunscreen. I have a terrible sunburn.

   _____

B　**结对练习**　与同伴轮流讲述自己曾经犯过的错误，以及原本可以避免犯错的方法。

Someone stole my wallet from my purse at a restaurant last weekend. I'd hung my purse on the back of my chair. If I hadn't put it on the back of my chair, no one would have stolen my wallet. If I had put my purse closer to me, I'd have my wallet now.

3 总结和回应型写作中的常用表达

词汇讲解

熟练的学术写作者在总结和回应型写作中，善于使用合适的表达来引出并表明观点。	The article **provides** a thorough introduction to the issues of privacy. The author **fails to address** more controversial concerns.

3.1 总结和回应型写作中的常用表达

A 可以用下列由主语 + 动词构成的常见表达来引出某个总结的核心观点。这些表达按使用频率由高到低的顺序排列如下：
the article + say, state, note, describe, mention, quote, report ...
the author + claim, explain, call, say, write, argue, cite, establish, start ...
在表示总结或回应的句子中，the article 作主语的频率比 the author 作主语的频率高很多。
注意：当这类句子的主语是 the author 时，谓语动词尽量避免使用 believe 或 think。

The article describes the problem of privacy and computers.

The article mentions ways that education can prevent problems with technology.

The author starts the article by saying that technology is part of everyone's lives.

The author claims that the experts he interviewed for this article were well known.
不说 The author ~~thinks~~ that the experts he interviewed for this article were well known.

B 以上常见表达通常用现在时，有时也用一般过去时或现在完成时。
（对转述动词的讲解见 Unit 14。）

The article quoted many well-known sources.
The author has argued that individuals are responsible for protecting their own privacy.

3.1　总结和回应型写作中的常用表达（续表）

C 可以用下列表达来说明原文作者的观点：	
discuss	**The article discusses** identity theft in detail.
go on to say	**The article goes on to say** that the problem is being addressed.
further state / explain	**The author further states** that regulations may be necessary in the future.
also state	**The author also states** that consumers need to become proactive on this issue.
according to the author	**According to the author**, the government has an important role in this debate.
D 可以用下列表达来总结原文作者的观点：	
in conclusion	**In conclusion**, the author predicts that Internet privacy will become one of the most important issues of the next decade.
in sum	
the author concludes	
summing up	**Summing up**, the author calls for people to be cautious when giving their personal information online.
E 在对原文作出回应时，可以用下面的表达来指出原作者忽略或未考虑到的内容：	
fail to address / mention	The author **fails to address** the idea that users are also to blame for identity theft.
not address / mention	The author **does / did not mention** that we are all responsible for protecting privacy.
注意：in my opinion 等第一人称短语很少用于学术写作中，而更常用于杂志文章等非正式文本中。	~~I think that the author~~ ... ~~In my opinion~~, the author could have ...

词汇应用

练习 3.1　总结信息

下面这个段落是对一篇谈论互联网时代隐私的文章的总结。阅读这段总结，圈出正确的选项。

John M. Eger, Chair of Communications and Public Policy at San Diego State University, [1] **addresses** / **claims**　the issue of privacy in the Internet age in his

article "Growing Concerns Over Internet."
He [2] **starts the article / further states** by
explaining the historical context of the
right to privacy in the United States and
[3] **cites / describes** how in 1928, a Supreme
Court decision was made to protect the right
to privacy. However, he [4] **concludes that / notes that** our online lives are
today being monitored in ways that most people do not even realize. He then
[5] **claims / goes on to explain** how websites use cookies to follow an Internet
user's every move. The author [6] **acknowledges that / thinks that** some
sharing of information may provide us with advertisements for things that may
be beneficial to us, but then he [7] **argues that / sums up that** data collectors
might collect and share health and financial information, and even connect our
names to our data. In addition, [8] **according to the article, / the article quotes**
there are currently no laws that adequately protect our right to privacy. Then,
while the author [9] **goes on to show / concludes** by saying that we need to
do something about this problem, he [10] **does not mention at all / further states**
what we can do to protect ourselves.

练习 3.2 更多练习：总结信息

 阅读下列句子，并听一段录音。录音内容为两个人谈论一篇关于互联网密码的文章。录音将播放两遍。听第一遍时，做好笔记；听第二遍时，补全句子。

1 *The author starts the article by saying that a website* was recently hacked.

2 _____ when they create their passwords.

3 _____ can break one password a second.

4 _____ shouldn't use the same password
for multiple accounts.

5 _____ says, "I always use the same
password for everything because otherwise I can't remember them."

6 _____ is abc123.

7 _____ is 123456.

8 _____ can do to create strong
passwords.

4 常见错误提示 ⚠️

1 在表示过去的非真实条件句的主句中，注意情态动词后接 have 和动词的过去分词。

                                                               avoided

If the company had installed secure systems, it would have ~~avoid~~ data theft.

2 在学术写作中，注意要用准确的学术词汇，而不要用短语动词或习语，例如：

find out	→	discover / learn	start off / out	→	start / begin
put up with	→	tolerate	look into	→	investigate

                                discovering

Social media users enjoy ~~finding out~~ what products and services their friends recommend.

                              tolerate

Older users will not ~~put up with~~ further invasions of privacy.

The article starts ~~off~~ with a presentation of both sides of the issue.

                  investigates

The author ~~looks into~~ recent developments in Internet security.

改错练习

下面的段落是对一篇关于隐私问题与社交网络的文章的总结，从中找出另外的语法错误和使用欠妥当的动词短语共 5 处并改正。

    In his article "Privacy and Security Issues in Social Networking" (2008),
                  investigates
Brendan Collins ~~looks into~~ the security and privacy problems associated with
social networks. He starts off by making the distinction between security issues
and privacy issues, highlighting that social networking sites (SNSs) provide ideal
5 opportunities for both types of violations. An example of a security violation that
Collins cites is the case of a hacker who shut down an SNS just for fun. Fortunately
the attack was harmless. If the attack had been malicious, the personal data of
millions of users would have be stolen. According to Collins, SNSs provide ideal
opportunities for break-ins because they have so much information, and because
10 so many people have access. As an example, he gives the case of Adrienne Felt,
a PhD student at U.C. Berkeley, who found out that there was a security flaw
in a major SNS. The program that allowed people to share photos and send
invitations also exposed their information to theft. If Felt had not looked into the
SNS, many users could have had their information stolen. Collins recommends
15 ways to limit the possibility of violations. Because SNSs are so big, it is impossible
to monitor them. Therefore users should take precautions with the information
that is shared. Collins concludes that there probably will never be a solution
to these issues and that we will have to put up with threats to our privacy and
security.

说服 1：非限制性关系从句；用于限制过度概括的表达

Violence in the Media

1 现实生活中的语法

阅读这篇讨论电视上的暴力镜头的文章。作者在文中提出，这一现象应该得到政府管控。这是一篇说服性写作的范例。

A 读前准备 你认为电视上的暴力镜头是否过多？谁应该负责管控儿童在电视上看到的暴力镜头的次数：父母、政府，还是两者都应该负责？阅读文章并思考：作者的主要论点是什么？

B 阅读理解 回答下列问题。

1 What evidence is given in the essay that violence on TV may negatively affect children's behavior?

2 Why might it be difficult in the United States for the government to regulate TV violence?

3 Do you agree with the writer that violence on TV should be regulated? Why or why not?

C 语法发现 回答下列问题，注意作者是如何使用关系从句来解释并支持自己的观点的。

1 比较第 13—17 行和第 63—65 行中关于儿童的两个句子。作者在哪个句子中指向所有的儿童？在哪个句子中指向一群特定的儿童？

2 阅读第 47—55 行中以 TV rating and program-blocking systems 开头的两个句子，观察这两个句子中的关系从句。这里的关系从句对于理解句意来说是必不可少的吗？关系从句为读者提供了什么信息？

TV Violence:
WHO IS RESPONSIBLE?

SHOULD VIOLENCE ON TV BE REGULATED?
This question has long been debated. Opponents defend the right to freedom of speech. Proponents believe that some
5 restriction is essential to protect young people from too much exposure to violence. Over a decade ago, in a controversial report, the Federal Communications Commission (FCC), which is the government agency
10 that regulates radio, TV, and Internet communications, advised the government to regulate violence on television to protect children. Since then, many reports have suggested that children who watch violent
15 TV shows and play violent video games are likely to exhibit more aggressive and violent behavior. They may also become "immune" to violence and begin to identify with the characters shown. The American Academy
20 of Family Physicians states that the average American child will have witnessed 200,000 acts of violence on screen by the age of 20. It is clear that the government should take immediate action and control violence on TV
25 through regulations.

Regulation by the government should protect the public, especially children, from overexposure to violence. In the past, courts have protected violent speech and depictions[1]
30 of violence under the First Amendment.[2] Nonetheless, the government regulates TV and film indecency.[3]

According to the FCC, the Supreme Court allows these restrictions so that children
35 are not so easily exposed to indecency. The parallel with violence in the media is obvious. Limiting media violence is much like limiting indecency in the media.

Government regulation will also help
40 parents monitor their children's exposure to violence. FCC Chairman Kevin Martin explained that while parents should always be the decision makers on how to best protect their children from violence, they alone
45 cannot be responsible. The main problem is that television violence seems to have a strong presence in most children's lives. TV rating and program-blocking systems, which are both tools to help parents control viewing,
50 are "not effective," according to the FCC, since networks may not consistently monitor TV shows for violent content. In fact, the Parents Television Council, which monitors TV shows for violent content, states that networks are
55 not doing a good job of rating TV shows. As a result, children have access to inappropriate content. Research conducted in 2017 by the Parents Television Council shows that gun violence has increased on primetime
60 television shows that are marketed as suitable for children's viewing.

Congress has resisted addressing this issue. However, not addressing it could put children, who have young minds that
65 are easily impressionable,[4] at risk. It could also put society at risk for aggressive acts committed by people influenced by violent media. Therefore, the government must act now to regulate media; otherwise, society will
70 have a difficult road ahead trying to control the negative effects of violent media on our children.

---

[1]**depiction:** an image 画面；描绘的景象
[2]**First Amendment:** an amendment in the United States Constitution that allows for freedom of speech in most situations 第一修正案
[3]**indecency:** behavior that upsets popular moral standards, usually as they relate to sexual behavior and nudity 下流行为
[4]**impressionable:** readily or easily influenced 易受影响的

2 非限制性关系从句

语法讲解

可以用非限制性关系从句（nonidentifying relative clauses）为名词短语补充额外信息。写作者常用这类从句来描述或指明所提及的专有名词，以增加所引用的专家、组织等的可信度。	The Federal Communications Commission (FCC), which regulates radio, TV, and Internet communications, has condemned violence in children's programming. Parents, who one could argue have the most influence on young children, must limit their children's exposure to violence.

2.1 非限制性关系从句

A 可以用非限制性关系从句为名词或名词短语补充更多细节信息。这类从句由关系代词 who，which，whose 或 whom 引导，而且前后均使用逗号。	The National Institute of Mental Health, 非限制性关系从句 which is a government agency, conducts research on the effects of violence on children.
B 非限制性关系从句包含的信息可以省略，而且省略之后句意仍然完整。	Brad J. Bushman and Craig A. Anderson, who are on the faculty of Iowa State University, have written extensively on violence in the media. Brad J. Bushman and Craig A. Anderson have written extensively on violence in the media.
C 非限制性关系从句多用于书面语中，较少用于口语中。	L. Rowell Huesmann, PhD, whose research on the effects of media violence on children is well-regarded, argues that there is a correlation between watching violent shows and aggressive behavior.
D 非限制性关系从句不可由 that 引导，而且其中的关系代词不可省略。	The American Academy of Pediatrics, which is a prominent group of medical professionals, has several suggestions about television violence. 不说 The American Academy of Pediatrics, ~~that~~ is a prominent group of medical professionals, has several suggestions about television violence. 不说 The American Academy of Pediatrics, ~~is a prominent group of medical professionals~~, has several suggestions about television violence.

2.1 非限制性关系从句（续表）

E 非限制性关系从句可用于人名、组织名称等专有名词之后，以增强信息来源的可信度。	Susan P. Leviton, **who is the president of the Advocates for Children and Youth**, is on the faculty of the University of Maryland Francis King Carey School of Law. The National Violence Survey, **which has examined violence on TV for many years**, released its report today.
描述专家资历时，可以用更简短的同位语代替非限制性关系从句。 （更多对同位语的讲解见 Unit 12。）	Adam D. Thierer, **a senior fellow at the Progress & Freedom Foundation**, believes that parents should decide whether their children play violent video games.

 语法应用

练习 2.1 非限制性关系从句

A 画出下列句子中的专家或组织的名称。用非限制性关系从句补充关于专家或组织的额外信息，写出新的句子。

1 <u>Jason Edwards</u> reports that the effect of violent content on adolescents depends on how it is portrayed.
   Additional information: Jason Edwards is an assistant professor of communication at Bradford College.
   Jason Edwards, who is an assistant professor of communication at Bradford College, reports that the effect of violent content on adolescents depends on how it is portrayed.

2 A child who watches two hours of TV a day is exposed to approximately 10,000 acts of violence a year, based on research by the Philips Family Foundation.
   Additional information: The Philips Family Foundation is a nonprofit organization that focuses on health-care issues.

   _____

   _____

3 Parents should discuss the content of TV advertising with their children, according to Joanna Moore.
   Additional information: Joanna Moore is the mother of five teenagers.

   _____

   _____

4 According to Pablo Silva, the best way for children to be active is to turn off the TV set.

Additional information: Pablo Silva studies the effects of TV on children's development.

_____

_____

5 In 2006, the American Academy of Child & Adolescent Psychiatry determined that children with excessive exposure to violence on television may "become 'immune' or numb to the horror of violence."

Additional information: The American Academy of Child & Adolescent Psychiatry provides resources about children's mental health.

_____

_____

6 Gerard Jones believes that effective use of media violence can help children vent their anger.

Additional information: Gerard Jones is a well-known comic book writer and the author of the article "Violent Media Is Good for Kids."

_____

_____

B **结对练习** 在练习 A 中，找出可以将关系从句转换为同位语的句子。说出关系从句被同位语替换后的句子，并给出你对这些信息的看法。

Jason Edwards, an assistant professor of communication at Bradford College, reports that the effect of violent content on adolescents depends on how it is portrayed. I think I agree. When violence is portrayed as something heroic or admired, then I think it is harmful because children always want to imitate their heroes.

练习 2.2 **更多练习：非限制性关系从句**

 A 听一段谈论媒体暴力对儿童的影响的访谈节目。边听录音边做笔记，记下讲话者的资历或背景信息，以及他们对问题的看法。再用非限制性关系从句描述每位讲话者。

1 Dr. Marc Richards

Marc Richards, who is a school psychologist, believes that exposure to violence in the media encourages young children to react violently when they're upset.

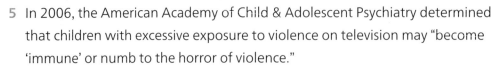

2 Kevin McDonald

_____

_____

3 Dr. Marcia Chan

_____

_____

4 Catherine Wong

_____

_____

5 Dr. Eric Lopez

_____

_____

6 Barbara Cramer

_____

_____

7 Noah Friedman

_____

_____

B **小组活动**　小组成员轮流选择一位练习 A 中的讲话者，介绍该讲话者的身份，总结该讲话者的观点，分享自己对其观点的看法，并邀请小组其他成员作出回应。

A *Marc Richards, who is a school psychologist, says that exposure to violence in the media causes children to react violently when they get upset. I'm not sure I agree with him. It's true that young children are impressionable, so they may think that the violent behavior on video games, for example, is appropriate, but I think family and friends are more influential.*

B *I think I agree with Dr. Richards more. When children see violent images over and over, I think it might make them more likely to use violence when they get angry.*

3 用于限制过度概括的表达

词汇讲解

<table>
<tr>
<td>在说服性文章中，写作者需要提供一些事实来支撑自己的论点和看法。然而，要谨慎选择表达观点的语言。有些表达可以对过度概括的陈述作出限制，增强陈述的准确度和可信度，这类表达也被称为模糊限制语（hedges）。</td>
<td>This statement **is likely to** cause arguments.
Television violence **seems to** be everywhere.
In most cases, parents try to control what their children watch on television.</td>
</tr>
</table>

3.1 用于限制过度概括的表达

<table>
<tr>
<td>**A** 可以用 "seem / appear / tend / be likely + 不定式" 这一结构来表示某种情况是可能的但不一定是确定无疑的，或表示某种情况并非总是正确的。其中，seem 是这类结构中最常用的动词。</td>
<td>Experts who study violence **seem to / appear to** disagree with one another's conclusions.（我们并不了解所有研究暴力现象的专家，但据我们所知，他们的意见并不一致。）
Children who watch many hours of TV every day **are likely to / tend to** be exposed to violent programs.（我们并不知道是否所有的孩子都会接触到暴力节目，但我们推测大多数情况是这样。）</td>
</tr>
<tr>
<td>**B** 当写作者认为某个现象是一种趋势，但却没有足够的证据来支撑这一看法时，可以使用 it seems that，it appears that 等 it 结构进行表达。</td>
<td>**It seems that** parents are becoming more cautious about what programs their children should watch on TV.</td>
</tr>
<tr>
<td>**C** 可以用下面的表达限制概括性的陈述：
in most cases，mainly，typically</td>
<td>**In most cases**, children can tell the difference between cartoon violence and real violence.
Children will **typically** show higher levels of aggression after watching violence on TV.</td>
</tr>
<tr>
<td>**D** according to 最常用于指明信息的具体来源。</td>
<td>**According to** the report, the television industry is not policing itself to the satisfaction of parents.</td>
</tr>
</table>

词汇应用

练习 3.1 用于限制过度概括的表达

A 下列句子谈论了媒体暴力可能产生的积极影响。根据括号中的信息，从 according to，appears，in most cases，likely，seem(s)，tend，typically 中选择合适的限制词语改写下列句子。每个词语仅可使用一次。有些句子要改变部分措辞。

1 Many parents and teachers believe children should not be exposed to any kind of violence in the media. (This is a trend, but there is not enough evidence to support this.)

It appears that many parents and teachers believe children should not be exposed to any kind of violence in the media.

2 Children are taught to deny their feelings of violence. (This is true of some children, but not all children.)

_____

3 Adults attempt to repress any violent reactions they have. (This seems to be true of many, but not all adults.)

_____

4 Media violence allows people to fantasize about releasing their aggression in a safe, nonthreatening environment. (Some experts believe this claim.)

_____

5 Violent video games provide players with an outlet for feelings of anger and frustration. (This is possible, but there isn't enough research to back this up.)

_____

6 Constant denial of violent feelings, rather than exposure to media violence, makes people react to problems with aggression. (It is very possible, but it is not certain that this is true.)

_____

7 Video games portray heroes as violent. (It is possible, but not true all the time.)

_____

B **结对练习** 结合下列话题，与同伴轮流给出过度概括的陈述，再努力说服对方，让他／她用限制过度概括的词语对所述观点进行限制。

- The effects of violent video games on teenagers
- Reasons that children like to play violent video games
- The effects of violence in cartoons and movies on children

A Violent video games always make children act violently.

B I think you're overgeneralizing. In some cases, some violent video games may make some children act violently, but you can't say that is true for all violent video games and all children unless you have research to back up your claims.

4 常见错误提示 ⚠

1 在非限制性关系从句中，注意要使用关系代词。

                            which

"Violent Video Games: Myths, Facts, and Unanswered Questions," ∧was published by the American Psychological Association, establishes the connection between violence in games and violent behavior.

2 注意关系代词 that 不用于引导非限制性关系从句。

                     which

The National Institute of Mental Health, ~~that~~ published the article, is an excellent source of recent studies on the effects of violence in the media.

3 当动词 seem 与 it 连用时，注意使用其单数形式。

  seems

It ~~seem~~ that not enough parents take responsibility for monitoring their children.

改错练习

下面是一篇文章的主体段落，文章讨论了媒体上的暴力内容。从中找出另外 8 处错误并改正。

Government's Role in Violence in the Media

There is a major reason that the government should not be involved in solving the

problem of violence in the media. Government control of the media is unconstitutional.

It seem that some people feel that the Federal Communications Commission (FCC),

is the government agency that regulates media such as TV and the Internet, is the

5 best tool for protecting children. However, many experts disagree. For example, the

American Civil Liberties Union (ACLU), that focuses on constitutional rights, believes that

government control of the media is a form of censorship. The First Amendment to the

U.S. Constitution, guarantees freedom of speech, gives us the right to media that are not

controlled by the government. A free and open media is the foundation of democracy in

10 the United States. However, it is important to protect children from violence. According

to the ACLU, protecting children is the responsibility of parents, although it seem that

many parents are unwilling to take on this responsibility. Caroline Fredrickson, is a

director of the ACLU's Washington Legislative Office, points out in her article, "Why

Government Should Not Police TV Violence and Indecency," was published in *The*

15 *Christian Science Monitor,* that parents "already have many tools to protect their children,

including blocking programs and channels, changing the channel, or simply turning

off the television." She adds that the Parents Television Council, that is a nonprofit

media monitoring organization, provides information on their website about television

programs that are appropriate for children. It seem that if parents take responsibility for

20 monitoring their children's television viewing, then we will be able to have free and open

media and protect children at the same time.

说服 2：特殊疑问词和 if / whether 引导的名词性从句；用于论证的表达

Living in an Age of Information Overload

1 现实生活中的语法

阅读这篇讨论网络信息便捷性的文章。作者在文中呈现了对立的观点。这是一篇说服性写作的范例。

A 读前准备 你通过何种渠道来获取大部分信息：纸质媒体还是电子媒体？阅读文章并思考：作者对于依赖网络获取信息这一现象有哪些担忧？

B 阅读理解 回答下列问题。

1 What are the two main points in favor of new technology mentioned by the writer?

2 Why does the writer believe that ease of access to information may not be such a good thing?

3 The writer offers readers a choice in the concluding paragraph. What point do you think the writer is making by offering a choice?

C 语法发现 在文中找到下列问题的答案，注意作者在论述观点时使用的语法。

1 阅读第 57—59 行中以 People who embrace 开头的句子，注意作者是如何使用由特殊疑问词引导的从句来帮助呈现争议的两个不同方面的。该争议的两个方面分别是什么？

2 在第 1 段中找到作者陈述反方观点并对其进行回应的句子。作者使用了哪个表达来引出反方的观点，然后进行了反驳？

So Much Information, So Little Time

WE LIVE IN AN AMAZING TIME, with access to almost unlimited information, entertainment, and opinions. Digital technology offers us new information
5 whenever we are "plugged in." Just the other day, I watched a baseball game on TV, texted a friend, and kept track of the details of my other friends' lives online. I also kept an eye on all the other sports scores as they were
10 happening. I did all this while also having a conversation with my brother. While it is true that digital technology has many benefits, they come at a cost, producing citizens who have fewer critical-thinking skills and weaker
15 social skills.

According to the proponents[1] of technology, easy access to information is one way that people benefit from new technology. When doing research, you do not have to
20 walk to a library, search for books, and read words on paper. Obviously, finding what we need from the Internet is faster, and online searches provide a broader range of sources. Often, however, when people are faced
25 with search-engine results in the thousands or more, their critical-thinking skills may be overwhelmed by the sheer volume of material to read. One study in the UK showed that students skimmed over most information
30 they found. According to this study, they rarely read more than a page or two when completing academic research.

Proponents also point out that technology has increased social connections.
35 People can stay in touch with friends more easily now, sending them birthday greetings, sharing complaints, and keeping each other informed, all online. Naturally, email and social networking websites have facilitated[2]
40 communication. Ironically,[3] though, the tools designed for increased online interaction may actually lead to people being less social. Students rarely need to engage in face-to-face interactions these days either with their
45 professors or their fellow students. Lonely librarians remember when students used to ask them questions in person. Now they more often respond to students' text queries via website help centers. At the end of the day,
50 workers come home exhausted by so much online interaction. Having made themselves accessible online 24 hours a day, they end up sacrificing family time at home as they prepare for the next round of virtual interaction.

55 Clearly, increased access to information results in added benefits, but it is also true that there is a cost. People who embrace new technology should reflect on what they lose as well as what they gain. There is a choice
60 between touching and smelling a flower grown in my garden and sharing it with one or two friends in the neighborhood, and instead photographing the flower, putting that image online, and reading the responses
65 of my worldwide set of "friends." Perhaps the touch of the real flower should rule.

---

[1] **proponent:** supporter 支持者
[2] **facilitate:** make easier 促进；使便利
[3] **ironically:** in a way that is different from what was expected 出乎意料的是

2 特殊疑问词和 if / whether 引导的名词性从句

语法讲解

在说服性的学术写作中，特殊疑问词和 if / whether 引导的名词性从句（noun clauses）很有用，尤其是在作者呈现不同的观点并对这些观点发表评论时。	Experts disagree on **what the benefits and drawbacks of Internet use are for students.** Nobody really knows **if children today have more difficulty with concentration.**

2.1 特殊疑问词引导的名词性从句

A 由特殊疑问词（who, what, where, when, why 和 how）引导的名词性从句在句中的功能相当于名词，可用作主语、动词宾语或介词宾语。在学术写作中，多用作动词宾语和介词宾语。

特殊疑问词引导的名词性从句遵循陈述句语序（即主语位于动词之前）。主语前无助动词或情态动词。

特殊疑问词引导的名词性从句

Readers have to decide <u>which</u> expert they trust.

Readers are concerned about <u>who</u> seems the most credible.

Students have to learn <u>how</u> they can evaluate sources.

不说 Students have to learn how ~~can they~~ evaluate sources.

B 特殊疑问词引导的名词性从句常跟在下列动词后面：

表达想法与观点的动词: agree, consider, disagree

与学习和认知相关的动词: know, remember, see, understand, wonder

We need to <u>consider</u> who our main market is.

I don't <u>remember</u> where I read that.

2.2 if / whether 引导的名词性从句

A if / whether 引导的名词性从句在句中的功能相当于名词，可用于表示在两者之中或者在是否之间作出选择。与特殊疑问词引导的名词性从句相同，if / whether 引导的名词性从句也遵循陈述句语序。

当表示在两者之中选择其一时，whether 的使用频率较高。

Students need to check **whether their online sources are current or out-of-date.**
（二选一：这些信息是时新的还是已经过时了？答案是二者之一。）

I don't know **if that website has accurate information.**
（是或否：网站的信息是否准确？答案为"是"或"否"。）

2.2 if / whether 引导的名词性从句（续表）

B 动词 know，see 和 wonder 常与 if / whether 引导的名词性从句连用。	Let's see if we can find an answer on this website. Some students wonder whether they should do research online or in the library. I don't know if there are computers available to do the research online.

 语法应用

练习 2.1 特殊疑问词和 if / whether 引导的名词性从句

下面的句子涉及信息过载对员工和职场的影响。用特殊疑问词、if 或 whether 引导的名词性从句将每对句子组合起来。有时正确答案不唯一。

1 How does information overload affect the workplace? Researchers are studying this.

Researchers are studying how information overload affects the workplace.

2 Does information overload make an employee more or less efficient? Researchers are trying to determine this.

_____

3 What do employees do when they are overwhelmed by too much information? Employers want to know this.

_____

4 Do employees ignore important facts or absorb more when they are overloaded with information? Employers wonder this.

_____

5 Do overloaded employees waste time? Corporations want to find this out.

_____

6 How does information overload affect employees' decision-making skills? Studies may determine this.

_____

7 When do employees feel overwhelmed by information? Researchers wonder this.

_____

8 Does information overload increase or decrease productivity? Researchers want to learn this.

_____

> **练习 2.2** 更多练习：特殊疑问词和 if / whether 引导的名词性从句

A 听一段关于信息过载的讲座。按照录音中特殊疑问词和 if / whether 引导的名词性从句出现的顺序，为下列疑问句编号。

_____ **1** What is the daily volume of new web content?

_____ **2** What can we do about information overload?

_____ **3** Do you really need to send out emails to people who don't need them?

_____ **4** Does each recipient of information really need the information that he or she receives?

__*1*__ **5** How does information overload impact us?

_____ **6** Do you have to look at that video that your friend sent you?

_____ **7** What are some of the causes of information overload?

_____ **8** What can you do to avoid being overwhelmed by information?

_____ **9** Can you spend a portion of your day disconnected from technology?

B **结对练习** 下面这一段落是对练习 A 中讲座内容的总结。与同伴一起，将练习 A 中的疑问句改写为特殊疑问词或 if / whether 引导的名词性从句，将此段落补充完整，再将答案分享给另一组同学。

First, the lecturer says that he wonders ^{1} ***how this information overload impacts us*** and ^{2}_____ . Then he says he is going to examine ^{3}_____ . Next, he tells us that people tend to distribute information without considering ^{4}_____ . The lecturer also wonders ^{5}_____ . Then he moves on to consider ^{6}_____ . His first suggestion is that people should see ^{7}_____ . Second, he tells his audience to focus on one source of information at a time. Third, he asks people to consider ^{8}_____ . Finally, he tells people to ask themselves ^{9}_____ .

3 用于论证的表达

词汇讲解

写作者可以使用特定的表达来给出一个相对立的观点。进行论证时，写作者可以先承认这个观点的可取之处，再进行反驳或给予反证。	It has been argued that the Internet has caused groups to form more quickly than in the past. Clearly, the Internet offers access to a wealth of information. However, some students need more guidance than others in using online resources.

3.1 用于给出一个相对立的观点的表达

A 可以用下列表达来给出一个相对立的观点： It has been argued that ... It is argued that ... It has been claimed that ... Some researchers disagree that ... 其中，argue 和 claim 为最常用的动词。	It has been argued that young people handle information in a much different way. It has been claimed that it is important for adolescents to spend time away from electronic devices.
B 当写作者不能提供潜在对立观点的确切来源时，可以使用下面的表达进行表述。其中的情态动词削弱了语气。 It might / could / may be argued that ... It might / could / may be claimed that ... 其中，might 和 could 的使用频率比 may 高。 （更多对 it 结构的讲解见 Unit 16。）	It could be argued that video games allow children to develop critical-thinking skills. It might be claimed that cell phone use can be addictive.

3.2 用于表达观点的逻辑连接词

下列副词为逻辑连接词，可用于引出某一特定的观点或相反的论点： clearly，naturally，obviously，of course	Clearly, increased access to information results in a benefit. Obviously, few want to return to the old system of information gathering. Internet research is different, of course, and it requires specific strategies to get proper results.

可以用下列表达来对一个观点进行反驳或表示异议：

However, …

It is not true that …

That may be so, but …

(Unfortunately,) this is (simply) not true.

While it is true that …

其中，This is (simply) not true. 最为常用。

对立观点
Some claim that violence on TV leads to
反驳
violence at school. **However, this is simply not true.**

对立观点
While it is true that well-designed video games can help children think creatively,
反驳
they do not replace physical interaction with others.

 词汇应用

练习 3.1　用于论证的表达

下文讨论了信息获取更便捷的同时一些随之而来的问题。圈出正确的选项。

^1 (While it is true that)/ However, it has been argued that　easy access to information allows people to learn almost anything they want at any time, there are some downsides to this accessibility. Some people believe that individuals are more productive when they multitask. ^2 **Naturally / Unfortunately**　, this is simply not true, according to recent studies. Attempting to do several things at once is less efficient than doing one thing at a time. People should attempt to focus on one source of information at a time and one piece of information at a time. ^3 **Clearly, / It has been claimed that**　people want to receive a lot of information, though. Otherwise, they wouldn't access so many different sources of information at once.

Also, ^4 **while it is true that / it has been claimed that**　social networks allow people to stay updated on their friends' activities, they also create a big distraction. The vast amount of information that we have to sift through cuts into time we could actually be spending with friends. ^5 **It is not true that / Obviously,**　individuals have to decide on their own priorities, but spending time with friends face-to-face might be more valuable than communicating with them online. A person would probably benefit greatly from trading time spent learning unimportant information for some time spent with friends. ^6 **It could be argued that / Of course,**　people will not remember the 20 status updates and 5 emails they read after work, but they will very likely enjoy and remember a dinner with a friend.

练习 3.2　更多练习：用于论证的表达

以下面的 A 为范例，根据 B 的中心论点，在一张纸上写出一个简短的段落，内容包括给出一个相对立的观点，对该观点部分认同以及对该观点加以反驳。在写作中注意使用前面讲到的用于论证的一些表达。

A　**Thesis Statement:** The college should provide more on-campus child care for students.

Opposing view: The college should not provide more on-campus child care.

Agreement with the opposing view: There are enough day-care facilities in the community to serve the students who need them.

Refutation: The majority of day-care centers do not have evening hours, and most students attend school at night.

Supporting information: Many students miss school because they do not have anyone to care for their children while they are at school.

Body Paragraph:　*Some college personnel may argue that the college should not provide more on-campus child care. Clearly, they believe that there are enough day-care centers in the community to serve the students who need them. However, the majority of day-care centers do not have evening hours, and most students attend school at night. Therefore, many students miss school because they do not have anyone to care for their children while they are at school.*

B　**Thesis Statement:** Students should turn off their electronic devices during class.

Opposing view:　Students should be allowed to have their devices on during class.

Agreement with the opposing view: Students may need to be in contact with family members or their jobs.

Refutation: Electronic devices can be a distraction in the classroom.

Supporting information: Students can become easily distracted by their devices and miss important information.

结对练习 与同伴一起从下列话题中选择一个，或使用一个老师认可的其他话题。从该话题涉及的两个对立观点中各选一方，使用前面讲到的用于论证观点的一些表达，写出为自己的立场进行辩护的句子，再与同伴进行角色扮演并展开辩论。

- Are parents who allow their children to spend all day using electronic devices negligent?
- Should people turn their cell phones off when they're out with friends?
- Is it acceptable to surf the Internet and check text messages during class?

A *It has been claimed that too much television is not good for young children. However, children can learn a lot from watching television. They can learn about cultures and families that are different from their own. And they can learn practical information like reading and numbers by watching educational shows.*

B *That may be so, but it is also true that children can learn even more by interacting with humans rather than with an "electronic babysitter."*

4 常见错误提示 ⚠

1 注意用 if 引导条件状语从句，而不用 whether。

                  if
E-books will be popular ~~whether~~ they are less expensive than print books.

2 or not 与 whether 连用时可直接跟在 whether 之后，与 if 连用时置于 if 引导从句的句尾。

                  whether
Experts can't decide ~~if~~ or not students retain enough information with online reading.
Experts can't decide if ~~or not~~ students retain enough information with online
         or not
reading⌄.

3 注意 whether 的拼写要正确。

                  whether
The instructors decide ~~weather~~ students bring laptops or smartphones to class.
                  whether
They have not decided ~~wether~~ laptops are helpful or a distraction.

改错练习

下面是一篇文章的主体段落，文章讨论了信息过载这一现象。从中找出另外 6 处错误并改正。

Information Overload

Opponents of online technology often point to the negative effects of the information age. They claim that ~~weather~~ *whether* individuals use the Internet for research or for social networking, they suffer from information overload. They believe that easy access to information has a negative effect on users' critical-thinking skills. They also cite the fact
5 that online readers understand and retain less than print readers. The fact is, however, that experts have not yet determined if or not there is a difference between reading online and reading print material. There haven't been enough studies to determine if or not there truly are negative effects of information overload. Furthermore, it is important for proponents of this argument to identify wether they are referring to the effects of
10 technology on older people or younger people. For example, their arguments may not be valid whether they consider how digital natives respond to technology. Digital natives are people who were born since the 1990s. They were born into a digital world, and they have been using technology since childhood. According to the author, Don Tapscott, digital natives process information differently than digital immigrants (people who
15 were born before the 1990s and learned how to use the Internet later in life than digital natives did). Tapscott cites a study designed to show whether digital natives retained more information from a traditional newscast or an interactive webcast. The study showed that digital natives remembered more from the interactive news source. Tapscott also points out that intelligence and aptitude test scores are rising, which further
20 indicates that digital natives' thinking styles have not suffered. Some wonder wether digital natives should adapt to traditional ways of processing information. However, if or not we like it, the information age is here to stay. Therefore, digital immigrants are going to have to adapt to digital ways of interacting with technology.

说服 3：表示将来的行为；说服性写作中的常用单词和短语

Social Media

1 现实生活中的语法

阅读这篇文章，文章谈论了社交媒体对大学生学业成绩的可能影响。在这篇说服性文章中，作者主张在大学校园的部分场所内禁止社交媒体网站的使用。

A **读前准备** 你和你的朋友经常使用哪些社交媒体网站？社交媒体可能带来什么负面影响？阅读文章并思考：作者认为社交媒体对学生的影响是积极的还是消极的？为什么？

B **阅读理解** 回答下列问题。

1 What positive things does the writer say about social media?

2 Why does the author want to limit or ban social media on campuses?

3 Do you agree or disagree with the writer's point of view? Why?

C **语法发现** 按照下列提示回答问题，注意作者在谈论未来可能发生的事件时所用的语法。

1 比较 should 在第 12 行与第 64 行的用法。should 的含义有何不同？

2 阅读第 60—63 行以 Based on these concerns 开头的句子，注意句中 is likely to 的使用。该动词短语指的是现在还是将来？

3 注意 would 在第 41 行与第 63 行的用法。would 指的是现在发生的事还是将来有可能发生的事？

Social Media on College Campuses

SOCIAL MEDIA HAS REVOLUTIONIZED the way we communicate with friends, colleagues, classmates, and even family members. It is now possible to interact and maintain a relationship with someone
5 without ever meeting in person. There are many positive aspects of these new types of interactions. However, the excessive use of such websites has created a distraction[1] for some users. Some college students spend hours a day "networking" instead
10 of focusing on their studies. To help these students be more successful, colleges and universities should block access to social media in most areas of their campuses.

Social media has been growing in popularity
15 at an astonishing rate. According to the Pew Research Center's Internet & American Life Project, it is estimated that at least 85 percent of college students in the United States use some type of online social media on a daily basis. In fact,
20 according to many instructors, college students are growing dependent on such networks. While there is no doubt that social media has created valuable new ways to communicate and share information, they have also become a distraction
25 for college students who spend time online instead of preparing for their future careers.

Some proponents claim that the social media phenomenon[2] can be positive. Students can join online groups in which everyone shares the same
30 interest, and they can learn how to communicate effectively in this digital age. It has been further argued that, when online, students will discuss current events and issues that they are less likely to discuss in "real life" interactions. In an ideal world,
35 this could indeed be a beneficial way to promote interaction with people from different cultures and backgrounds. Opponents argue that, in reality, some discussions provide a less rigorous platform for ideas because of the lack of monitoring and
40 the informal nature of the format. It is therefore difficult to argue that these postings would add significantly to the students' knowledge base.

Colleges and universities should consider strong policies on the use of social media on campus because students waste valuable study time on it. In fact, some studies report a link between time on social media and grades. For
50 example, an Ohio State University survey indicates that students who regularly use social media study less than five hours per week and have an average GPA between 3.0 and 3.5. In contrast, students who do not use these websites study 11 hours or
55 more per week and have an average GPA between 3.5 and 4.0. In addition, teachers are increasingly concerned about social media use in class. They complain that students are "messaging friends or posting ... status updates from their laptops instead
60 of paying attention to lectures." Based on these concerns, establishing clear policies for use of these websites on campus is likely to help students focus on their studies. They would spend more time studying, and their grades should improve as
65 a result.

Social media presents a new way to find, organize, and share information and contacts. These visually stimulating, highly interactive websites attract many college students. However,
70 their addictive nature can potentially disrupt[3] student life to the degree that colleges and universities have to take action and ban access to social media in some areas on campuses.

[1]**distraction:** something that takes your attention away from where it should be focused 使人分心的事物
[2]**phenomenon:** something that is noticed because it is unusual or new 现象
[3]**disrupt:** change the normal direction and create disorder 扰乱

2 表示将来的行为

语法讲解

写作者可以用 will，be going to 和其他一些情态动词或表达来表示对将来的计划、预测和期望。	Students **will not** be able to access social media sites if colleges ban them. Blocking social media on campus **would** help students focus on their studies.

2.1　用 will，be going to 等表示将来的行为

A will 和 be going to 可用于表示对未来的计划或预测。在学术写作中，will 的使用频率比 be going to 高。	The Internet **will continue to allow** for a greater exchange of ideas. Some colleges **are going to ban** access to social media on campuses.
B 情态动词 could，might 和 may 可用于表示将来某事可能发生。	The use of social media by recruiters for jobs **could increase** in the next few years.
C 情态动词 should 可用于表示对某事的预期。	New technology **should make** communication more efficient.
D 情态动词 would 可用于表示（在某个已明确说明或未明确说明的条件下）对某事的预期或设想。	Banning note-taking on laptops **would prevent** students from using the Internet during classes. If the school implements the ban now, it **would see** major benefits within the next few months.

2.2　其他描述将来行为的表达

A 以下表达可用于描述在不久的将来有可能会发生的事件： is due to is about to	The new version of the phone **is due to come** out by next year. The company **is about to introduce** a new app.

2.2 其他描述将来行为的表达（续表）

B 以下表达也可用于描述将来可能会发生的事件：
it is / seems / looks likely that + 从句

某事 / 某人 is (are) / seem(s) / look(s) likely to + 动词
某事 / 某人 is / are considering + 动词 -ing 形式
anticipate + 动词 -ing 形式（表示某事很有可能发生）

It seems likely that younger teachers will be more comfortable with educational technology.
Younger teachers **are likely to be** more comfortable with using technology.
The school **is considering prohibiting** all unauthorized Internet access on campus.
We **anticipate focusing** only on student performance scores, not other factors.

C 以下动词（后接不定式）可用于表示对将来的计划，且常用一般现在时形式：
hope to：尚未确定但希望发生的事件
intend to：尚未确定但有望发生的事件

plan to：预先安排好的、将要发生的事件

The students **hope to maintain** their high school friendships online.
The university **intends to investigate** the effects of technology on student performance.
Large technology companies **plan to move** many applications to phones and other digital devices.

语法应用

练习 2.1 将来的可能性

A 一家设计类杂志的管理者们注意到，在工作时间使用社交媒体的员工越来越多。阅读下面的博客文章以及员工对此问题的评论，圈出正确的选项。

Friday, May 8

It has been noted that some employees are spending a lot of time on social media during work hours, and productivity has gone down. We really need everyone to be focused right now because we [1] **(are about to)**/ are considering ___ launch our new website, and we [2] **plan to get / anticipate getting** ___ a lot of new business as a result. Because of this, management [3] **is likely to block / is considering blocking** ___ social media websites from the office. However, we'd like to hear what you all think about this. We welcome your comments. We [4] **anticipate having / will have** ___ a meeting next Friday at 2:00 to discuss this issue. All employees are welcome. We [5] **plan to / hope to** ___ see all of you there.

COMMENTS:

Marta G.: Not everyone spends a lot of time on the sites. Most of us check the sites a couple of times a day. Why punish everyone? It ⁶ <u>should be / seems likely</u> that people who waste time ⁷ <u>should / will</u> find other ways to waste time if they can't get on social media.

Erin W.: I like this idea. It's frustrating when my team members don't complete their work because they have spent too much time online. This change ⁸ <u>would / is going to</u> prevent them from spending half the workday online. And my team's productivity ⁹ <u>intends to / could</u> increase.

Tomas K.: I use social media to update my clients on the latest design trends. Some of my clients contact me during the day on this site. If I couldn't use the site at work, I ¹⁰ <u>should / might</u> lose some of my clients. I ¹¹ <u>intend / am not likely</u> to protest this policy if it goes through.

Kevin L.: Friday's a bad day for this meeting. A lot of people ¹² <u>don't plan / are not likely</u> to attend because they telecommute that day. You should change the day.

B 结对练习 假设你和同伴是两位小型企业的经理，你们对于工作时间使用社交媒体持不同态度。根据下面的情景进行角色扮演式对话。角色扮演过程中要回答下列问题：作为管理者，你考虑如何解决这个问题？你将采取的政策对员工会有什么影响？员工会作何反应？你计划如何应对员工的反应？注意用上表示将来行为的情态动词和表达。

Student A You are seriously considering banning the use of social media through the company's computers and implementing strict rules about not accessing them on smartphones during work hours. You strongly believe that these sites cause employees to waste time, do poor quality work, and be irresponsible.

Student B You do not believe that social media should be banned at work because you believe that this will create a lot of anger and resentment from employees. You want to work with employees to create a set of policies that everyone can agree with.

A *I'm seriously considering banning the use of social media sites at my workplace because I think they're a major distraction for my employees.*

B *I feel differently. I agree that there might be a need to have policies regarding their use, but I'm not sure that banning is the right solution. There may be other solutions. You're going to get a lot of criticism, you know.*

A *I know I am. I'm planning to hold several meetings about it …*

练习 2.2 更多练习：将来的可能性

两位大学生 Lisa 和 Ben 在谈论社交媒体。听录音，如果句子与录音内容一致，标记 T；如果不一致，标记 F。修正与录音内容不一致的句子。

_F_ 1 Their college *is considering blocking* ~~has recently blocked~~ Internet access to social media sites in some areas on campus.

_____ 2 Ben thinks blocking access might help students study more.

_____ 3 Lisa is going to demonstrate against it if the school blocks access.

_____ 4 Ben will demonstrate against it if the school blocks access.

_____ 5 One popular social media site is about to charge people to use their site.

_____ 6 Lisa thinks a lot of people might delete their accounts if the popular social media site charges people.

_____ 7 Ben thinks that people will pay to use a popular site.

_____ 8 Lisa might use a social media if she has to pay.

3 说服性写作中的常用单词和短语

词汇讲解

上一单元介绍了在说服性写作中常用于给出相对立的观点的表达。本单元将介绍在说服性及其他类型的学术写作中的其他常用词汇。	According to the **proponents** of technology, easy access to information is one way that people benefit from new technology. Some educators **claim** that the networking phenomenon can be positive.

3.1 说服性写作中的常用词汇

A 说服性写作中常用以下名词： 可以用这些名词来指人： advocates, opponents, proponents, supporters 可以用这些名词来指事实或观点： argument, belief, claim, conclusion, evidence, fact, information, problem(s)	**Opponents** of social media argue that these communities deter face-to-face interactions. The main **argument** used by **proponents** of social media is that it allows contact with people from all over the world. Some critics see students' dependence on social media as a **problem**, but there is little **evidence** of this.
B 说服性写作中常用以下动词： acknowledge, admit, advocate, argue, believe, claim, control, estimate, oppose, project, refute, support	Some people **believe** that children should not be allowed to text in class. A number of parents **support** banning text messaging from schools.
C 说服性写作中常用以下形容词： better, illogical, important, incomplete, little, true, unproved, valid	It is **important** to be familiar with the latest technology. It is **true** that some people spend too much time in front of the computer. The arguments supported by these researchers are **illogical**.
D 说服性写作中常用以下短语： be in favor of (something) be against (something)	Many instructors **are in favor of** receiving homework online. Many teachers **are against** the use of social media in schools.

词汇应用

练习 3.1 说服性写作中的词汇

阅读下列关于网络欺凌的句子，选择正确的单词或短语填空。每个单词或短语只可使用一次。

| argue | ~~claim~~ | in favor of | opponents | proponents |

1 Cyberbullying occurs when people, often teenagers, are teased or humiliated by others on the Internet. Many parents and psychologists *claim* that it can cause permanent emotional damage to children and teenagers.

2 Some people _____ that cyberbullying should be categorized as a criminal offense.

3 _____ of the idea that cyberbullying be classified as a criminal offense are _____ the approach because they believe it will decrease the amount of cyberbullying among teenagers.

4 _____ of making cyberbullying a criminal offense do not believe that criminalizing cyberbullying would be effective.

| acknowledge | against | evidence | a valid point |

5 While some people _____ that cyberbullying needs to be criminalized, they worry that the law will be ineffective because it is difficult to track the perpetrators.

6 The difficulty of tracking perpetrators is _____ , but the point may not be convincing in the near future since tracking devices are rapidly improving.

7 Some people who are _____ the criminalization of cyberbullying say that creating laws making it a crime violates free speech.

8 Some researchers have found that there is _____ that educational programs in early grades are effective in reducing the incidence of bullying.

结对练习　与同伴一起从下列话题中选出一个，讨论你们对该话题的看法。注意用上说服性写作中的常用词汇。

- Should children under 12 be allowed to use social media?
- Should parents have access to their children's and teenagers' social media accounts?
- Should people be "friends" with their coworkers and managers on social media?

I believe that children under 12 should be allowed to use social media. I acknowledge that children can get into trouble, but if they use the sites responsibly, they can learn a lot about socializing and computer skills …

4 常见错误提示 ⚠

1 注意 claim 既可用作动词，也可用作名词。

        claim
The ~~claiming~~ that social media is dangerous is illogical.

2 注意动词 argue 的名词形式是 argument。

        argument
The main ~~arguing~~ against using social media to communicate with people is that it is superficial.

3 注意要用 according to，而不要用 according for 或 according with。

        to
According ~~for~~ a recent study, young people are losing interest in social media.

        to
According ~~with~~ Smith, social media is useful as an educational tool.

改错练习

下面是一篇关于社交媒体的文章的主体段落，从中找出另外 6 处错误并改正。

Social Media

One of the main ~~arguing~~ *arguments* against social media is that people sometimes reveal information on them that often should be kept private. Recently another development has provided more support for this arguing: College admissions committees are now using social media as part of the application process. According for a survey by Kaplan
5 Test Prep, over 80 percent of college admissions officers use social media to communicate with students. The claiming that many colleges make is that they use these sites to attract new students or to stay in contact with former students. However, some colleges admit that they are also using social media as part of the admissions process. The main arguing for using social media is that it helps colleges evaluate candidates at a time when these
10 colleges are experiencing large numbers of applicants. According with many admissions officers, colleges need all the information they can get about applicants in order to make decisions because the admissions process has become very competitive. One college interviewer in a recent survey reported that if she has to choose between two students who are equally qualified in terms of grades and test scores, she looks at their online
15 profiles to make the final decision. In addition, applicants also use social media against each other. According for another admissions officer, his office often receives anonymous messages with links to sites that have negative information on or pictures of other applicants. Many colleges and universities do not have official policies yet on whether to use social media as part of the application process. Until these policies become clearer,
20 prospective college students should keep their social media pages private or remove anything that might make them look less attractive to admissions committees.

索引

Art Credits

The authors and publisher acknowledge the following sources of copyright material and are grateful for the permissions granted. While every effort has been made, it has not always been possible to identify the sources of all the material used, or to trace all copyright holders. If any omissions are brought to our notice, we will be happy to include the appropriate acknowledgements on reprinting and in the next update to the digital edition, as applicable.

The following images are sourced from Getty Images.

U1: LeoFFreitas/Moment; Gabriel Grams; JayLazarin/iStock Unreleased; U2: Jim Craigmyle/Corbis; Darryl Estrine/UpperCut Images; U3: RapidEye/E+; Martin Barraud/Caiaimage; Zinkevych/iStock; U4: Aaaaimages/Moment; AFP Contributor; MyrKu/iStock; JENS SCHLUETER/DDP; U5: WPA Pool; Brooks Kraft/Corbis Historical; Carsten Koall; Jessica Peterson/Tetra images; Scott Barbour; H. Armstrong Roberts/ClassicStock/Archive Photos; U6: nito100/iStock; Hero Images; U7: Maskot; Hero Images; Hirurg/E+; U8: FatCamera/E+; Juice Images; U9: Anthony Barboza/Archive Photos; Hemant Mehta/IndiaPicture; Rubberball Productions; Astrid Stawiarz; Martin Mills/Hulton Archive; Oliver Gerhard/imageBROKER; U10: Drew Angerer; Francis Dean/Corbis Historical; Tom Stoddart Archive/Hulton Archive; U11: Chris Ryan/Caiaimage; Kevin Dodge/Tetra images; Chris Ryan/Caiaimage; Alexsl/E+; U12: View Stock; Hero Images; Kristina Kohanova/EyeEm; J. Countess; C Flanigan/WireImage; Mint/Hindustan Times; Rawpixel/iStock; U13: Brunorbs/iStock; Fancy/Veer/Corbis; EmirMemedovski/E+; Pinghung Chen / EyeEm; U14: Coldsnowstorm/iStock; Digital Vision/Photodisc; U15: Ariel Skelley/DigitalVision; Andresr/E+; Maskot; Maskot; U16: Natali_Mis/iStock; Adam Hester/Tetra images; Weedezign/iStock; Tein79/iStock; Wavebreakmedia/iStock; U17: Artisteer/iStock; Gajus/iStock; U18: Vladans/iStock; Robert Daly/OJO Images; Miguel Sotomayor/Moment; U19: Busakorn Pongparnit/Moment; AJ_Watt/E+; U20: DragonImages/iStock; Halfdark/fStop; Hill Street Studios/Blend Images; KatarzynaBialasiewicz/iStock.

Images from other sources

U5: Hine, Lewis Wickes, 1874–1940/Library of Congress; U10: Calamy stock images/Alamy Stock Photo;
U11: BDoss928/Shutterstock.